I0570222

LAUREN GREEN

A Guide to Avoiding Miscommunications
when Speaking English with North Americans

WRONGLISH
—— 콩글리쉬 잘못됫쉬 ——
KONGLISH

북미사람들과 대화 할 때 자주 할 수 있는
오해를 막아주는 가이드북

TRANSLATED BY YIRE LEE 이이레

This publication is designed to provide accurate information in regard to the subject matter covered. It is sold with the understanding that neither the author nor the publisher is engaged in rendering legal, investment, or other professional services. While the publisher and author have used their best efforts in preparing this book, they make no representations or warranties with respect to the accuracy or completeness of the contents of this book and specifically disclaim any implied warranties of merchantability or fitness for a particular purpose. No warranty may be created or extended by sales representatives or written sales materials. The advice and strategies contained herein may not be suitable for your situation. You should consult with a professional when appropriate. Neither the publisher nor the author shall be liable for any loss of profit or any other commercial damages, including but not limited to special, incidental, consequential, personal, or other damages.

For privacy reasons, some names, locations, and dates may have been changed. Examples situations, sentences, and conversations are intended for educational purposes only and do not necessarily reflect the personal views of the author, translator, and publisher.

Copyright © 2024 Lauren Green and Yire Lee

All rights reserved. No part of this book may be reproduced or used in any manner without the prior written permission of the copyright owner except for the use of brief quotations in a book review. For more information, address: LaurensLanguageLessons@gmail.com

Library of Congress Number: 2024910104

First paperback edition November 2024

ISBN 979-8-9899078-0-9 (Paperback)
ISBN 979-8-9899078-2-3 (Hardcover)
ISBN 979-8-9899078-1-6 (eBook)

Lauren's Language Lessons, LLC
Houston, Texas, USA
www.LaurensLanguageLessons.com

TABLE OF CONTENTS

INTRODUCTION: WHY I WROTE THIS BOOK
서론: 내가 이 책을 쓴 이유

I once had a student from Korea who told me her son was an officer. For months, I thought her son was a police officer in Korea. At one point, we were talking about him, and I asked, "Is it dangerous to be an officer in Korea?" She looked really confused. "Of course not." I later found out he worked for a government agency in the finance department and that "officer" did not mean the same thing to Koreans as it did to me. Something had been lost in translation.

During my early years of teaching English to Koreans, I noticed that students would often say English words that didn't fit into the context of our conversation and didn't make sense. "He did overeat yesterday, so he can't come to class today." I'd feel confused and try to ask clarifying questions to understand their meanings. "I don't understand why the amount he ate yesterday is related to whether he is coming to class today…" Students would feel frustrated, wondering why I didn't understand the English they were speaking. One student even said quite bluntly in exasperation, "I am speaking English, why don't you understand me? Is it my accent?" In reality, he was speaking Konglish.

Konglish, or Korean-style English, includes Koreanized English words with similar meanings and sometimes just slightly different pronunciations (*pizza*). However, Konglish also includes hundreds of English words that have completely different meanings in Konglish than they do in American English (*consent*). Sometimes, there are even words that are neither Korean nor English (*Pierrot*). There are many others that are technically English but in practicality don't exist at all (*salaryman*) while others are creative abbreviations of English words that are not used or understood outside of Korea (*DC*).

In many ways, Konglish often provides a sense of identity for the Korean community within the United States and other countries, building unity and connection. In South Korea, Konglish reflects a piece of Korea's unique culture and serves as a fascinating and evolving example of the ever-changing world of language and our ever-growing global connectedness. However, outside of Korean communities themselves, the Korean version of English gets lost in translation, and misunderstandings abound.

The purpose of this book is to serve as a guide for Koreans learning American-style English and to help avoid some of the miscommunications that are often encountered from using certain Konglish words that don't mean the same thing in American English.

You will learn what many Konglish words actually mean to Americans and what you should say instead in order to be properly understood. You will also find a few words that aren't true Konglish but are common confusing mistakes that Korean speakers often make when speaking English. My hope is that this book will help you speak English more like a native speaker and avoid some of the miscommunications and frustrations I've seen many of my Korean students experience when speaking to Americans!

Special Note: Language is constantly changing! Even in the years of writing and putting together this book, new Konglish words have been adopted; older Konglish words have become outdated; and some previously obscure Konglish words have become mainstream and commonly used even in American English circles.

It's also important to keep in mind that English itself is extremely diverse. This book focuses on American English and does not address the differences that may be found between Konglish and other varieties of English, but even within the United States, there can be regional differences in certain word choices as well as differences based on your age, generation, socioeconomics, life experiences, subculture, ethnic background, field of work, and much more. For example, people in the South and West are more likely to say "tennis shoes" while those in the Northeast are more likely to say "sneakers," and those under the age of 25 are more likely to use the newly abbreviated term "sus" to describe someone or something as "suspicious."

For some terms, there are far too many meanings and nuances to include every single use case. Since this book is not meant to serve as a complete dictionary, I have just included the most common, useful, or relevant information. With those caveats, I have done my best to make this book as extensive as possible, knowing that because of the diversity of English and the ever-changing nature of language, it will never be completely possible for it to be truly all-inclusive.

예전에 한국에서 온 한 학생이 그녀의 아들이 "officer"라고 말했습니다. 몇 달 동안 저는 그녀의 아들이 한국의 경찰이라고 생각했습니다. 그 아들에 대해 이야기하고 있을때, "한국에서 경찰일이 위험한가요?"라고 물었습니다. 그녀는 매우 혼란스러워 보였습니다. "물론 그렇지 않습니다." 나중에 그가 재무 부서의 정부 기관에서 일했다는 것과 내가 알고 있는 있었던 "officer"가 한국 사람들에게는 같은 의미가 아니라는 것을 알게 되었습니다.

한국인들에게 영어를 가르치는 초기 몇 년 동안, 한 학생이 대화의 맥락에 맞지 않고 이해가 되지 않는 영어 단어를 자주 말하는 것을 알아챘습니다. "그는 어제 과식을 해서 오늘 수업에 올 수 없습니다." 저는 혼란을 느끼고 의미를 이해하기 위해 명확한 질문을 하려고 노력했습니다. "저는 그가 어제 먹은 양이 왜 그가 오늘 수업에 오는지와 관련이 있는지 이해할 수 없습니다..." 그 학생은 왜 그들이 말하는 영어를 제가 이해하지 못하는지 궁금해하며 좌절감을 느낄 수도 있을 것입니다. 한 학생은 심지어 꽤 직설적으로 "저는 영어로 말하고 있는데, 왜 제 말을 이해하지 못하나요? 제 억양인가요?"라고 말했습니다. 실제로 그는 콩글리시를 말하고 있었습니다.

콩글리시, 즉 한국식 영어에는 비슷한 의미, 때로는 약간 다른 발음(피자)을 가진 한국화된 영어 단어들이 포함되어 있지만, 미국 영어(동의)와는 완전히 다른 의미의 콩글리시 영어 단어 수백 개도 포함되어 있습니다. 때로는 심지어 한국어도 아니고 영어도 아닌 단어들(피에로)도 있습니다. 엄밀히 말해 영어 단어로 만들어졌지만 실제로 존재하지 않는 단어들(샐러리맨)도 많고, 다른 것들은 한국 밖에서는 사용되지 않거나 이해되지 않는 영어 단어들(DC)의 줄임말들도 있습니다.

여러 면에서 콩글리시는 종종 미국과 다른 나라들에 사는 한국인들에게 통일성과 유대감을 형성하는 정체성을 제공합니다. 한국에서 콩글리시는 한국의 독특한 문화의 일부를 반영하며 끊임없이 변화하는 언어의 세계와 계속해서 증가하는 세계적인 연결성의 흥미로운 진화하는 예로 작용합니다. 그러나 한국인 공동체 그 자체 밖에서 한국어 버전의 영어는 잘 이해되지 못하고 많은 오해를 일으킵니다.

이 책의 목적은 미국식 영어를 배우는 한국인들에게 가이드 역할을 하고, 미국 영어에서 같은 의미가 아닌 특정 콩글리시 단어를 사용함으로써 자주 접하는 잘못된 의사소통을 피할 수 있도록 돕는 것입니다.

여러분은 많은 콩글리시 단어들이 실제로 미국인들에게 무엇을 의미하는지, 그리고 제대로 이해되기 위해서는 여러분이 대신 무엇을 말해야 하는지 배울 것입니다. 여러분은 또한 진정한 콩글리시는 아니지만 한국인들이 영어를 말할 때 자주 하는 흔한 실수들을 알 수 있을 것입니다. 저는 이 책이 여러분이 원어민처럼 영어를 더 많이 말하고 제가 봐왔던 많은 한국학생들이 미국인들과 대화할 때 겪는 오해와 좌절을 피할 수 있도록 도와주기를 바랍니다!

특별 참고: 언어는 계속해서 변화하고 있습니다! 이 책을 쓰고 정리한 몇 년 동안에도, 새로운 콩글리쉬 단어들이 사용되었고, 오래된 콩글리쉬 단어들은 구식이 되었습니다. 이전에 잘 알려지지 않은 일부 콩글리쉬 단어들은 주류가 되었고 심지어 미국 영어권에서조차 흔하게 사용되고 있습니다.

또한 영어 자체가 매우 다양하다는 것을 명심해야 합니다. 이 책은 미국 영어에 초점을 맞추고 콩글리시와 다른 종류의 영어 사이에서 발견될 수 있는 차이점을 다루지 않지만, 미국 내에서도 특정 단어 선택의 지역적 차이뿐만 아니라 나이, 세대, 사회경제, 삶의 경험, 하위 문화, 민족적 배경, 직업 분야 등에 따른 차이가 있을 수 있습니다. 예를 들어, 남부와 서부 사람들은 "테니스 신발"이라고 말할 가능성이 더 높은 반면, 북동부 사람들은 "운동화"라고 말할 가능성이 더 높으며, 25세 미만의 사람들은 누군가 또는 어떤 것을 "suspicious" 것으로 묘사하기 위해 새로 약칭된 "sus"라는 용어를 사용할 가능성이 더 높습니다.

어떤 용어들은 사용 사례를 일일이 다 포함하기에는 의미와 뉘앙스가 너무 많습니다. 이 책은 완전한 사전 역할을 하는 것이 아니기 때문에, 가장 일반적이고 유용하고 적절한 정보를 포함했습니다. 이런 주의 사항을 고려하여, 영어의 다양성과 언어의 변화하는 특성 때문에, 이 책이 진정으로 모든 것을 포괄하는 것은 결코 가능하지 않을 것이라는 것을 알고, 가능한 한 광범위하게 이 책을 만들기 위해 최선을 다했습니다.

NOTE ABOUT QR CODES: Scan the QR code located on each chapter title page to hear audio for English pronunciation of the words included in each chapter! For a continuous playlist of all chapters and words included in this book, scan this QR code →

각 챕터 제목 페이지의 링크를 클릭하면 각 챕터에 포함된 단어의 영어 발음 오디오를 들을 수 있습니다. 이 책에 포함된 챕터와 단어의 연속 재생 목록을 보려면 아래 링크를 클릭하세요.

1

ABBREVIATIONS
줄임말

Scan for Audio!

APPL 어플

Meaning in American English:
미국식 영어로 의미:

Sounds like apple
사과처럼 들림

Say Instead:
미국식 영어로 말할려면:

App

Konglish Sentence	American English
The Kakao *appl* is the most widely used in Korea.	The Kakao *app* is the most widely used in Korea.

카톡 어플이 한국에서 제일 많이 쓰인다.

A/S AFTER SERVICE
에이 에스 / 에프터 서비스

Meaning in American English:
미국식 영어로 의미:

Doesn't exist

이 단어는 존재하지 않습니다

Say Instead:
미국식 영어로 말할려면:

Warranty

Konglish Sentence	American English
I just bought this phone one week ago, but it is not working correctly. Do you have *A/S*? 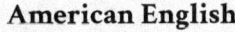	I just bought this phone one week ago, but it's not working correctly. Does it have a *warranty*? / Is it under *warranty*?

일주일전에 전화기를 샀는데 작동하지 않아요. A/S 되나요?

Real Life Story:
실화:

I once had a student who moved to the United States and bought a couch. A week later, she found a small rip in one of the cushions. She went to the store and asked if they had A/S on her sofa purchase. The store employees looked at her kind of strangely and eventually went to get a manager to help. "A/S. After service," she asked again, "Do you have after service for my couch?" Still, no one at the store understood. She left the store feeling sad and defeated and thought maybe her accent was too thick for people to understand. She was sure she was speaking correct English.

미국으로 이주해 온 친구가 소파를 산적이 있다. 일주일 후에 소파가 조금 찢어진 것을 알게 되었다. 그래서 친구는 가게에 가서 소파 A/S 를

해달라고 점원에게 물어보았다. 가게 직원은 그녀를 이상하게 바라
보았다. 친구는 다시 물었다. 다른 직원도 친구가 요청하는 것을 알아듣지
못했다. 친구는 "A/S 애프터 서비스, 구입한 소파 애프터 서비스
해주세요"라고 물었다. 그러나 그녀가 말하는 것을 아무도 알아듣는
직원이 없었다. 친구는 발음을 정확히 영어로 말했다고 생각 했었다.

BGM 비지엠

Meaning in American English:
미국식 영어로 의미:

Doesn't exist

이 단어는 존재하지 않습니다

Say Instead:
미국식 영어로 말하려면:

Background music

Konglish Sentence	American English
That CF is famous for its *BGM*.	That commercial is famous for its *background music*.
이 씨에프(CF)는 배경음악으로 유명해요.	

BJ 비제이

Meaning in American English:

미국식 영어로 의미:

1. BJ or B.J. can be a male name. There's a famous TV show writer in the US
   with this name as well as a famous restaurant chain.

   BJ 나 B.J.는 남성 이름으로 사용될 수 있다. 미국에는 이 이름을 가진
   유명한 미국 드라마 작가로 일하고 있는 사람이 있을 뿐만 아니라 이
   이름을 가진 유명한 레스토랑 체인점이 있다.

2. BJ also has an inappropriate meaning

   BJ 는 일반명사로 사용될 때 부적절한 의미를 가진다.

Say Instead:

미국식 영어로 말하려면:

YouTuber, YouTube streamer, Live streamer

Konglish Sentence	American English
My friend is a *BJ* on YouTube.	My friend is a *YouTube streamer*. My friend is a *live streamer*.

내 친구는 유튭 비제이이다.

Origins:

기원:

BJ comes from the English words *broadcast* and *jockey*. The author guesses this
may come from a mixing of the terms *broadcast announcer* or *radio broadcasting*
and *disc jockey (DJ)*.

BJ 는 broadcast jockey 라는 영어 단어에서 왔다. 필자는 이것이 '방송
아나운서' 또는 '라디오 방송'과 '디스크 자키(DJ)'라는 용어가 혼합된
것으로 추측한다.

CF 씨 에프

Meaning in American English:
미국식 영어로 의미:

Doesn't exist

이 단어는 존재하지 않습니다

Say Instead:
미국식 영어로 말하려면:

Commercial

Konglish Sentence	American English
That *CF* is famous for its BGM.	That *commercial* is famous for its background music.

이 씨에프(CF)는 배경음악으로 유명해요.

D/C 디씨

Meaning in American English:
미국식 영어로 의미:

Many people use DC to mean Washington
D.C., the capital city of the United States.
많은 사람은 미국 수도 Washington
D.C. 대신 DC 를 사용한다.

Say Instead:
미국식 영어로 말할려면:

Discount

Konglish Sentence	American English
Please give me some *D/C.* ⟹	I'd like a *discount*, please.
디씨(디스카운트) 좀 해주세요.	

How Americans use DC:
미국인들이 "DC"를 사용하는 법:

D Dad

> Our plane just landed in DC

Awesome, I'll pick you up at baggage claim!

J Julia

How long are you planning to be in New York? I'd love to see you!

> We'd love to see you too! We're coming to NYC from Wednesday to Monday. Might do a quick trip to **DC** on Saturday/Sunday

OST 오에스티

Meaning in American English:
미국식 영어로 의미:

This is not a common abbreviation. It can mean a specific type of data file, but this is not common. You may find some people who understand *OST* to mean "soundtrack" (it stands for original soundtrack), but most people will not understand this abbreviation.

일반적인 축약어는 아니다. 특정 종류의 데이터 파일을 의미할 수 있지만, 이는 일반적이지 않다. OST 를 한국어처럼 배경음악을 의미하는 것으로 이해하는 사람들을 볼 수 있지만, 대부분의 사람들은 이 축약어를 이해하지 못할 것이다.

Say Instead:
미국식 영어로 말할려면:

Soundtrack

Konglish Sentence	American English
Korean dramas use famous singers for their *OSTs*.	Korean dramas use famous singers for their *soundtracks*.

한국 드라마는 유명한 가수의 OST 가 많다.

PT 피티

Meaning in American English:
미국식 영어로 의미:

1. Physical therapy
   물리치료

2. Part time work (only when written)
   아르바이트 (글로 쓸 경우에만)

3. Personal trainer (much less common)
   개인 트레이너 (일반적이지 않음)

4. A patient (used in medical terminology)
   환자 (의학 용어에 사용됨)

Say Instead:
미국식 영어로 말할려면:

Personal trainer

Presentation

Konglish Sentence		American English
I have a class with my *PT* teacher today. / I have a *PT* class today.		I have a session with my *personal trainer* today.

오늘 나 피티(P.T)선생님하고 수업 있어.

Real Life Story:
실화:

One day, I was teaching a business English class for several Korean businessmen. As they were arriving for my class, one student said, "Mr. Kim has a PT first today."

Thinking he meant that Mr. Kim had been hurt and perhaps had a physical therapy session that overlapped with our class, I asked, "Oh really? So will he miss our class today? Is he OK?"

The student looked confused. "No, he is here. He will do a PT first... the homework you gave us." I scratched my head. The only homework I had given them was to do a business-related PowerPoint presentation.

Turns out, that's what he meant! And before we started our presentations, I taught them that *PT* does not mean "presentation" in American English. They were all shocked to learn this new information, and I was shocked to learn that in Korea, *PT* can mean "presentation."

내가 한국 회사원에게 영어를 가르칠 때였다. 어느날, 한 분이 "미스터 김이 오늘 먼저 PT 를 할거예요."라고 . 그래서 난 그 분이 어디 다쳤거나 물리 치료를 받으러 간다고 생각했다. 수업시간 시작중에 "오늘 못 오신다고요? 괜찮으신가요?"라고 물었더니 다른 분들은 의아해하는 눈치였다. "아니요. 올꺼예요. 오늘 숙제 내주신 PT 먼저 할꺼예요."라고 말했고 난 이해가 되지 않았다. 내가 내준 숙제는 비지니스 관련 파워포인트 프리젠테이션이었다.

알고 보니, 그들이 말하는 의도가 바로 그것이었다. 프레젠테이션을 시작하기 전에 그들에게 PT 가 미국 영어로 '프레젠테이션'을 의미하는 것이 아니라는 것을 가르쳤다. 그들은 이 새로운 정보를 알고 모두 충격을 받았고, 나도 한국에서 PT 가 '프레젠테이션'을 의미할 수 있다는 것을 알고 충격을 받았다.

How Americans use PT:
미국인들이 "PT"를 사용하는 법:

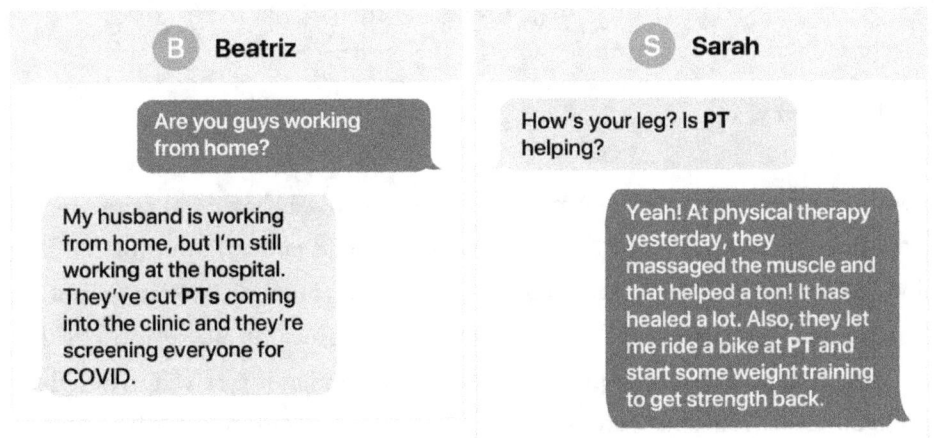

PPT 피피티

Meaning in American English:
미국식 영어로 의미:

Doesn't exist

이 단어는 존재하지 않습니다

Say Instead:
미국식 영어로 말할려면:

PowerPoint, PowerPoint presentation, Presentation

(*when talking about a presentation for a meeting or presenting information* 미팅 프리젠테이션에 대해 이야기하거나 정보를 제공할 때 쓰는 단어들)

Slideshow, Presentation slideshow

(*when talking about a slideshow that turns the slide automatically, often used for showing pictures at events on a loop* 슬라이드를 자동으로 돌리는 슬라이드 쇼에 대해 설명할 때 사용되거나, 이벤트에서 사진이 나올 때 사용되는 단어들)

Konglish Sentence	American English
He is going to prepare a *PPT* for the meeting.	He is going to prepare a *PowerPoint presentation* for the meeting.

그는 미팅을 위해 PPT 를 준비할 것이다.

Real Life Story:
실화:

Recently, one of my Korean-American friends who was born and raised in the United States went back to Korea with her husband and children for the first time in more than 20 years for a wedding and family reunion. Though she speaks Korean, her husband and children don't speak Korean at all, so most of her cousins speak to them in English. When my friend's family arrived in Seoul for the family reunion and were greeted by relatives, one of her cousins proudly explained that he had prepared a wonderful *PPT* for their family reunion. None of them knew what this meant, but they were excited to find out. It turns out, the cousin had put together a heart-warming slideshow of family pictures throughout the years, including pictures of cousins, aunts, and uncles back into their childhoods.

최근, 미국에서 태어나고 자란 제 한국계 미국인 친구 중 한 명이 지인 결혼식과 가족 모임을 위해 20 여 년 만에 처음으로 남편과 아이들과 함께 한국으로 돌아갔다. 그녀는 기본적인 수준의 한국어를 말할 수 있지만, 그녀의 남편과 아이들은 한국어를 전혀 하지 못해서 그녀의 사촌들 대부분은 영어로 그들과 이야기했다. 친구의 가족이 가족 모임을 위해 서울에 도착해서 친척들로부터 인사를 받았을 때, 그녀의 사촌 중 한 명이 그들의 가족 상봉을 위해 멋진 피피티를 준비했다고 자랑스럽게 말했다. 그들 중 아무도 이것이 무엇을 의미하는지 몰랐지만 그것이 무엇일까 기대하고 있었다. 알고 보니, 그 사촌은 그들의 어린 시절의 사촌, 이모, 삼촌들의 사진을 포함하여 수년 동안 가족 사진을 모아 감동적인 슬라이드쇼를 준비했던 것이었다.

SF 에스에프

Meaning in American English:
미국식 영어로 의미:

SF often means San Francisco.
SF 는 주로 샌프란시스코를
의미합니다.

Say Instead:
미국식 영어로 말할려면:

Science fiction, Sci-fi

Konglish Sentence	American English
I love a *SF* novel.	I love *science fiction* books. I love *sci-fi* novels.

나는 에스에프(S.F)소설을 좋아해.

Additional Info:
그 외:

SF is not a widely used or recognized abbreviation for Americans. Many people might guess San Francisco. It can sometimes be used for a variety of very specific abbreviations in unique fields. For example, *sf* can be used to show "square feet" in a measurement of area when written; however, people would still say "square feet" when reading it rather than the abbreviation. There also seem to be some very small groups of people in the United States who use SF in written English online in very specific fan groups of science fiction. This is a small minority of people. I have never personally come across an American speaking the letters "SF" to mean "science fiction." It is much more common to say "sci-fi." Most Americans would not understand what you are trying to say if you say "SF."

SF 는 미국인들에게 널리 쓰이거나 알려진 약어가 아니다. 많은 사람이 샌프란시스코(San Francisco)라는 뜻으로 사용한다. 그것은 때때로 독특한 분야에서 매우 구체적인 다양한 약어로 사용될 수 있다. 예를 들어, SF 는 면적 측정에서 '평방 피트'를 나타내기 위해 사용될 수 있다. 이 약어를 사용한다고 해도, 그것을 읽을 때 약어 대신 "평방피트"라고 말할 것이다. 미국에는 아마도 매우 구체적인 공상과학 팬 그룹에서 온라인에서 쓰인 영어로 SF 를 사용하는 매우 작은 그룹의 사람들이 있을 수 있다. 이것은 소수의 사람이다. 저는 개인적으로 공상과학을 의미하기 위해 "SF"라는 글자를 사용하는 미국인을 만나 본 적이 없다. "sci-fi"라고 말하는 것이 훨씬 더 일반적이다. 만약 여러분이 "SF"라고 말한다면 대부분의 미국인은 여러분이 말하려고 하는 것을 이해하지 못할 것이다.

How Americans use SF:
미국인들이 "SF"를 사용하는 법:

29

Kk ㅋㅋ

Meaning in American English:

미국식 영어로 의미:

K or Kk can mean "okay"

오케이라는 뜻

Say Instead:

미국식 영어로 말할려면:

Haha(hahaha) or Lol

Konglish Sentence	American English
Kkkkkkk.	*Hahahahahaha.*
ㅋㅋㅋㅋㅋㅋㅋ.	

TT OR TT TT ㅠㅠ

Meaning in American English:

미국식 영어로 의미:

Doesn't exist

이 단어는 존재하지 않습니다

Say Instead:

미국식 영어로 말할려면:

:(

Konglish Sentence		American English
I'm sorry TT.	⟹	I'm sorry :(
미안해 ㅠㅠ.		

Meaning in American English:
미국식 영어로 의미:

  ^^ Look up at something already previously written
  ^^ 이미 작성한 것을 다시 체크하다

Say Instead:
미국식 영어로 말할려면:

  :)

Konglish Sentence		American English
Hello ^^.	⟹	Hello :)
안녕하세요^^.		

Real Life Story:
실화:

I once had a Korean boss. She emailed me some important information and wrote ^^ in a sentence at the end of the email. I kept rereading the whole email trying to find what details she wanted me to look at again. I couldn't find anything I might have been missing. I finally asked a Korean friend what ^^ meant, and she told me it was basically a smiley face. We started laughing as I told her I was so stressed trying to figure out what information "above" in the email my boss wanted me to find. I had no idea my boss was just being friendly and typing a :) to me.

예전에 한국인 사장과 일한 적이 있었다. 그녀는 나에게 몇 가지 중요한 정보를 이메일로 보냈고 이메일 끝에 문장으로 ^^라고 표시했다. 그녀가 나에게 어떤 세부 사항을 다시 체크해 보기를 원하는지 찾기 위해 이메일을 계속 읽어보았지만 무엇을 놓쳤는지 찾을 수 없었다. 결국 한국 친구에게 ^^가 무엇을 의미하는지 물어봤는데 웃는 표정을 표현한 거라고 말해주었다. 직장 상사가 위 내용을 다시 읽어보라는 줄 알고 스트레스받았다고 말했을 때 우리는 웃기 시작했다. 나는 상사가 단지 친절하게 :) 이모티콘을 사용한 것인지 전혀 몰랐다.

2

FOOD & DRINKS
음식 & 음료

▶ Scan for Audio!

AMERICANO 아메리카노

Meaning in American English:
미국식 영어로 의미:

A specific type of espresso drink made by adding water to espresso
에스프레소에 물을 타서 만든 특정 종류의 에스프레소 커피 종류

Say Instead:
미국식 영어로 말할려면:

Coffee, Drip coffee

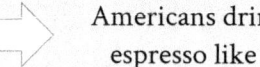

Konglish Sentence	American English
Americans drink *Americano*, not espresso like many Koreans.	Americans drink *drip coffee*, not espresso like many Koreans.

미국 사람들이 마시는 아메리카노는 한국사람들이 마시는 에스프레소 같지 않다.

Life & Culture in the USA:
미국의 삶과 문화:

Stories say that the name *Americano* came from World War II. When the American soldiers went to Europe to fight with the Allies, most Europeans they encountered, especially Italians, drank espresso, which was much stronger than what the Americans were used to. To solve this problem, they added water to the espresso to make it weaker tasting. They started calling this new drink an *Americano* because it's what the American soldiers usually preferred to drink.

'아메리카노'라는 단어는 제 2 차 세계 대전때 유래되었다고 합니다. 미국 군인들이 다른 동맹국들과 싸우기 위해 유럽으로 갔을 때, 대부분의 유럽 군인들, 특히 이탈리아인들은 미국인들에게 익숙한 커피 보다 훨씬 더 진한 에스프레소를 마셨습니다. 이 문제를 해결하기 위해 에스프레소에

물을 타서 맛이 덜 진하도록 만들었습니다. 이 새로운 음료를 아메리카노라고 부르기 시작했는데 그 이유는 그 커피를 미군들이 더 좋아했기 때문입니다.

Real Life Story:
실화:

Once, a student went to a coffee shop and ordered an iced Americano. An American lady walked up to her and said, "What's that?" Shocked that the American didn't know what an Americano was, my student answered, "It's an iced Americano, of course." The American still didn't know what an Americano was. "Is it good?" she asked. At this point, the barista said to the American lady, "An Americano is two shots of espresso with hot water added. Don't drink it. It's really bitter and doesn't taste good." While some Americans drink Americanos, it is not the most popular drink. Many Americans drink coffee brewed in a machine (drip coffee). Then many people add cream and/or sugar. The process for American style coffee is a bit different than espresso. Even if you add water to your espresso, the taste will be slightly different if you compare an *Americano* with an American drip coffee. But of course, many Americans have different preferences as to how they like their coffee.

한 학생이 커피숍에 가서 아이스 아메리카노를 주문한 적이 있습니다. 한 미국인 여성이 다가와서 "그게 뭐죠?"라고 말했고 그 미국인이 아메리카노가 무엇인지 모른다는 사실에 충격을 받은 제 학생은 "당연히 얼음 들어있는 아메리카노요"라고 대답했습니다. 그 미국인은 여전히 아메리카노가 무엇인지 몰랐습니다. "맛있나요?"라고 그녀가 물었습니다. 이때 바리스타가 그 미국인 여성에게 "아메리카노는 에스프레소 두 샷에 뜨거운 물을 부은 것입니다. 정말 쓰고 맛이 없으니 마시지 마세요."라고 말했습니다. 일부 미국인은 아메리카노를 마시지만, 미국에서는 대중적이지 않은 커피입니다. 많은 미국인은 커피 기계로 우려낸 커피(드립 커피)를 마시며 보통 설탕이나 크림을 넣어 마십니다. 미국식 커피는 에스프레소와는 만드는 과정이 조금 다릅니다. 에스프레소에 물을 넣는다고 해도 드립 커피와 맛의 차이가 있습니다. 물론 많은 미국인들이 커피를 좋아하는 것에 대해 다른 선호를 가지고 있습니다.

BAR 바 (술집)

Meaning in American English:
미국식 영어로 의미:

A place that serves drinks and alcohol. This can include a drinks-only bar like a bar at a beach where you can order alcoholic drinks. This can also include traditional bars or family-friendly bars where you can order a drink and some bar food (like burgers, wings, fries, nachos). This can also include more modern bar and grills where you can order a drink and food - basically like a restaurant that is open late and has a good alcoholic drink menu.

This can also include beer gardens, a growing trend in the US that is styled off of German-style beer gardens, where you can order drinks from an incredible beer list and specialty food (depending on the particular place) and enjoy the beautiful outdoor (and sometimes indoor) seating area often with games, scenery, plants, and lots of tables. Basically a bar is anywhere where the alcohol is the main item. A bar can also mean the bar area of a restaurant, where you can sit on stools in front of the bar counter rather than at a proper table or booth.

음료와 술을 제공하는 곳. 술을 주문할 수 있는 해변의 바와 같은 음료 전용 바를 포함할 수 있습니다. 이것은 음료와 약간의 음식(햄버거, 닭날개, 감자튀김, 나초등)을 주문할 수 있는 전통적인 바 또는 가족 친화적인 바도 포함할 수 있습니다. 늦은 시간까지 문을 열고 좋은 술 메뉴가 있는 레스토랑같은 음료와 음식을 주문할 수 있는 더 현대적인 바와 그릴도 포함할 수 있습니다.

미국에서 증가하고 있는 독일식 스타일 맥주 정원도 포함할 수 있으며, (특정 장소에 따라) 아주 많은 맥주 종류와 특별한 음식과 음료를 주문하고 게임, 풍경, 식물 및 많은 테이블이 있는 아름다운 야외 좌석 공간(때로는 실내)을 즐길 수 있습니다. 기본적으로 술이 주 메뉴인 곳이라면 어디든 바라고 할 수 있습니다. 바는 레스토랑의 바 구역을 의미할 수 있는데, 식탁이나 부스 대신 카운터 앞 의자에 앉을 수 있는 곳을 뜻합니다.

Say Instead:
미국식 영어로 말하려면:

Lounge, Club, Over 21 bar, Adults-only bar

Konglish Sentence	American English
I was shocked when an American friend told me you can take your kids to the *bar*, but when we went I realized it was just a hop.	I was shocked when an American friend told me you can take your kids to the *lounge/club*, but when I went, I realized it was just a bar and grill for all ages.

친구가 당신이 아이들을 바에 데려가도 된다고 말했을 때 나는 충격을 받았지만, 우리가 갔을 때 나는 그것이 단지 음료수를 파는 곳임을 깨달았다.

How Americans use Bar:
미국인들이 "Bar"를 사용하는 법:

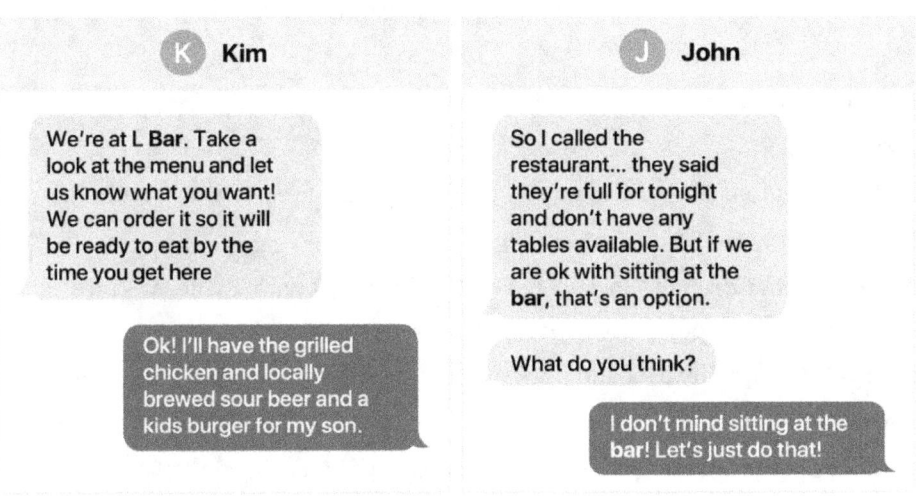

Kim

We're at L **Bar**. Take a look at the menu and let us know what you want! We can order it so it will be ready to eat by the time you get here

Ok! I'll have the grilled chicken and locally brewed sour beer and a kids burger for my son.

John

So I called the restaurant... they said they're full for tonight and don't have any tables available. But if we are ok with sitting at the **bar**, that's an option.

What do you think?

I don't mind sitting at the **bar**! Let's just do that!

BBQ 비비큐

Meaning in American English:
미국식 영어로 의미:

Correct for writing, but B-B-Q is rarely spoken. People say "barbecue."
BBQ 라고 쓸수는 있지만 말할때 절대 사용하지 않으며 "barbecue"라고
말합니다.

Say Instead:
미국식 영어로 말할려면:

Barbecue

Konglish Sentence	American English
We ate *B-B-Q*.	We ate *barbecue*.
우리는 바베큐를 먹었다.	

Additional Info:
그 외:

Different regions have different styles of BBQ. Here are a few characteristics:

Texas - usually beef, usually served with a spicy, smoky, garlicy sauce

North & South Carolina - usually pork, usually served with a vinegar sauce

Memphis - usually pork, usually served without sauce

Kansas City - usually beef and pork, usually served with a sweet tangy sauce
with a ketchup base

각 주마다 BBQ 의 스타일이 다릅니다. 몇 가지를 소개합니다:

텍사스 - 보통 쇠고기, 매콤하고 숯향이 나는 마늘 소스와 함께
제공됩니다

노스 & 사우스 캐롤라이나 - 보통 돼지고기, 식초 소스와 함께
제공됩니다

멤피스 - 보통 돼지고기, 소스 없이 제공됩니다

캔자스 시티 - 보통 쇠고기와 돼지고기, 케첩 베이스와 새콤달콤한
소스와 함께 제공됩니다

CAN MAEKJU 캔맥주

Meaning in American English:
미국식 영어로 의미:

Doesn't exist

이 단어는 존재하지 않습니다

Say Instead:
미국식 영어로 말할려면:

Canned beer

Konglish Sentence	American English
Do you prefer *can maekju*, bottled beer, or live beer?	Do you prefer *canned beer*, bottled beer, or beer on tap?

당신은 맥주, 병맥주, 아니면 생맥주 중 어느 것을 더 좋아합니까?

CHICKEN 치킨

Meaning in American English:
미국식 영어로 의미:

The live animal chicken or any food from
this animal
살아있는 닭 또는 닭고기

Say Instead:
미국식 영어로 말할려면:

Fried chicken

Konglish Sentence	American English
We always eat *chicken* on Fridays.	We always eat *fried chicken* on Fridays.

우린 금요일마다 치킨을 먹는다.

How Americans use Chicken:
미국인들이 "Chicken"을 사용하는 법:

 Wife

Don't buy eggs at the
store! I have some!

What? How did you get
eggs? I thought you
were at Callie's house?

Callie & Ted have 10
chickens they're raising
in their backyard! They
gave me a dozen fresh
eggs to take home!

 Shante

We're finally going to try
L's Grill this weekend!
What did you like there?

Their garlic grilled
chicken is sooooo good!

CHOCO(L) 초코 (초콜)

Meaning in American English:
미국식 영어로 의미:

Doesn't exist; the pronunciation of 초콜 sounds a bit like "charcoal" which means the black carbon blocks used to start a fire or grill

이 단어는 존재하지 않습니다. 불을 피우거나 구울 때 사용되는 검은 탄소 덩어리를 의미하는 "charcola"과 발음이 약간 비슷하게 들립니다.

Say Instead:
미국식 영어로 말할려면:

Chocolate

Konglish Sentence	American English
Do you want a *choco* bar?	Do you want a *chocolate* bar?
초코바 먹을래?	

CIDER 사이다

Meaning in American English:
미국식 영어로 의미:

1. *Hard cider* is an alcoholic drink from apples
    Hard cider 는 사과로 만든 알코올이 들어간 음료
2. *Hot cider* is a winter holiday drink - often homemade and made from apple juice and spices simmered together
    Hot cider 는 겨울 특별 음료- 주로 집에서 직접 만들고 향신료와 함께 끓여 만든 사과 주스
3. *Apple cider* is an unfiltered and less-processed version of apple juice
    Apple cider 는 여과되지 않고 가공되지 않은 사과 주스

Cider could be any of these depending on the context.
'사이더'는 상황에 따라 이 중 하나일 수 있습니다.

Say Instead:
미국식 영어로 말할려면:

Sprite, 7UP

Konglish Sentence	American English
Cider is great because it doesn't have alcohol and can help your stomach feel better. It's also great for kids. Americans often drink *cider* when they are sick.	*Sprite* is great because it doesn't have alcohol and can help your stomach feel better. It's also great for kids. Americans often drink *Sprite* or *7UP* when they are sick.

사이다는 알코올이 들어가 있지 않기 때문에 소화에 도움을 준다. 아이들에게도 좋다. 미국에서는 배가 아플때 사이다를 먹기도 한다.

Real Life Story:
실화:

I once had a student who often golfed with colleagues on the weekend when he lived in the United States, and they all had an ongoing friendly competition. One particular day he was determined to win, so he devised a simple plan. While his colleagues all ordered beer, he would order cider. "All my colleagues will be affected by the alcohol, but I will have an advantage since cider isn't alcoholic," he schemed proudly to himself. When he received the bottle of *cider*, he saw that the bottle looked similar to a beer bottle and thought, "Wow, I guess cider in the United States has a glass bottle! It must be much nicer here!"

After a few bottles of cider, he noticed that his score hadn't improved much, and he was feeling a little tipsy. "It must be the heat outside today," he guessed. He had no idea that *cider* in the United States isn't a Sprite-like drink and sometimes has around 4-5% alcohol, similar to beer. Needless to say, he didn't have much of an advantage in golfing that day.

예전에 한 학생이 말해준 이야기입니다. 어느날 미국에 있는 몇몇 동료들과 함께 퍼팅 레인지에 골프치러 갔습니다. 그와 그의 동료들은 계속해서 시합을 했습니다. 그는 경기에서 반드시 이기고 싶어했고 좋은 생각을 하게 되었습니다. 그의 동료들이 모두 맥주를 주문하는 동안, 그는 사이다를 주문했습니다. '모든 동료들이 그 술에 영향을 받겠지만, 사이다는 알코올 성분이 없기 때문에 나는 유리한 점이 있을 것이다'라고 자신을 자랑스럽게 생각했습니다. 그가 사이다 병을 받았을 때, 그 병이 맥주병과 비슷하게 생긴 것을 보고, '와, 미국에선 사이다도 유리병에 주는구나! 진짜 좋다.'라고 생각했습니다.

사이다를 몇 병 마시고 나서 점수가 별로 좋아 지지 않았고 약간 취기를 느꼈습니다. '오늘 날씨가 더워서 그런거야'라고 생각했습니다. 그는 미국에서 사이다가 스프라이트 같은 음료가 아니라 알코올이 4-5% 들어간 것 술이라는 것을 몰랐습니다. 말할 것 도 없이 그 날 골프를 칠 때 유리한 점이 별로 없었습니다.

COLA/KOLA 콜라

Meaning in American English:
미국식 영어로 의미:

Doesn't exist alone

이 단어는 존재하지 않습니다

Say Instead:
미국식 영어로 말할려면:

Coke, Coca-Cola

Konglish Sentence	American English
I'd like a *cola* to drink.	I'd like a *coke* to drink.

콜라 주세요.

Life & Culture in the USA:
미국의 삶과 문화:

In the USA, there are some regional differences for talking about these drinks:

Soda - in the West and Northeast

Pop - in the Midwest and West

Soda pop - in New York and some places in the West

Cold drink - some places in the South

Soft drink - in the South and some places on the East coast

Coke - the South. (This is the most confusing. "Do you want a coke?" "Yes, please. What kind do you have?" "We have Coke, Sprite, Fanta,...")

미국에서는 이러한 음료를 지역에 따라 다르게 말합니다:

소다 - 서부와 북동부 지역

팝 - 중서부와 서부

소다팝 - 뉴욕과 서부의 몇몇 지역

콜드 드링크 - 남부의 몇몇 지역

소프트 드링크 - 남부 및 동해안 일부 지역

코크 - 남부. (이게 제일 헷갈리네요. "콜라 드릴까요?" "네, 어떤 종류가 있나요?" "콜라, 사이다, 환타,...")

COMBI 콤비

Meaning in American English:
미국식 영어로 의미:

Doesn't exist

이 단어는 존재하지 않습니다

Say Instead:
미국식 영어로 말할려면:

Supreme pizza

Half [cheese] half [pepperoni]

A good pair or a good combo

Konglish Sentence	American English
My favorite pizza is *combi* pizza.	My favorite pizza is *supreme* pizza.

내 최애는 콤보 피자이다.

COMBO SET 콤보세트

Meaning in American English:
미국식 영어로 의미:

> *Combo* can have the same meaning, but *set* is usually used for something that isn't food. For example, *a combo tool set* is a set of tools with some combinations of different items in the set. For food or a meal, *combo set* would sound confusing.
>
> '콤보'는 같은 의미를 가질 수 있지만, '세트'는 보통 음식이 아닌 것에 사용됩니다. 예를 들어, 콤보 도구 세트는 여러가지 도구가 묶음으로 되어있음을 뜻합니다. 음식이나 식사의 경우, '콤보 세트'는 혼란스럽게 들릴 것입니다.

Say Instead:
미국식 영어로 말하려면:

> Combo, Meal

Konglish Sentence	American English
Thanks for your hamburger order at LBurger. Would you like to make that a *combo set* or just the burger?	Thanks for your order at LBurger. Would you like to make that a *meal/combo* or just the burger?

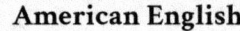

LBurger 시켜주셔서 감사합니다. 콤보로 시키겠어요, 아님 햄버거만 드시겠어요?

CREAM PASTA 크림 파스타

Meaning in American English:
미국식 영어로 의미:

Doesn't exist

이 단어는 존재하지 않습니다

Say Instead:
미국식 영어로 말할려면:

Alfredo pasta, Fettuccine Alfredo, Pasta with creamy sauce

Konglish Sentence	American English
That restaurant has a good *cream pasta.*	That restaurant has good *Alfredo pasta.*

그 레스토랑은 크림 파스타가 맛있다.

HOP/HOF 호프

Meaning in American English:
미국식 영어로 의미:

1. (Noun) Hop - A little jump
   (명사) 작은 점프
2. (Verb) To make a short jump or leap
   (동사) 짧게 뛰거나 도약하기
3. (Noun) Hops - the specific flowers
   you use to make beer
   (명사) 홉 - 맥주를 만들 때 사용하는 특정 꽃

Say Instead:
미국식 영어로 말할려면:

Bar, Pub

Konglish Sentence	American English
We like going to *hop* after work.	We like going to *bars* after work.
일 끝나고 호프집에 가는 걸 좋아한다.	

How Americans use Hop:
미국인들이 "Hop"를 사용하는 법:

 Shariq's Birthday Plans

> Hey! What's the plan for tonight?

We have dinner reservations at 7:15 and then afterwards, we will bar **hop** downtown.

 TJ

> How's life in New York?!

I love living in NYC! But I really miss having a car and the freedom to **hop** in and drive anywhere I want!

*Note: A bar hop or bar hopping is an activity where a group of people visits several different bars in a short time period, usually having one drink at each bar before going on to the next place.

참고사항: 바 홉 또는 바 호핑에서는 여러 개의 다른 바를 짧을 시간에 다닐 수 있고 다음 바로 가기 전에 한 잔정도 마시고 가능 경우가 많다.

HOT DOG 핫도그

Meaning in American English:
미국식 영어로 의미:

A sausage in a soft bun, usually with condiments like mustard and ketchup and other toppings
보통 머스타드와 케첩과 다른 토핑을 얹은 부드러운 빵에 들어가 있는 소시지

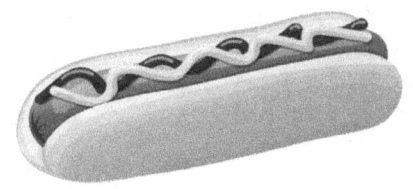

Say Instead:
미국식 영어로 말할려면:

Corn dog, Korean hot dog, Korean corn dog

Konglish Sentence		American English
I love *hot dogs* because they are on a stick and are easy to eat.		I love *corn dogs* because they are on a stick and are easy to eat.

나는 핫도그가 막대기에 달려있어 먹기 쉬워서 좋다.

Additional Info:
그 외:

Typical hot dog topping are mustard, ketchup, mayo, cheese, relish, onions, sauerkraut or coleslaw, and sometimes chili. Obviously you can be as creative as you'd like, but some combination of these (not usually all of those together) is most common.

전형적인 핫도그 토핑은 머스타드, 케첩, 마요네즈, 치즈, 렐리쉬, 양파, 사우어크라우트 또는 콜슬로, 그리고 때때로 칠리입니다. 원하는 것을 넣어서 먹을 수 있지만, 이것들의 일부 섞어 먹는것이 가장 일반적입니다 (일반적으로 모든 것을 다 함께 먹는 것은 아님).

ICE BAR 아이스 바

Meaning in American English:
미국식 영어로 의미:

Doesn't exist

이 단어는 존재하지 않습니다

Say Instead:
미국식 영어로 말할려면:

Popsicle, Ice cream bar

Konglish Sentence	American English
Ice bars are really popular for kids in Korea in the summer.	*Popsicles* are really popular for kids in Korea in the summer.

한국에선 여름에 아이스바가 아이들에게 인기가 좋다.

JELLY 젤리

Meaning in American English
미국식 영어로 의미:

Similar to jam
잼과 유사합니다

Say Instead:
미국식 영어로 말할려면:

Gummies, Gummy bears, Jello

Konglish Sentence		American English
Kids love *jelly*.	⟹	Kids love *gummies/jello*.
애들은 젤리를 좋아한다.		

Konglish Sentence		American English
I love taking *jelly* vitamins.	⟹	I love taking *gummy* vitamins.
난 젤리 비타민을 좋아한다.		

Additional Info:
그 외:

Many Americans aren't totally sure of the difference between jelly and jam. Some people use these words interchangeably. Technically, jelly is made with no seeds or pieces of fruit. Jam, on the other hand, can have small pieces of fruit or seeds.

미국인들 대부분은 젤리와 잼의 차이점에 대해 잘 모릅니다. 어떤 사람들은 이 단어들을 바꿔서 사용합니다. 엄밀히 말하자면, 젤리는 씨앗이나 과일 조각이 없는 것이고 잼은 작은 과일 덩어리나 씨앗이 들어 있을수 있습니다.

How Americans use Jelly:
미국인들이 "Jelly"를 사용하는 법:

Jenny

I made peanut butter and **jelly** sandwiches to take with us for lunch on our hike today.

Awesome! I can bring some fruit and nuts to snack on

BFF

What are you going to bring tomorrow?

I think I'm going to bring some cream cheese mixed with jalapeno **jelly** with crackers.

LIVE BEER 생맥주

Meaning in American English:
미국식 영어로 의미:

Doesn't exist; sounds like beer that is alive
이 단어는 존재하지 않습니다. 마치
살아있는 맥주처럼 들립니다.

Say Instead:
미국식 영어로 말할려면:

Draft beer, Beer on tap

Konglish Sentence	American English
That bar has good *live beer*. $\Longrightarrow$	That bar has good *draft beer*.
이 바는 맛있는 생맥주가 있다.	

Konglish Sentence	American English
I'd like to order *live beer*. $\Longrightarrow$	I'd like to order a *draft beer*.
생맥주 주세요.	

Konglish Sentence	American English
What *live beers* do you have? $\Longrightarrow$	What beers do you have *on tap*?
어떤 생맥주 있나요?	

LUNCHBOX 런치박스

Meaning in American English:
미국식 영어로 의미:

The box where you put your lunch for work or school, but this is only the reusable box or bag, not necessarily the food

직장이나 학교에서 도시락을 넣어 두는 박스. 재사용 가능한 상자나 가방이지 반드시 음식은 아닙니다.

Say Instead:
미국식 영어로 말할려면:

Lunch

Konglish Sentence	American English
He brought his *lunchbox* to work. ⟹	He brought his *lunch* to work.
런치박스를 일하는 곳에 가져왔다.	

How Americans use Lunchbox:
미국인들이 "Lunchbox"를 사용하는 법:

 Oldest Son

> Son, where's your **lunchbox**? I can't find it.

> Sorry... I left it in my locker at school today

> Ok. I'll pack your lunch in a paper bag tomorrow. Make sure you bring your **lunchbox** home plz

 Youngest Son

> Mom, I found a dinosaur **lunchbox** online. It's fire and only $20. Can I buy it?

> No. Maybe for your birthday present...

MENU 메뉴

Meaning in American English:
미국식 영어로 의미:

The whole list of food items and drinks offered by a restaurant. In English, it doesn't make sense to say, "What menu did you order?"
식당에서 제공하는 음식과 음료의 전체 목록. 영어로 "어떤 메뉴를 주문했어?"라고 말하면 이해하지 못합니다.

Say Instead:
미국식 영어로 말할려면:

What did you order? Name of item on a menu

Konglish Sentence	American English
What *menu* did you order?	What did you order?

무슨 메뉴 시키셨어요?

Additional Info:
그 외:

It's common for a Korean student to say, "What menu did you order at that restaurant?" This is a very confusing question for an American. There is only one menu. The menu is the list of all items and dishes that you can order. So it doesn't make sense to ask, "What menu did you order?" If you want to ask this question, you can ask, "What did you order?" or "What did you get?"

한국 학생들이 자주하는 말 "What menu did you order?" 이런 질문은 미국인에게 매우 혼란스러운 질문입니다. 메뉴는 오직 하나입니다. 메뉴는 주문할 수 있는 모든 품목과 요리의 목록입니다. 그래서 "What menu did you order?"라고 묻는 것은 말이 되지 않습니다. 이 질문을 하고 싶다면 "What did you order?" 또는 "What did you get?"라고 물을 수 있습니다.

How Americans use Menu:
미국인들이 "Menu"를 사용하는 법:

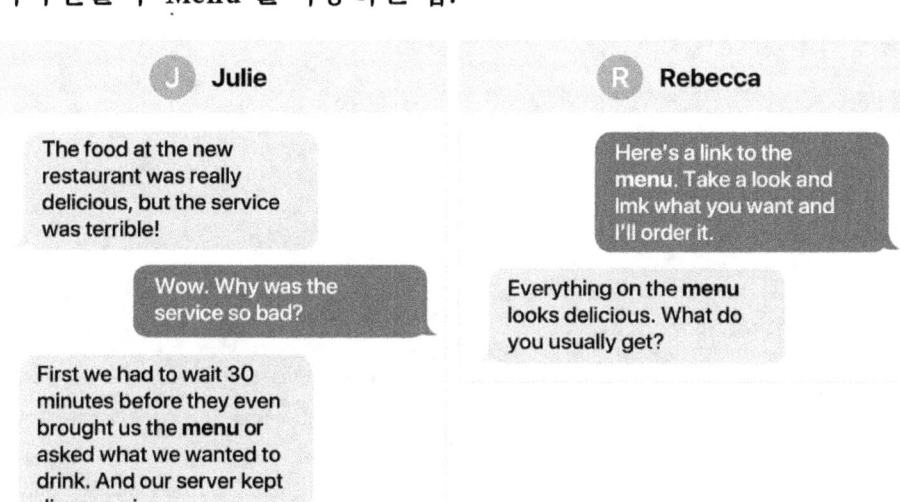

ONE SHOT 원샷

Meaning in American English:
미국식 영어로 의미:

Literally means one shot (not two or three or four...)

말 그대로 한 잔을 의미합니다 (두 세 네 잔이 아니라...)

Say Instead:
미국식 영어로 말할려면:

Chug (*for beer or bigger drinks* 맥주 또는 더 큰 음료)

Shoot (*for a shot* 한 방에)

Do a shot, Take a shot

Cheers!

Konglish Sentence		American English
You have to drink soju *one shot*.		You have to *take a shot* of soju. You have to *do a shot* of soju.
소주는 원샷이다.		

SAND 샌드

Meaning in American English:
미국식 영어로 의미:

The sand at the beach
모래

Say Instead:
미국식 영어로 말할려면:

Stuffed cookie, Sandwich cookie, Chocolate Sandwich cookie,...

Egg sandwich, tofu sandwich, ... *(for sandwiches, say the full name* 샌드위치를
말할 때 어떤 것인지 이름 전체를 말해야한다)

Konglish Sentence	American English
At the beach, they sell good *sand*.	At the beach, they sell good *ice cream sandwiches/ sandwich cookies/ stuffed cookies.*
해변가에서 좋은 샌드를 판다.	

How Americans use Sand:
미국인들이 "Sand"를 사용하는 법:

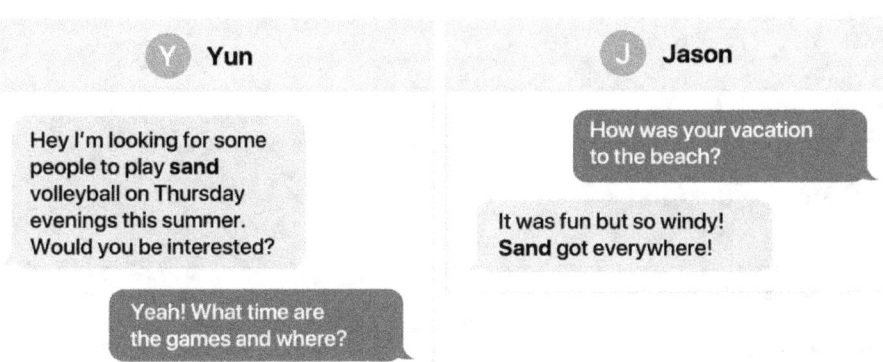

Yun

Hey I'm looking for some people to play **sand** volleyball on Thursday evenings this summer. Would you be interested?

Yeah! What time are the games and where?

Jason

How was your vacation to the beach?

It was fun but so windy! **Sand** got everywhere!

(SALAD) SAUCE (샐러드) 소스

Meaning in American English:
미국식 영어로 의미:

Sauce is a large category of tasty liquids that are often used for dipping food, pouring over food, or as the liquid that a dish is cooked in to give it flavor. It almost never refers to something you put over salad. That is specifically called *dressing* or *salad dressing*. For example, some dipping sauces would include soy sauce to eat with sushi or soy bean paste (*ssamjang*) eaten with meat. For pouring over food, an example would be a chimichurri *sauce* poured over a steak or a Hollandaise *sauce* poured over an eggs benedict breakfast. Food cooked in *sauce* would include spaghetti made with tomato *sauce,* or a meat dish might be cooked in a wine reduction *sauce*.

소스는 음식에 담그거나, 음식 위에 붓거나, 이미 요리된 음식에 맛을 내기 위해 사용되는 맛있는 액체를 뜻합니다. 샐러드 위에 얹는 것이라고 거의 사용하지 않고 그것은 구체적으로 '드레싱' 또는 '샐러드 드레싱'이라고 불립니다. 예를 들어, 찍어먹는 소스 중엔 초밥과 함께 먹는 간장이나 고기와 함께 먹는 쌈장이 있습니다. 음식 위에 붓는 소스의 예로는 스테이크 위에 부어 먹는 치미추리 소스나 계란 베네딕트 아침식사 위에 부어 먹는 홀란드제 소스가 있습니다. 소스로 요리된 음식은 토마토 소스로 만든 스파게티를 말하거나, 와인 소스를 담궈 만든 고기요리도 있습니다.

Say Instead:
미국식 영어로 말할려면:

Salad dressing (for salad)

Konglish Sentence		American English
Do you put *sauce* on your salad? I always use *sauce*.		Do you put *salad dressing* on your salad? I always use *dressing*.
샐러드에 소스 넣는 걸 좋아하나요? 저는 항상 넣어요.		

How Americans use Sauce:
미국인들이 "Sauce"를 사용하는 법:

Roommate

Hey! I already left but there are some dumplings in the fridge!

> Wow! Thanks! That sounds amazing!

I also made some **sauce** to go with them. It's brown-ish and in a small container in the fridge

Yvonne

How do you usually cook salmon?

> I usually pan-sear it on the stove or bake it in foil in the oven

> And I make a lemon butter **sauce** to drizzle over it before serving

SAUCE CHICKEN 양념치킨

Meaning in American English:
미국식 영어로 의미:

Doesn't exist

이 단어는 존재하지 않습니다

Say Instead:
미국식 영어로 말할려면:

Korean-style wings, Korean-style fried chicken with sauce, Korean chicken

Konglish Sentence	American English
We love eating *sauce chicken* after work.	We love eating *Korean-style wings / fried chicken with sauce* after work.

우리는 일 끝나고 양념치킨 먹는 걸 좋아한다.

YOGURT 요구르트

Meaning in American English:
미국식 영어로 의미:

Yogurt
요거트

Say Instead:
미국식 영어로 말할려면:

Probiotic yogurt drink, Liquid probiotic yogurt

Konglish Sentence	American English
I noticed that many stores in the USA only sell Yoplait but not *yogurt.*	I noticed that many stores in the USA only sell yogurt and not *liquid probiotic yogurt.*

미국에선 요거트는 팔지만 요구르트는 없다.

YOPLAIT 요플레

Meaning in American English:
미국식 영어로 의미:

One brand of yogurt

요거트 제품 브랜드

Say Instead:
미국식 영어로 말할려면:

Yogurt

Konglish Sentence	American English
I noticed that many stores in the USA only sell *Yoplait* but not yogurt.	I noticed that many stores in the USA only sell *yogurt* and not liquid probiotic yogurt.
미국에선 요거트는 팔지만 요구르트는 없다.	

ZERO COLA 제로 콜라

Meaning in American English:
미국식 영어로 의미:

Doesn't exist

이 단어는 존재하지 않습니다

Say Instead:
미국식 영어로 말할려면:

Diet Coke, Coke Zero

Konglish Sentence	American English
Do you have a *zero cola*?	Do you have a *Diet Coke*?
제로 콜라 있나요?	

3

CLOTHING & FASHION
옷과 패션

Scan for Audio!

BIG SIZE 빅사이즈

Meaning in American English:
미국식 영어로 의미:

  Big

  크다

Say Instead:
미국식 영어로 말할려면:

  Plus size

Konglish Sentence	American English
Do you sell *big size* here?	Do you sell *plus size* clothes here?

큰 사이즈 있나요?

BURBERRY / BURBERRY CHECK MUNI
버버리 / 버버리 체크무늬

Meaning in American English:
미국식 영어로 의미:

The specific brand Burberry

특정 브랜드 버버리

Say Instead:
미국식 영어로 말할려면:

Trench coat

Konglish Sentence	American English
I love her *Burberry.*	I love her *trench coat.*
그 여자 버버리 멋있다.	

COMBI-STYLE 콤비 스타일

Meaning in American English:

미국식 영어로 의미:

Doesn't exist

이 단어는 존재하지 않습니다

Say Instead:

미국식 영어로 말하려면:

Pants with different colored jacket/blazer

Sports coat and slacks

Slacks and a jacket/blazer

Business casual

Konglish Sentence	American English
What should men wear to the party? *Combi-style* is good.	What should men wear to the party? *Slacks and a jacket* is good.

남자는 그 파티에 어떻게 입고 가야할까? 콤비 스타일이면 좋지.

COUPLE LOOK 커플룩

Meaning in American English:
미국식 영어로 의미:

Doesn't exist

이 단어는 존재하지 않습니다

Say Instead:
미국식 영어로 말할려면:

They match.

They are matching.

They have matching outfits.

Konglish Sentence	American English
Oh cute! I like their *couple look*!	Oh cute! They are *matching*! I like their *matching outfits*!

너무 귀엽다! 커플룩이 넘 이뻐보여!

DRESS 드레스

Meaning in American English:
미국식 영어로 의미:

The general word for all types of women's
dresses including casual dresses
바지가 아닌 모든 유형의 드레스: 드레스,
원피스

Say Instead:
미국식 영어로 말할려면:

Formal dress or specific name (wedding dress)

Konglish Sentence	American English
You shouldn't wear a *dress* to a casual restaurant.	You shouldn't wear a *formal dress* to a casual restaurant.

캐주얼한 레스토랑에는 드레스를 입으면 안돼.

Additional Info:
그 외:

In American English, a dress is a broad category of clothing. It includes all styles from very casual to very formal.

If you are really into fashion, there are hundreds of names for specific styles of dresses in English. However, the general public typically doesn't use most of them.

A few that every woman should know, per the author's opinion, include: casual dress, cocktail dress, backless dress, formal dress, evening gown, knee-length dress, floor-length gown, lace dress, tunic dress, strapless dress, sleeveless dress, maxi dress, sun dress, and seer-sucker.

미국 영어에서 드레스는 광범위한 뜻을 가지고 있다. 매우 캐주얼한 것부터 매우 격식 있는 것까지 모든 스타일을 포함합니다.

만약 여러분이 정말로 패션에 관심이 있다면, 영어로 된 특정 스타일의 드레스 이름들이 수 백 개가 있습니다. 하지만, 일반 적으로 다 사용하지는 않습니다.

제 생각에 모든 여성이 알아야 할 몇 가지는 캐주얼 드레스, 칵테일 드레스, 백리스 드레스, 정장 드레스, 이브닝 드레스, 무릎까지 오는 드레스, 바닥까지 오는 드레스, 레이스 드레스, 튜닉 드레스, 스트랩리스 드레스, 민소매 드레스, 맥시 드레스, 선 드레스, 사각형 무늬 드레스입니다.

FREE SIZE 프리 사이즈

Meaning in American English:
미국식 영어로 의미:

Doesn't exist

이 단어는 존재하지 않습니다

Say Instead:
미국식 영어로 말할려면:

One size fits all

Konglish Sentence	American English
These one pieces are *free size*.	These dresses are *one size fits all*.

이 원피스는 프리 사이즈야.

Real Life Story:
실화:

Once, I was shopping in Hawaii at a swap meet or flea market. I came across a vendor with cute dresses. I loved the designs. I asked the Korean owner, "What sizes do you have in these?"

"Free size," he answered. Confused, I looked at my husband expecting him to know. He's Hawaiian. I thought maybe it was a Hawaiian phrase. But he didn't know either.

"Only one size," the shop owner said. "One size for everybody." I understood. He meant, "One size fits all."

The next week back in Houston, a Korean student said the same phrase, "free size." This time, I knew what it meant.

하와이에 있는 벼룩시장에서 쇼핑한 적이 있습니다. 귀여운 드레스를 입은 노점상을 우연히 발견했습니다. 저는 그 드레스 디자인들이 마음에 들었습니다. 한국인 주인에게, "이것들은 어떤 사이즈들이 있나요?"라고 물었습니다. "프리 사이즈"라고 그는 대답했습니다. 저는 약간 혼란스러워서 남편이 알기를 기대하며 쳐다보았습니다. 남편은 하와이 사람입니다. 저는 그것이 하와이에서 사용되는 표현이라고 생각했습니다. 그러나 그도 역시 몰랐습니다. "한 사이즈만"이라고 가게 주인은 말했습니다. "모두를 위한 한 사이즈". 주인의 말은, "한 사이즈가 모두에게 맞습니다"라는 것이었습니다. 그다음 주 휴스턴에서, 한 한국 학생이 "프리 사이즈"라고 말했습니다. 이번에는 그것이 무엇을 의미하는지 알았습니다.

GOLDEN/CORDON PANTS 골덴바지

Meaning in American English:

미국식 영어로 의미:

Doesn't exist; pants that are gold in color

이 단어는 존재하지 않습니다. 황금색 바지

Say Instead:

미국식 영어로 말할려면:

Corduroy pants

Konglish Sentence	American English
Golden pants aren't very popular these days. 	*Corduroy pants* aren't very popular nowadays.
요즘 골덴바지는 그렇게 유행하지 않는다.	

GOWN 가운

Meaning in American English:

미국식 영어로 의미:

1. A very nice formal dress
   정장, 드레스
2. A hospital gown for patients
   병원 환자 가운
3. A night gown
   잠옷 가운

Say Instead:

미국식 영어로 말할려면:

Robe

Doctor's coat, Lab coat, White coat

Konglish Sentence		American English
The doctor looked professional in his *gown*.		The doctor looked professional in his *white coat*.
그 의사 가운이 멋있어 보인다.		

Konglish Sentence		American English
She always wears a *gown* at home on the weekends.		She always wears a *robe* at home on the weekends.
그녀는 항상 집에서 가운을 입고 있는다.		

How Americans use Gown:
미국인들이 "Gown"을 사용하는 법:

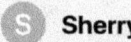 **Sherry**

What classifies as "formal attire"? I have no idea what to wear this weekend to the wedding.

A lot of people have been asking because that usually means ball **gowns** and tuxedos.

I asked John. He said it's more like semi-formal. Look nice, but no need to wear a fancy **gown** or tux.

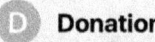 **Donation Center**

What types of items does the medical charity need most right now?

They're asking for donations for any PPE: masks, caps, and **gowns**

HALF COAT 하프코트

Meaning in American English:

미국식 영어로 의미:

Doesn't exist

이 단어는 존재하지 않습니다

Say Instead:

미국식 영어로 말할려면:

Coat

Konglish Sentence	American English
I got a new *half coat* for the winter.	I got a new *coat* for the winter.
나 이번 겨울에 새로운 하프코트 샀어.	

JACKU 자크

Meaning in American English:
미국식 영어로 의미:

Doesn't exist

이 단어는 존재하지 않습니다

Say Instead:
미국식 영어로 말할려면:

Zipper

Konglish Sentence		American English
My *jacku* is broken.	⇒	My *zipper* is broken.
내 자크가 고장났어.		

JUMPER 점퍼

Meaning in American English:
미국식 영어로 의미:

1. A girls' outfit that is a dress with a shirt underneath
   점퍼스커트; 밑에 셔츠가 있는 드레스인 여아 옷

2. A person who jumps
   점프하는 사람

3. Jumper cables help jump start your car if it breaks down
   자동차가 점프 시동을 걸 수 있도록 도와주는 점퍼 케이블

Say Instead:
미국식 영어로 말할려면:

Jacket, Coat

Konglish Sentence		American English
I really like your *jumper*. Where did you get it?		I really like your *jacket*. Where did you get it?
네 점퍼가 이쁘다. 어디서 샀어?		

MUFFLER 머플러

Meaning in American English:
미국식 영어로 의미:

An important part in your car that helps make it more quiet

자동차의 머플러 (소음기)

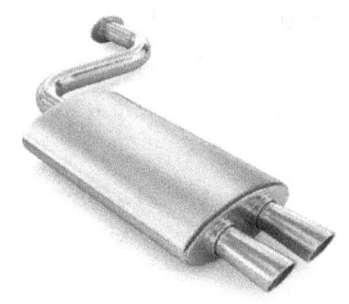

Note: There are some areas of the US where muffler is also used to mean a winter scarf; however, a large number of Americans are not familiar with this and would understand a car part instead.

*참고: 미국에는 머플러가 겨울 스카프라는 뜻으로 사용되는 지역도 있지만, 많은 미국인들이 이에 대해 잘 모르며 대신 자동차 부품으로 이해할 것입니다.

Say Instead:
미국식 영어로 말할려면:

Scarf

Konglish Sentence		American English
I'm going to give her a *muffler* for her birthday.		I'm going to give her a *scarf* for her birthday.
그녀에게 머플러를 생일 선물로 줄 것이다.		

Real Life Story:
실화:

In college, I had a great Korean friend. One year, for my birthday, she told me that she had asked her mom to mail me a special gift from Korea, but it hadn't arrived on time. She said she couldn't find the style in the U.S. that she liked, so she had her mom pick out a muffler for me from Korea. I smiled and thanked her for her kind thought and reassured her that I didn't mind waiting for it to arrive.

When I thought about it later that evening, all I could think was, "What is a muffler?" The only kind of muffler I knew about was the kind that is in your car. I wasn't even totally sure what *that* muffler was. I just knew that you didn't want it to break. Obviously, she wasn't mailing me a car part for my birthday. Maybe it was a special kind of Korean mittens for the winter?

Later, when the gift arrived, I opened the box and found a beautiful winter scarf.

대학생 때 친한 한국 친구가 있었습니다. 어느 해 제 생일을 맞아 그녀 어머니에게 한국에서 특별한 선물을 저에게 우편으로 보내달라고 부탁했지만, 그것은 제시간에 도착하지 않았다고 말했습니다. 친구는 여기에서 자신이 좋아하는 스타일을 찾을 수 없어서, 어머니에게 한국에서 머플러를 골라달라고 했습니다. 저는 미소를 지으며 어머니의 친절한 생각에 감사를 표했고, 머플러가 도착하기를 그날 저녁 늦게 생각해 보았는데, 오직 떠오르는 것은 '머플러란 무엇인가?'뿐이었습니다. 제가 아는 유일한 종류의 머플러는 차 부품입니다. 심지어 그 머플러가 무엇인지 완전히 확신하지 못했습니다. 친구는 그것이 부서지는 것을 원하지 않았습니다. 분명히 친구는 제 생일을 위해 자동차 부품을 우편으로 보내는 것이 아니었습니다. 아마도 그것은 겨울을 위한 특별한 종류의 한국식 벙어리 장갑이었던 것일까요?

나중에 선물이 도착했을 때, 저는 상자를 열었고 아름다운 겨울 스카프를 발견했습니다.

How Americans use Muffler:
미국인들이 "Muffler"를 사용하는 법:

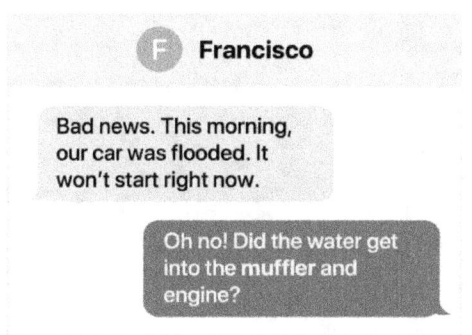

ONE PIECE 원피스

Meaning in American English:
미국식 영어로 의미:

Swimsuit that is all one, not a bikini
비키니가 아닌 하나로 된 수영복

Say Instead:
미국식 영어로 말할려면:

Dress

Konglish Sentence	American English
She's wearing a one piece to the party.	She's wearing a *dress* to the party.

그녀는 파티에서 원피스를 입고있습니다.

Real Life Conversation:
실생활 대화:

Here is a conversation I once had with a Korean student:
한국 학생과 나눈 대화는 다음과 같습니다:

Me - What are you going to wear to the party tomorrow?
나 - 내일 파티에 뭐 입을 거예요?

Student - I'm going to wear a one piece.
학생 - 원피스를 입을 거예요.

Me - Oh? It's a swimming party?
나 - 어? 수영 파티라고요?

Student (looking confused) - No. It's not a swimming party.
학생 (혼란스러운 표정) - 아니요. 수영 파티가 아닙니다.

Me (looking confused) - It's not? Then why are you wearing a swimsuit if it's not a swimming party?

나 - 아니야? 근데 왜 수영복을 입고 간다고 했어? 수영 파티도 아닌데?

Student (more confused) - I'm not wearing a swimsuit tomorrow!

학생 (더 헷갈림) - 내일 수영복 안 입어요!

Me (more confused) - What? I'm confused. You said you were wearing a one piece tomorrow?

저 (더 혼란스러움) - 뭐라고요? 헷갈리네요. 내일 원피스를 입고 오신다고요.

PADDING 패딩

Meaning in American English:
미국식 영어로 의미:

Extra cushion, usually from soft material like cloth, crumbled paper products like paper towels, tissues, or newspaper, or any other soft fluffy material. It is usually used to provide protection or comfort or *padding* around an object. For example, "We don't want the nice glass vase to break during the move. Let's make sure we put a lot of padding around it for protection. We can wrap it in paper towels and then wrap it in a blanket."

여분 쿠션은 보통 천과 같은 부드러운 소재, 종이 타월, 티슈, 신문지와 같은 바스러진 종이 제품, 또는 다른 부드러운 솜털 소재로 만들어집니다. 그것은 보통 보호나 편안함을 제공하거나 물체에 '패딩'을 하기 위해 사용됩니다. 몇 가지 예는 "우리는 이동 중에 좋은 유리 꽃병이 부서지는 것을 원하지 않습니다. 보호를 위해 많은 패딩을 그 주변에 넣읍시다. 꽃병을 종이 타월로 감싼 다음 담요로 감쌀 수 있습니다."

Say Instead:
미국식 영어로 말할려면:

Puffer jacket, Puffy jacket, Down jacket

Konglish Sentence	American English
I'm surprised that people here are wearing Burberrys. In Korea, we usually wear *paddings* in this weather.	I'm surprised that people here are wearing trench coats. In Korea, we usually wear *puffer jackets* / *down jackets* in this weather.
여기 사람들은 버버리 입고 있어서 깜짝 놀랐어. 이 날씨에 한국에서는 패딩을 입는데 말이야.	

Additional Info:
그 외:

Down jacket - specifically a jacket that is filled with down, a soft fluff from ducks or geese

다운 재킷 - 특히 오리나 거위의 부드러운 솜털, 다운으로 채워진 재킷

Puffy or puffer jacket - this can be similar to a down jacket but can also use synthetic filling instead of down feathers from animals. This kind of jacket uses the stitching to make different rows of quilted pockets or segments that help give it the fluffy puffy look.

퍼피 재킷 - 이것은 다운 재킷과 비슷할 수 있지만 또한 동물에서 나오는 것 대신 합성 충전재를 사용할 수도 있습니다. 이런 종류의 재킷은 바느질을 사용하여 누빔 주머니 또는 부분의 다양한 열을 만들어 폭신하고 부풀어오게 합니다.

Padded jacket - not used much in American English

패딩 재킷- 미국 영어에서 많이 사용되지 않음.

How Americans use Padding:
미국인들이 "Padding"을 사용하는 법:

M **Moving Company**

Do you use moving blankets or bubble wrap to protect the furniture?

Our company provides **padding** and wrapping for all large items

---

to: Me <Camper@greatcampingtrips.com>

subject: Camping at the Canyons

We look forward to hosting you on the Canyons Camping Trip. Below you will find some information about what to expect and what to bring.

We provide all guests with sleeping bags and mats for the overnight camping. Many of our guests bring their favorite pillow for comfort at night, and others bring extra *padding* to go underneath their sleeping bags. You are always welcome to pack your own sleeping gear if you wish to use your own rather than ours.

PANTY 팬티

Meaning in American English:
미국식 영어로 의미:

Typically only women's underwear (and always plural: panties)

일반적으로 여성만을 위한 속옷 (그리고 항상 복수로 사용)

Say Instead:
미국식 영어로 말할려면:

Panties (*for women* 여성에게만)

Underwear, briefs, boxers (*for men* 남성에게만)

Konglish Sentence	American English
These are my husband's *panty*.	These are my husband's *underwear/boxers*.

이거 내 남편 속옷이야.

Other English Uses:
기타 영어 사용:

To *get your panties in a bunch* is an idiom that means to become upset about or overly emotional or worried about something meaningless and trivial.

"It's really stupid and not a big deal, but for some reason my panties are still in a bunch about it all. It's really bothering me."

의미 없고 사소한 것에 대해 화를 내거나 지나치게 감정적이거나 걱정하는 것을 의미하는 관용구이다.

"진짜 바보같고 암껏도 아닌데 그것 때문에 계속 화가나. 진짜 신경쓰여."

PANTY STOCKINGS 팬티 스타킹

Meaning in American English:
미국식 영어로 의미:

Doesn't exist

이 단어는 존재하지 않습니다

Say Instead:
미국식 영어로 말할려면:

Pantyhose, Stockings

Konglish Sentence	American English
In the USA, *panty stockings* were really popular in the 1980s, but now they aren't very popular.	In the USA, *pantyhose/stockings* were really popular in the 1980s, but now they aren't very popular.

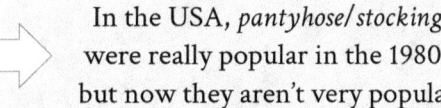

미국에서 팬티 스타킹은 1980 년도에 유행했지만 지금은 그렇지 않다.

Additional Info:
그 외:

Pantyhose - These are usually quite thin and go up to your waist. They are usually footed and fit over your feet.

Pantyhose 는 보통 상당히 얇고 발부터 허리까지 올라갑니다.

Stockings - These are similar to pantyhose but usually only go to the top of each leg. They are worn separately on each leg, like very tall socks.

Stockings - 팬티스타킹과 비슷하지만 보통 각 다리의 윗부분까지만 올라가며 매우 큰 양말처럼 각 다리에 따로 신습니다.

Tights - These are similar to pantyhose but are usually much thicker (e.g., ballet tights). They are often worn in dance or under other clothes, but aren't usually worn by themselves.

Tights - 이것들은 팬티스타킹과 비슷하지만 보통 훨씬 더 두껍습니다 (예:

발레 타이즈). 그것들은 종종 춤출때 입거나 다른 옷 안에 입지만, 보통 혼자 입지는 않습니다.

Leggings - These are the thickest options. They are un-footed and do not cover the feet. Nowadays, many women wear leggings in the place of pants for every day comfortable use.

Leggings- 제일 두껍다. 발까지 이어지지 않는다. 요즘 일상에서 바지 대신 많이 입는다.

POLAR T 폴라티

Meaning in American English:
미국식 영어로 의미:

Doesn't exist

이 단어는 존재하지 않습니다

Say Instead:
미국식 영어로 말할려면:

Turtleneck

Konglish Sentence	American English
Some people think *polar Ts* are fashionable, but I don't agree.	Some people think *turtlenecks* are fashionable, but I don't agree.

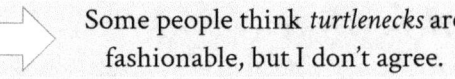

어떤 사람들은 폴라티가 멋있다고 하지만 난 그렇게 생각 안 해.

SCHOOL JUMPER 학교 점퍼

Meaning in American English:

미국식 영어로 의미:

A girls' school uniform (see Jumper)

여자 아이 유니폼 (점퍼 단어 참조)

Say Instead:

미국식 영어로 말할려면:

Letter jacket

Konglish Sentence	American English
The high school students were all wearing their *school jumpers* at the party.	The high school students were all wearing their *letter jackets* at the party.

고등학교 학생들이 파티 때 학교 점퍼를 입었다.

Life & Culture in the USA:

미국의 삶과 문화:

In the US, a letter jacket, or sometimes letterman jacket, is considered an honor to be earned. To earn and get a letter jacket from your school, you have to "letter" or achieve a certain award or level before you can receive the patch and buy the jacket. Sports are one of the most common ways to earn this jacket. In most schools, if you make a varsity level sports team, you can earn a "letter" and buy this letter jacket. However, there are many other awards that can help you qualify - for example, achievements in band, orchestra, academic competition teams, and other clubs and activities. Traditions can vary by state and school.

미국에서 레터 재킷, 또는 레터맨 재킷은 수상의 영광으로 여겨집니다. 학교에서 레터 재킷을 받기 위해 패치를 받고 재킷을 살 수 있기 전에 상을 받거나또는 특별한 수준을 달성해야 합니다. 스포츠는 이 재킷을 얻을 수 있는 가장 일반적인 방법 중 하나입니다. 대부분의 학교에서 대표팀으로 선발 된다면 레터 재킷을 살 수 있습니다. 밴드, 오케스트라, 학술 경시대회 팀, 그리고 다른 클럽과 활동에서의 성과와 같은 여러분의 자격을 갖추는데 도움을 줄 수 있는 많은 다른 상들이 있습니다. 주와 학교에 따라 전통이 다를 수 있습니다.

SEPARATE CODI 세퍼레이트 코디

Meaning in American English:
미국식 영어로 의미:

Doesn't exist

이 단어는 존재하지 않습니다

Say Instead:
미국식 영어로 말하려면:

Mix and match (colors and styles)

Konglish Sentence	American English
Spring is the season when people love to do *separate codi* with vibrant colors.	Spring is the season when people love to *mix and match vibrant colors and styles.*

봄은 사람들이 색이 선명한 코디를 분리하는 것을 좋아하는 계절이다.

S SIZE

Meaning in American English:
미국식 영어로 의미:

S is used only in writing. When speaking, people say Small.

S 는 영어에서 말로 표현하지 않고 글로만 사용됩니다.

Say Instead:
미국식 영어로 말할려면:

Small

Konglish Sentence	American English
She wears *S size*.	She wears a *small*.

그녀는 스몰 사이즈를 입는다.

M SIZE

Meaning in American English:
미국식 영어로 의미:

M is used only in writing. When speaking, people say Medium.

M 은 영어에서 말로 표현하지 않고 글로만 사용됩니다.

Say Instead:
미국식 영어로 말할려면:

Medium

Konglish Sentence	American English
I need *M size*.	I need a *medium*.

나는 미디엄 사이즈가 필요해요.

L Size

Meaning in American English:
미국식 영어로 의미:

L is used only in writing. When speaking, people say Large.

L 은 영어에서 말로 표현하지 않고 글로만 사용됩니다.

Say Instead:
미국식 영어로 말할려면:

Large

Konglish Sentence	American English
Can you buy *L size* for my dad? $\implies$	Can you buy a *large* for my dad?
아빠를 위해 라지 사이즈 살 수 있어?	

LL Size or 2L

Meaning in American English:
미국식 영어로 의미:

Doesn't exist

이 단어는 존재하지 않습니다

Say Instead:
미국식 영어로 말할려면:

Extra Large (XL)

Konglish Sentence	American English
Do you sell this shirt in *LL size*? $\implies$	Do you sell this shirt in *XL*?
엑스트라 특대 사이즈 티셔츠는 있나요?	

LLL SIZE OR 3L

Meaning in American English:
미국식 영어로 의미:

Doesn't exist

이 단어는 존재하지 않습니다

Say Instead:
미국식 영어로 말할려면:

Extra extra large (XXL or 2XL)

Konglish Sentence	American English
His shirt size is *3L/LLL*.	His shirt size is *2XL*.

그의 셔츠 사이즈는 3L 이다.

SHORT PANTS 반바지

Meaning in American English:
미국식 영어로 의미:

1. Pants that are too short
   짧은 바지

2. An older term for shorts. Most people will probably understand this, and there are certainly people who still use it; however, it sounds unnatural to many people as "shorts" is much more common.
   Shorts 의 오래된 용어입니다. 대부분의 사람들은 아마 이것을 이해할 것이고, 아직도 그것을 사용하는 사람들이 있습니다. 그러나 대부분의 사람들에게 'shorts'가 훨씬 더 일반적이기 때문에 그것은 부자연스럽게 들립니다.

Say Instead:
미국식 영어로 말할려면:

Shorts

Konglish Sentence	American English
You should wear your *short pants* to the zoo today.	You should wear *shorts* to the zoo today.
짧은 반바지 입고 동물원 오세요.	

SINGLE STYLE SUIT 수트

Meaning in American English:
미국식 영어로 의미:

Doesn't exist

이 단어는 존재하지 않습니다

Say Instead:
미국식 영어로 말할려면:

Suit

Konglish Sentence	American English
He usually wears a *single style suit* to the office.	He usually wears a *suit* to the office.

그는 보통 수트입고 출근한다.

SLIPPERS 슬리퍼

Meaning in American English:
미국식 영어로 의미:

Soft warm shoes that you only wear
inside the house, often in winter.
겨울에 가끔 집 안에서만 신는
부드럽고 따뜻한 신발입니다.

그것들은 한국 화장실에서 신는 신발과 다릅니다. 그것들은 보통 천이나
양모로 만들어졌고 방수가 되지 않습니다.

Say Instead:
미국식 영어로 말할려면:

Slides, Sandals

Konglish Sentence		American English
Please wear these *slippers* in the bathroom.		Please wear these *sandals/ slides* in the bathroom.
슬리퍼는 화장실에서만 쓰세요.		

How Americans use Slippers:
미국인들이 "Slippers"를 사용하는 법:

Ⓢ **Sister**

I'm thinking about getting dad a nice pair of warm **slippers**. Supposed to be one of the best for men, and he is always wearing **slippers** around the house. Do you think he'll use them if they are comfortable and warm?

Yeah! Great idea!

Ⓢ **Sandra**

I have the same bunny **slippers** as you!

Yay! So comfy!!

TRAINING BOK 트레이닝복

Meaning in American English:
미국식 영어로 의미:

Doesn't exist

이 단어는 존재하지 않습니다

Say Instead:
미국식 영어로 말할려면:

Track suit, Sweat suit, Jogging suit

Konglish Sentence	American English
I really like her new *training*.	I really like her new *track suit*.
나는 그 분의 새로운 훈련복이 정말 마음에 든다.	

TWO PIECE 투피스

Meaning in American English:
미국식 영어로 의미:

A bikini swimsuit

비키니 수영복

Say Instead:
미국식 영어로 말할려면:

Women's suit, Pantsuit, Skirt suit

Konglish Sentence	American English
She wore a *two piece* to the office for her first day of work.	She wore a *skirt suit* / *pantsuit* for her first day of work.

그녀가 처음으로 투피스입고 첫출근했어.

How Americans use Two Piece:
미국인들이 "Two Piece"를 사용하는 법:

 Adela

> Looking forward to the beach next week!

Same! I'm not wearing a **two piece**, but I'll bring a one piece and plenty of cover-ups to wear!

WALKER 워커

Meaning in American English:
미국식 영어로 의미:

A device that an older person uses to help them walk

보행보조기; 나이든 사람들이 걷는 것을 돕기 위해 사용하는 것

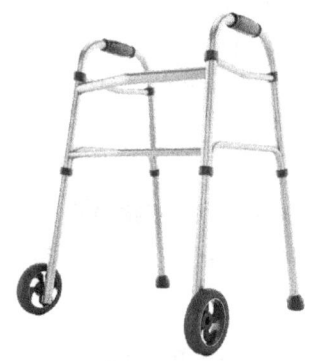

Say Instead:
미국식 영어로 말할려면:

Military style boots, Combat boots, Military boots

Konglish Sentence	American English
He has cool *walkers*.	He has cool *combat boots*.

그는 멋있는 워커가 있다.

How Americans use Walker:
미국인들이 "Walker"를 사용하는 법:

B Bianca

> What did y'all get for the baby shower gift?

> We bought them the baby **walker** from their gift registry

C Cousin

> How was the weekend with grandma?

> It was fun. I think we need to get her a new **walker**. She said she doesn't want a new one, but hers is basically falling apart at this point

Y SHIRT 와이 셔츠

Meaning in American English:
미국식 영어로 의미:

Doesn't exist

이 단어는 존재하지 않습니다

Say Instead:
미국식 영어로 말할려면:

Dress shirt, Button-up shirt, Button-down shirt

Konglish Sentence	American English
I can't find my *Y shirt*. I need it for work tomorrow.	I can't find my *white dress shirt*. I need it for work tomorrow.

나 와이셔츠 못 찼겠어. 내일 출근할 때 필요한데 말야.

4

ACCESSORIES
액세서리

CROSS BAG 크로스백/핸드백

Meaning in American English:
미국식 영어로 의미:

Doesn't exist

이 단어는 존재하지 않습니다

Say Instead:
미국식 영어로 말할려면:

Crossbody (bag)

Konglish Sentence	American English
I love her *cross bag*.	I love her *crossbody (bag)*.

난 크로스백을 좋아한다.

HAIR BAND 헤어 밴드

Meaning in American English:
미국식 영어로 의미:

Ponytail holder, hair tie
머리끈

Say Instead:
미국식 영어로 말할려면:

Headband

Sweatband

Konglish Sentence	American English
I want to buy that *hair band*. ⟹	I want to buy that *headband*.
나 저 헤어밴드 사고싶어.	

How Americans use Hair Band:
미국인들이 "Hair Band"를 사용하는 법:

 Jessica

> Do you remember who from the other team scored goals during the game last night?

> I can't remember for sure, but I know that the girl with the green **hair band** scored 2.

 Michelle

> The cat has stolen my **hair band** from my dresser 4 nights in a row, and I have no idea what she's doing with them or where she's taking them.

> Hahaha! My cat does the same thing! So crazy.

HAIR PIN 헤어 핀

Meaning in American English:
미국식 영어로 의미:

A bobby pin for your hair or one
specifically for hair styling
머리를 위한 바비핀 같은 납작한 것
또는 헤어 스타일링을 위한 것

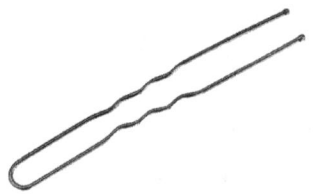

Say Instead:
미국식 영어로 말할려면:

Clip
Bobby pin
Barrette

Konglish Sentence	American English
Your *hair pin* is so nice. 	Your *hair clip* is so cool. I really like your *hair clip*.

너 헤어핀 예쁘다.

RIBBON 리본

Meaning in American English:
미국식 영어로 의미:

A long and narrow strip of fabric or material that is used to tie or make a bow or used for decoration
나비 모양으로 묶거나 만들 때나 장식에 사용되는 길고 좁은 천 또는 소재의 조각

Say Instead:
미국식 영어로 말할려면:

Bow, Hairbow
Bow tie

Konglish Sentence	American English
The pink *ribbon* in that baby's hair is so cute.	The pink *bow* in that baby's hair is so cute.

저 아기가 하고 있는 핑크 리본 귀여워.

How Americans use Ribbon:
미국인들이 "Ribbon"을 사용하는 법:

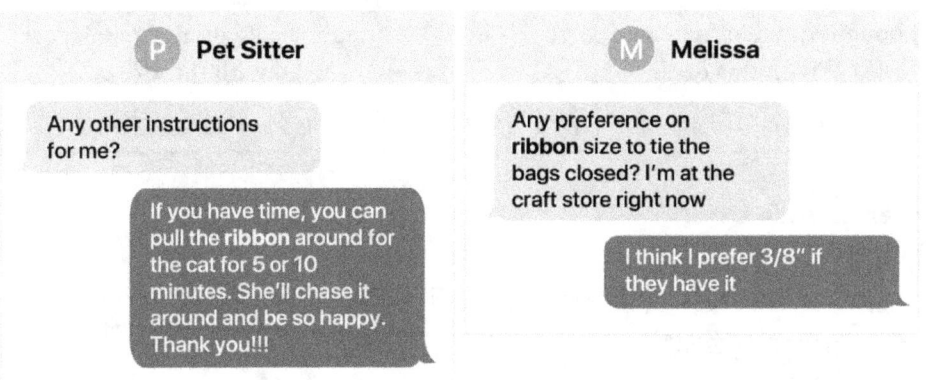

P Pet Sitter

Any other instructions for me?

If you have time, you can pull the **ribbon** around for the cat for 5 or 10 minutes. She'll chase it around and be so happy. Thank you!!!

M Melissa

Any preference on **ribbon** size to tie the bags closed? I'm at the craft store right now

I think I prefer 3/8" if they have it

SACK 쌕

Meaning in American English:
미국식 영어로 의미:

A large bag, usually without handles, usually doesn't close, usually very basic, not very nice, maybe dirty (e.g., a sack of potatoes, a sack of groceries, Santa's sack of toys)

보통 손잡이가 없는 큰 가방은 보통 닫히지 않습니다. 보통 아주 기본적인 거나 좋지 않거나 더럽습니다 (예: 감자 한 봉지, 식료품 한 봉지, 산타 갖고 다니는 장난감 한 봉지)

Say Instead:
미국식 영어로 말할려면:

Fanny pack, Crossbody fanny pack, Small backpack

Konglish Sentence	American English
I bought a cute orange *sack* to go with this dress.	I bought a cute orange *fanny pack* to go with this dress.
나는 이 드레스에 어울리는 귀여운 오렌지 색의 쌕을 샀다.	

Other English Uses:
기타 영어 사용:

There is an American idiom "Hit the Sack" that means "Go to bed"
'잠자러 가다'는 의미의 미국 관용구 'Hit the Sack'이 있습니다.

How Americans use Sack:
미국인들이 "Sack"을 사용하는 법:

 Community Center

Make sure your kids wear closed-toe shoes to the festival and clothes that can get dirty! There will **be sack** races for the kids and some other fun games. This is a traditional American activity where kids stand inside large burlap potato **sacks** and hop in a race to the finish line.

 Mira

Do you use a sleep **sack** for your baby?

Yes! We always use it during nap time!

5

MAKEUP & SKINCARE
매이크업 & 스킨케어

CUSHION 쿠션

Meaning in American English:
미국식 영어로 의미:

1. A pillow or soft pad usually used to sit on. For example, you might buy cushions to put on top of hardwood chairs to make them more comfortable. You can also buy a cushion-top mattress, a mattress that has a special cushioning pad on the top to make it softer and more comfortable.
    베게나 폭신한 방석같이 앉을 때 사용됩니다. 예를 들어, 나무 의자 위에 올려놓을 쿠션을 사서 의자를 더 편안하게 만들 수도 있습니다. 쿠션 탑 매트리스를 살 수도 있는데, 그것은 더 부드럽고 편안하게 만들기 위해 특별한 쿠션 패드가 있는 매트리스입니다.

2. A cushion can also be any soft thing that provides a softer barrier against something hard. You might buy cushion inserts for your shoes to make them softer and more comfortable.
    단단한 것에 대해 더 부드러움을 제공하는 것이 될 수 있습니다. 신발을 더 부드럽고 편안하게 만들기 위해 쿠션 삽입물을 구입할 수 있습니다.

Say Instead:
미국식 영어로 말할려면:

Wet dry foundation
Korean cushion foundation

Konglish Sentence	American English
I need to buy a new *cushion*. The maker I like discontinued the product.	I need to buy a new *Korean cushion foundation / wet dry foundation* for my face. The brand I like discontinued their product.

나 새 쿠션 사야해. 그 제품을 이제 만들지 않아.

How Americans use Cushion:
미국인들이 "Cushion"을 사용하는 법:

 Pet Sitter

We are going to your house now to feed the pets

Thank you!!! I left the house key under the **cushion** of the chair on the right side of the front door

 Alex

When you camp, do you just use a sleeping bag, or do you put anything under it like a mat?

We usually use a sleeping mat – it keeps you warmer and also gives you more **cushion** and makes it more comfortable so you aren't lying directly on the hard ground

EYE REMOVER 아이 리무버

Meaning in American English:
미국식 영어로 의미:

Doesn't exist; sounds like something torturous that will remove your eyes
이 단어는 존재하지 않습니다. 눈을 빼내는 고문할 때 쓰는 도구처럼
들립니다

Say Instead:
미국식 영어로 말할려면:

Makeup remover, Eye makeup remover

Konglish Sentence	American English
I usually use *eye remover* at night to take off my makeup.	I usually use *(eye) makeup remover* at night to take off my makeup.
밤에 화장을 지우기 위해 아이 리무버를 사용한다.	

MANICURE 매니큐어

Meaning of Manicure in American English:
미국식 영어로 의미:

The cosmetic treatment process of getting your nails done, usually at a nail salon. It includes cleaning, trimming, painting, filing, and sometimes massage. It could also include getting fake nails or tips or any other nail art.

보통 네일샵에서 손톱을 손질하는 미용 과정입니다. 손톱 청소, 손질, 색칠, 파일링, 그리고 가끔 마사지도 포함됩니다. 가짜 손톱이나 팁, 또는 다른 네일 아트를 받는 것도 포함될 수 있습니다.

Say Instead:
미국식 영어로 말할려면:

Nail polish

Konglish Sentence	American English
I like your *manicure* color a lot.	I like your *nail polish* a lot.
Your *manicure* color is so nice.	I love that *nail (polish)* color.

너 메니큐어 색깔 엄청 예뻐.

How Americans use Manicure:
미국인들이 "Manicure"를 사용하는 법:

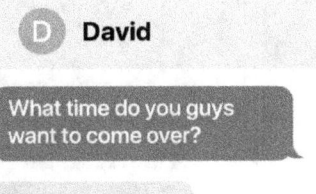

David

> What time do you guys want to come over?

The girls have a **manicure** in the morning, so we could go to your house after lunch. Does that work?

PACK 팩

Meaning in American English:
미국식 영어로 의미:

1. To put your things in boxes or suitcases for a move or a vacation
   이사나 휴가를 위해 상자나 여행 가방에 물건을 넣는 것
2. A group of products sold together in bulk (a pack of cigarettes, a pack of pencils, a pack of tissues)
   대량으로 함께 판매되는 제품(담배 한 갑, 연필 한다발, 휴지 한다발)

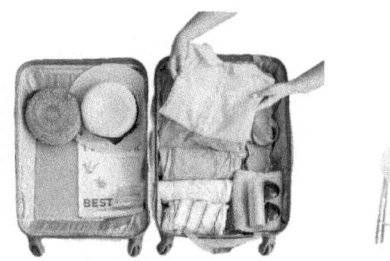  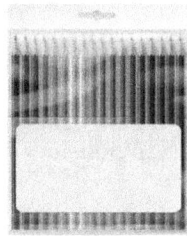

Say Instead:
미국식 영어로 말할려면:

To wrap (gifts), Face mask, Sandwich bag

Konglish Sentence		American English
Let's *pack* all the Christmas presents!		Let's *wrap* all the Christmas presents!
크리스마스 선물을 다 싸자!		

Konglish Sentence		American English
Korea is famous for its rejuvenating *packs*.		Korea is famous for its rejuvenating *facial masks*.
한국은 미용팩이 유명하다.		

Konglish Sentence	American English
Let's put the fruit in a *pack*.	Let's put the fruit in a *sandwich bag*.

우리 과일 팩에 넣자.

How Americans use Pack:
미국인들이 "Pack"을 사용하는 법:

 Alyssa

Should I **pack** shampoo and conditioner? Or do you think they'll have some at the hotel?

They'll probably have some at the hotel... or we can always just buy some once we're there...

 Marissa

I just ordered a **pack** of 100 masks, so let me know if you want any of them!

Yeah! Can we split the **pack** with you? We'll pay for half

RINSE 린스

Meaning in American English:
미국식 영어로 의미:

(Verb) To wash something lightly using only water. (E.g., "Rinse the soap off your hands after washing them." "Rinse the dishes before you wash them.")

(동사) 물만 사용하여 가볍게 씻는 것. (예. "손을 씻은 후 비누를 헹구세요." "설거지하기 전 물로 가볍게 헹구세요.")

Say Instead:
미국식 영어로 말할려면:

Conditioner

Konglish Sentence		American English
Some men don't use *rinse* for their hair.		Some men don't use *conditioner* for their hair.
어떤 남자들은 머리 감을 때 린스를 쓰지 않는다.		

How Americans use Rinse:
미국인들이 "Rinse"를 사용하는 법:

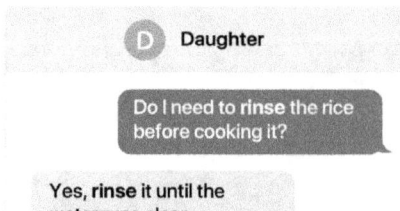

D Daughter

Do I need to **rinse** the rice before cooking it?

Yes, **rinse** it until the water runs clear

Make sure you rinse the dishes thoroughly after you wash them to make sure there's no soap left on them!! THANKS!

ROUS/ROUGE 루즈

Meaning in American English:
미국식 영어로 의미:

Doesn't exist

이 단어는 존재하지 않습니다

Say Instead:
미국식 영어로 말할려면:

Lipstick

Konglish Sentence	American English
I love your *rouge* color.	I love your *lip color*. I love your *lipstick color*.

네 루즈 색깔이 이쁘다.

SKIN 스킨, 토너

Meaning in American English:
미국식 영어로 의미:

The stuff that covers your body

피부

Say Instead:
미국식 영어로 말할려면:

Toner

Konglish Sentence	American English
My mom told me I should always use *skin* on my face at night.	My mom told me I should always use *toner* on my face at night.

우리 엄마는 밤에 스킨을 꼭 사용하라고 말씀하셨다.

How Americans use Skin:
미국인들이 "Skin"을 사용하는 법:

D Dinner Guests

Do you have a preference for chicken with the **skin** on or skinless chicken? I can make the dish either way

Either is ok! Whatever you think will taste better!

D Damian

I have to take my son to the doctor. He has some **skin** issues, so I think he might have eczema or an allergy to something

Oh no! that's the worst! Hopefully they can figure out what's causing it!

6

BODY & PHYSICAL APPEARANCE
몸 & 겉모습

BLACK EYES 블랙 아이

Meaning in American English:
미국식 영어로 의미:

Black is not usually used to describe eye color. If someone has very dark eyes, we usually describe them as "dark brown" but not black. Black eyes sounds like a robot with solid black eyes. Black eyes can also mean an injury to your eye when you get a bruise around your eye area. If we say, "He has a black eye," it sounds like maybe he got punched in the face or maybe hit with an item near his eye.

검은색은 보통 눈색깔을 표현하는데 사용되지 않습니다. 만약 누군가가 매우 어두운 눈을 가지고 있다면, 그것들을 "다크 브라운"이라고 표현하지만 검은색은 아닙니다. 검은 눈은 진한 검은 눈을 가진 로봇처럼 들릴지도 모릅니다. 검은 눈은 눈 주변에 멍이 들었을 때 눈의 부상을 의미할 수 있습니다. 만약 "그는 검은 눈을 가지고 있다"고 말한다면, 아마도 그가 얼굴에 주먹을 맞았거나 눈 근처를 어떤 물건에 맞았다는 것처럼 들릴 것입니다.

Say Instead:
미국식 영어로 말할려면:

Dark brown eyes

Konglish Sentence	American English
She has brown hair and *black eyes*.	She has brown hair and *dark brown eyes*.
그녀는 갈색 머리와 까만 눈동자를 가졌다.	

How Americans use Black Eyes:
미국인들이 "Black Eyes"를 사용하는 법:

 Friend

> She told me she's thinking about getting plastic surgery on her nose.

What? She has a nice nose! Also, I heard that if you have plastic surgery on your nose, you will have **black eyes** afterwards for a while...

 Bethany

> Great pics! What happened to your eye?!

My son elbowed me in the eye when I was picking him up the other day. Now I have a **black eye**

BODYLINE 바디라인

Meaning in American English:
미국식 영어로 의미:

Doesn't exist

이 단어는 존재하지 않습니다

Say Instead:
미국식 영어로 말할려면:

Figure, Shape

Konglish Sentence	American English
She has a good *bodyline*.	She has a good *figure*.
저 여자는 몸의 곡선이 예쁘다.	

Konglish Sentence	American English
I need to exercise to improve my *bodyline*.	I need to exercise to improve my *figure*.
나는 운동을 해서 이쁜 몸선을 만들어야 한다.	

DOUBLE EYELID 쌍커풀

Meaning in American English:
미국식 영어로 의미:

Literally means 'two eyelids.' This is a relatively new term and is becoming more widely accepted in the United States. Many people may still not be familiar with this term, and it may sound unnatural, perhaps like a deformity where someone has an extra eyelid or an extra eyelid membrane like dogs and cats have.

말 그대로 두 개의 눈꺼풀을 뜻한다. 미국에서 비교적 새롭게 뜨는 단어이다. 보통 사람들에게 익숙하지 않은 단어이고 강아지나 고양이의 여분의 눈꺼풀같이 기형처럼 눈꺼풀이 하나 더 있다고 들릴 수 있다.

Say Instead:
미국식 영어로 말할려면:

Eyelid crease, Crease in eyelid, Clearly-defined eyelid

Konglish Sentence	American English
I want to have *double eyelids* like Western people.	I want to have a *crease in my eyelid* like non-Asians.

난 외국 사람들처럼 쌍커풀이 있었으면 좋겠다.

Real Life Story:
실화:

A Korean friend of mine used to work as a hospital translator at a famous Korean hospital. Many times, Asian-Americans would come to this hospital in Korea to get eyelid surgery. My friend translated into English. "You are here for your double eyelid surgery." More than once, the American patients didn't know this term and felt afraid that maybe they had been scheduled for the wrong surgery.

내 친구 중 한 명은 한국의 유명한 병원에서 번역일을 했었다. 많은 아시아계 여성들이 그 곳에 와서 눈을 크게 만드는 수술을 했다고 한다. 영어로 번역할 때 "쌍커풀 수술 하러 오셨군요." 라고 말하면 미국 사람들은 이해하지 못하고 잘못된 수술을 잡은 건 아닌가 걱정했다고 한다.

GLAMOUR 글래머

Meaning in American English:

미국식 영어로 의미:

Beauty or charm or riches or fame, often that makes a person or place desirable or eye-catching

눈을 사로잡는 아름답거나 매력이거나 부유하거나 명성이 있는 사람이나 장소

Say Instead:

미국식 영어로 말할려면:

Curvy

Konglish Sentence		American English
People love *glamour* women nowadays.		People love *curvy* women nowadays.

요즘엔 글래머한 여성이 인기가 많다.

How Americans use Glamour:

미국인들이 "Glamour"를 사용하는 법:

Perla

I just got a job doing investment trading with a big company.

Wow! Fancy!

Haha, it's not as **glamorous** as it sounds

Diana

Here are some of the photos!

Wow! Those photos look so good! They look like **glamour** shots!

HIP 힙

Meaning in American English:
미국식 영어로 의미:

You have two hips on the sides. It includes the bones and joints where your femur connects to your pelvis. The back part is not usually called your hip.

옆구리에 두 개의 고관절이 있습니다. 이는 대퇴골이 골반과 연결되는 뼈와 관절을 포함합니다. 뒷부분(엉덩이)은 'hip'이라고 불리지 않습니다.

Say Instead:
미국식 영어로 말할려면:

Butt, Buttocks, Bottom, Behind, Backside, Derriere

Konglish Sentence	American English
She has a big *hip*.	She has a big *butt/behind*.
그녀는 큰 엉덩이를 가지고 있다.	

How Americans use Hip:
미국인들이 "Hip"을 사용하는 법:

 **Volunteer Buddy**

> Are you available to volunteer at the shelter next week?

Maybe... My aunt broke her left **hip** and might need **hip** replacement surgery. Waiting to find out the surgery date...

 Amir

> Do you ever bring your dog to the dog park?

Not really. Our dog was diagnosed with **hip** dysplasia and another disease that affects the **hips** and back legs so we can't let him do a lot of running :(

LOSE MY/YOUR WEIGHT 다이어트

Meaning in American English:
미국식 영어로 의미:

Doesn't exist

이 단어는 존재하지 않습니다

Say Instead:
미국식 영어로 말할려면:

Lose weight

Konglish Sentence

Did you *lose your weight*?
You look thin.

American English

Did you *lose weight*?
You look thin.

살 빠졌어? 말라보여.

Life & Culture in the USA:
미국의 삶과 문화:

In American culture, it is not usual to discuss or comment on weight. Although it can be common in Korean culture to make greeting comments like, "Did you lose weight? You look thin," or "You look healthy," this is not common in the U.S. It can be offensive or confusing and is considered inappropriate in work or professional settings. There are times when people talk about weight, and people will sometimes comment on their own weight; however, as a general rule, if you aren't sure, don't mention weight. It's a topic that's best to avoid.

미국 문화에서는 체중에 대해 토론하거나 언급하는 것이 일반적이지 않습니다. 한국 문화에서는 "살이 빠졌나요? 날씬해 보여요" 또는 "건강해 보여요"와 같은 인사말을 하는 것이 일반적일 수 있지만 미국에서는 일반적이지 않습니다. 이는 모욕적이거나 혼란스러울 수 있으며 직장이나 전문직 환경에서 부적절하다고 여겨집니다. 가끔 체중에 대해 말할 때가 있고, 때때로 자신의 체중에 대해 언급하기 도 합니다. 그러나 일반적으로 체중에 대해 언급하지 마십시오. 피하는 것이 가장 좋습니다.

OUTLOOK 아웃룩

Meaning in American English:
미국식 영어로 의미:

1. Attitude and view towards life and the future. "She has a positive outlook on things even though she has cancer and the situation is bad."
   인생과 미래에 대한 당신의 태도와 관점. "그녀는 암에 걸렸고 상황이 좋지 않음에도 불구하고 긍정적인 태도을 가지고 있습니다."

2. A viewpoint or place from which to see a good view
   좋은 경치를 볼 수 있는 장소

Say Instead:
미국식 영어로 말할려면:

Appearance, [He/she] looks...

Konglish Sentence		American English
Her *outlook* is bad today. Did she even take a shower?		She *looks* bad today. Did she even take a shower?

오늘 그녀의 아웃룩은 별로이다. 샤워를 하긴 한거야?

How Americans use Outlook:
미국인들이 "Outlook"을 사용하는 법:

Things to do in Panama:

- Old Town
- Pretty outlook point over the skyline
- Canal
- Rainforest

Thanks for being positive yesterday. I needed that. I hope you always keep your positive outlook on life. It makes me a better person.

S-LINE 에스라인

Meaning in American English:
미국식 영어로 의미:

Doesn't exist

이 단어는 존재하지 않습니다

Say Instead:
미국식 영어로 말할려면:

Hourglass figure

Konglish Sentence	American English
She has a perfect *S-line*.	She has an *hourglass figure*.

그녀는 완벽한 s 라인이 있다.

132

V-LINE 브이라인

Meaning in American English:
미국식 영어로 의미:

Doesn't exist

이 단어는 존재하지 않습니다

Say Instead:
미국식 영어로 말할려면:

Thin cheeks and a pointed chin, Heart-shaped face

Konglish Sentence		American English
Many [Korean] celebrities have plastic surgery to get a *V-line*.		Many Korean celebrities have plastic surgery to get *thinner cheeks and a pointed chin.*

많은 연예인들은 v 라인을 갖기 위해 성형 수술을 하다.

VISUAL 비주얼

Meaning in American English:
미국식 영어로 의미:

(Adjective) Related to seeing or being able to see. For example, a visual learner
is someone who learns best by seeing pictures, illustrations, or examples
(형용사) 시각과 관련이 있습니다. 예를 들어, 시각적 학습자는 그림,
삽화 또는 예시를 봄으로써 가장 잘 배우는 사람입니다

Say Instead:
미국식 영어로 말할려면:

Appearance, [He/she] looks...

Konglish Sentence	American English
His *visual* is really good today.	He *looks* really good today. His *appearance* is really sharp.

오늘 그의 비주얼은 최고다.

How Americans use Visual:
미국인들이 "Visual"을 사용하는 법:

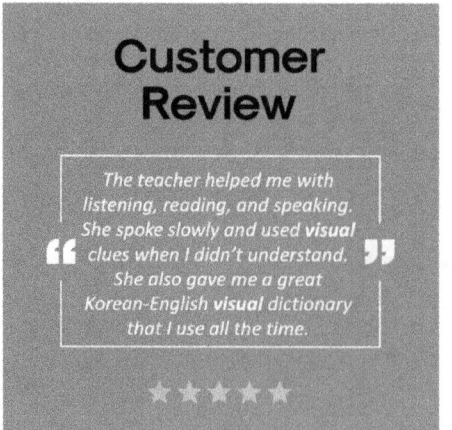

Customer Review

*The teacher helped me with listening, reading, and speaking. She spoke slowly and used **visual** clues when I didn't understand. She also gave me a great Korean-English **visual** dictionary that I use all the time.*

★★★★★

B Boyfriend

Did you watch the video of the comedian I sent?

Well, I read the transcript. I couldn't watch it bc the internet at the airport was too slow. Reading it wasn't very funny...

Yeah, you gotta have visuals when comedians are involved. Watch it later!

7

HEALTH
건강

Scan for Audio!

BALANCED MEAL 균형잡힌 식단

Meaning in American English:
미국식 영어로 의미:

One meal that has the right balance of nutrients and vitamins

영양소와 비타민의 균형이 잘 맞는 한끼

Say Instead:
미국식 영어로 말할려면:

Balanced diet

Konglish Sentence	American English
A *balanced meal* is good for health.	A *balanced diet* is good for you.
균형있는 식단은 몸에 좋다.	

BAND 밴드

Meaning in American English:
미국식 영어로 의미:

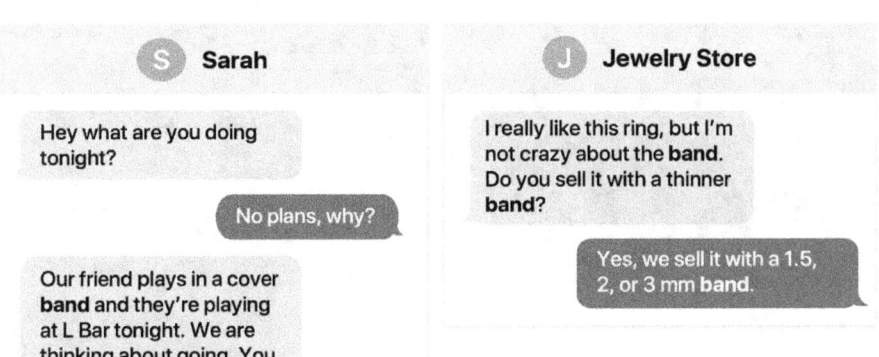

1. A musical group
   노래 그룹

2. A band can also be something flat or thin that wraps around something else (e.g., rubber band, watchband, wedding band).
   밴드는 무언가를 감싸는 평평하거나 얇은 것일 수도 있습니다. (예: 고무줄, 시계줄, 결혼반지 등).

Say Instead:
미국식 영어로 말할려면:

Band-Aid

Konglish Sentence	American English
Your cut is bleeding. Do you need a *band*?	Your cut is bleeding. Do you need a *Band-Aid*?

베인 곳에 피가 나오고 있어. 밴드 필요해?

How Americans use Band:
미국인들이 "Band"를 사용하는 법:

S Sarah

Hey what are you doing tonight?

> No plans, why?

Our friend plays in a cover **band** and they're playing at L Bar tonight. We are thinking about going. You should come with us too!

J Jewelry Store

I really like this ring, but I'm not crazy about the **band**. Do you sell it with a thinner **band**?

> Yes, we sell it with a 1.5, 2, or 3 mm **band**.

CHECK UP 첵엎

Meaning in American English:
미국식 영어로 의미:

Same meaning as in Korean, but it can only be used as a noun
한국어에서도 같은 의미지만, 오직 명사로만 사용될 수 있습니다

Say Instead:
미국식 영어로 말할려면:

Get a checkup

Konglish Sentence	American English
I *checked up* when I was in Korea because it's much cheaper to visit a doctor there.	I *got a checkup* when I was in Korea because it's much cheaper to go to the doctor there.

한국에서는 의료 검진이 더 싸기 때문에 검사 받고 왔어.

How Americans use Checkup:
미국인들이 "Checkup"을 사용하는 법:

 Steven

> Hey, are you busy next Tuesday? Grandpa has his yearly **checkup**. Can you drive him to his appointment?

> Sure! As long as I don't have a meeting, I can take him

 Grandma

> How's my great grandbaby?

> Good! Yesterday was her 6 month **checkup**. She's healthy and all updated on her vaccines.

CONDITION 컨디션

Meaning in American English:
미국식 영어로 의미:

- *Condition* can be used to describe things. (E.g., This chair for sale is in good condition. That house is in bad condition.)

  Condition 은 물건을 묘사하는 데 사용될 수 있습니다. (예: 이 판매용 의자는 상태가 좋습니다. 그 집은 상태가 좋지 않습니다.)

- *Condition* can be used to describe people only for long-term conditions, not just for today.

  Condition 은 오늘의 상태뿐만 아니라 장기적인 상태에 대해 사람들을 묘사하는 데 사용될 수 있습니다.

  - E.g., (*She has cancer and is looking thin and weak, and her hair is falling out*) "She is in pretty bad condition. We don't know if she will survive."

    예: (그녀는 암을 앓고 있고 매우 말랐으며 힘이 없어 보이고, 머리카락이 빠지고 있습니다.) "그녀 상태가 매우 좋지 않습니다. 그녀가 살 수 있을지는 아직 알 수 없습니다."

  - E.g., (*Someone had a bad car wreck and has many broken bones and is in the hospital*) "He is in bad condition, but we expect he will make a full recovery."

    예: (누군가가 나쁜 자동차 사고를 당했고 많은 뼈가 부러졌고 병원에 입원해 있습니다.) "그는 상태가 좋지 않지만 완전히 회복할 것이라고 예상합니다."

  - E.g., (*Someone recently had a heart attack and emergency surgery. He is recovering well in the hospital. The doctor is giving the family a report*) "He is in stable, good condition and should recover quickly. With a healthier diet in the future, he has a good prognosis."

    예: (누군가가 최근에 심장마비를 일으켰고 응급 수술을 받았습니다. 그는 병원에서 잘 회복하고 있습니다. 의사는 가족에게 보고를 하고 있습니다.) "그는 안정된 좋은 상태이며 빨리 회복 할 것으로 예상 됩니다. 향후 건강한식사를 하면 좋아 질 것입니다."

Say Instead:
미국식 영어로 말할려면:

How do you feel? / How are you feeling?

I am feeling better. / I feel great!

I don't feel very well today. / I am feeling under the weather.

Konglish Sentence		**American English**
What's your *condition?* My *condition* today is not good.		*How do you feel* today? *I don't feel very well* today. *I'm feeling a bit under the weather* today.

너의 상태는 어때? 내 상태는 안 좋아.

How Americans use Condition:
미국인들이 "Condition"을 사용하는 법:

 Seller

Hi, I'm interested in buying the used couch you're selling for $100. What **condition** is it in?

> Hi, the couch is in excellent **condition.** We bought it new around 6 months ago.

---

to: Me <TravelLover@theinternet.com>

subject: Tips for Traveling to Iceland

I'm so excited to hear you're going to Iceland! We've been there 3 times now and love it! Here's a few tips from our trips there:

1. Rent a Car!
This will allow you to get around easily and you can go all around the island, depending on how long you plan to stay. The Iceland government has a website devoted to driving safety where you can check road and weather **conditions** around the country. I highly recommend checking it daily because the **conditions** can change rapidly (and there are some places you don't want to be driving if things are bad). That being said, we had no issues driving and highly recommend renting a car!

DIET 다이어트

Meaning in American English:
미국식 영어로 의미:

1. *(Go/be) on a diet* means changing or restricting the foods you usually eat for medical reasons, healthier habits, or for weight loss. (E.g., she has diabetes, so she needs to go on a low-sugar *diet*; someone with high cholesterol might need to go on a low-sodium *diet*.)
   '다이어트중 입니다.' 또는 '다이어트 하세요'는 의학적인 이유, 더 건강한 습관 또는 체중 감량을 위해 보통 먹는 음식을 바꾸거나 제한하는 것을 의미합니다. 예를 들어, 그녀는 당뇨병이 있어서 저당식다이어트를 해야 합니다. 콜레스테롤이 높은 사람은 저염 분 다이어트를 해야 할 수도 있습니다.

2. *Diet* can also mean foods one usually eats. (E.g., A typical Korean *diet* includes rice and kimchi.)
   '다이어트'는 평소에 먹는 음식을 의미할 수도 있습니다. (예: 한국의 대표적인 식단에는 쌀과 김치가 포함됩니다)

Say Instead:
미국식 영어로 말하려면:

Trying to lose weight

Konglish Sentence	American English
I'm going to the gym because I'm on a *diet*.	I'm going to the gym because I'm *trying to lose weight*. I'm trying to get in shape.

다이어트 해야해서 헬스장에 가야한다.

How Americans use Diet:
미국인들이 "Diet"를 사용하는 법:

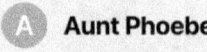 **Aunt Phoebe**

> How do you get rid of your eczema?

Medication and an anti-inflammatory **diet**

> What is an anti-inflammatory **diet**?

A **diet** low in simple carbohydrates basically. Simple sugars cause a lot of systemic inflammation and can make things like eczema worse

 Rachel

> Any dietary restrictions?

Mark's on a **diet** and isn't eating any bread or red meat right now

 Babe

> What did the vet say?

She said the dog weighs too much and we need to put him on a **diet** and try to give him more exercise

DISK 디스크

Meaning in American English:
미국식 영어로 의미:

1. A round, flat object (like a CD or a frisbee)
   둥글고 납작한 물건 (CD 나 프리스비 같은 것)
2. A normal healthy spinal disk (intervertebral disc)
   정상적인 건강한 척추 디스크 (추간 디스크)

- ◀— Normal Disc
- ◀— Degenerative Disc
- ◀— Bulging Disc
- ◀— Herniated Disc
- ◀— Thinning Disc
- ◀— Disc Degeneration with Osteophyte formation

Say Instead:
미국식 영어로 말할려면:

Slipped disk, Herniated disk, Ruptured disk

Konglish Sentence	American English
She hurt her back. She has a *disk*.	She hurt her back. She has a *slipped disk / herniated disk.*

그녀는 허리를 다쳤다. 디스크가 있다.

Real Life Story:
실화:

A student once told me, "I can't come to class this week because I have a disk." I was very confused. A disk? A DVD? A desk? A frisbee? I couldn't understand why he would need to miss one week of class for any reason related to "a disk." I saw his wife the next day, and when I asked about her weekend, she said, "It was terrible. We had to go to the hospital. My husband has a disk." Still confused, I realized *disk* might mean something medical. I asked more questions. She told me he hurt his back, and I finally understood that she meant he had a "slipped disk" or "herniated disk."

한 학생이 "디스크가 있어서 이번 주 수업에 올 수가 없어요."라고 말했습니다. 저는 매우 혼란스러웠습니다. 디스크? DVD? 책상이라고요? 프리스비? 그가 왜 그런 이유로 일주일 동안 수업을 빠져야 하는지 이해할 수가 없었습니다. 다음날 학생의 아내를 만났고 그녀에게 잘 지냈냐고 물어보았습니다. "정말 끔찍했어요. 남편이 디스트가 있어서 병원에 가야 했어요."라고 말했습니다. 여전히 혼란스러웠지만, 저는 "디스크"가 의학적인 의미일 수도 있다라고 생각했습니다. 저는 더 물어 보았습니다. 그녀는 남편이 허리를 다쳤다고 했고 그제서야 디스크가 무엇을 뜻하는지 알게되었다.

How Americans use Disk:
미국인들이 "Disk"를 사용하는 법:

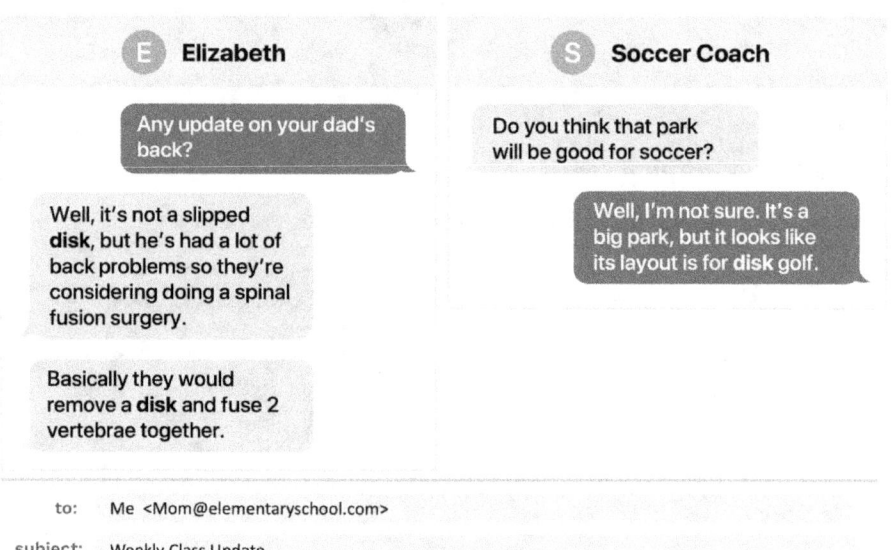

E **Elizabeth**

> Any update on your dad's back?

Well, it's not a slipped **disk**, but he's had a lot of back problems so they're considering doing a spinal fusion surgery.

Basically they would remove a **disk** and fuse 2 vertebrae together.

S **Soccer Coach**

> Do you think that park will be good for soccer?

Well, I'm not sure. It's a big park, but it looks like its layout is for **disk** golf.

to: Me <Mom@elementaryschool.com>

subject: Weekly Class Update

This week, we started reading a book about the space missions in the 1970s. This is a blend of our reading and science units. The book talked about making a *disk* with images and sounds of life on earth in case it was ever found in space.

The kids have been placed in groups of 4 for their project this week. Their project is to create a *disk* with images and audio files to show pictures and sounds of life and imagine this *disk* will be found by people thousands of years in the future, maybe on another planet.

EAT MEDICINE 약을 먹다

Meaning in American English:
미국식 영어로 의미:

Eat medicine in English sounds like you are eating the medicine like food
영어로 약을 먹는다고 하면 약을 음식처럼 먹는 것처럼 들립니다.

Say Instead:
미국식 영어로 말할려면:

Take medicine

Konglish Sentence	American English
If you have a cough, you should *eat* cough *medicine*.	If you have a cough, you should *take* cough *medicine*.

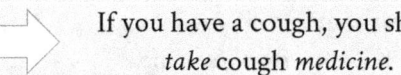

감기하면 감기약을 먹어야 한다.

FITNESS 헬스장

Meaning in American English:
미국식 영어로 의미:

The practice of being physically fit and healthy; never a place
신체적으로 건강함의 몸 상태; 결코 장소가 아님

Say Instead:
미국식 영어로 말하려면:

Gym, Fitness center

Konglish Sentence	American English
He works at a *fitness*, so he can exercise for free any time.	He works at a *gym*, so he can exercise for free any time.

그는 헬스장에서 일해서 무료로 운동할 수 있다.

How Americans use Fitness:
미국인들이 "Fitness"를 사용하는 법:

 LL Apartments

You have received a package. Your package is located in locker 15 in the hallway across from the **fitness** room.

This is an automated message. Please contact your leasing office with any additional questions.

 Volleyball Coach

What do you have in mind for volleyball practice today?

I want to start practice with at least 30 minutes of **fitness**. Maybe have the team warm up and do some **fitness** stuff first

GARGLE 가글

Meaning in American English:
미국식 영어로 의미:

The action of swishing something in the back
of your mouth and spitting it out; only a verb.
입 안에서 무언가를 헹구며 뱉어내는
동작. 동사로만 사용됩니다.

Say Instead:
미국식 영어로 말할려면:

Mouthwash

Konglish Sentence	American English
I need to buy some *gargle*.	I need to buy some *mouthwash*.
가글을 사고 싶다.	

How Americans use Gargle:
미국인들이 "Gargle"을 사용하는 법:

 Frank

> Hey, how's your throat?

Sore, but they gave me a
huge bottle of medicine
and lidocaine to **gargle**
with. They also said I can
gargle with salt water too

GOOD FOR ME 굿 포 미

Meaning in American English:
미국식 영어로 의미:

Good for me personally and that's it (not generally speaking)
나에게 단순히 좋다는 의미입니다. (보통 사용하지 않음).

Say Instead:
미국식 영어로 말할려면:

Good for you (general you)

Konglish Sentence	American English
Broccoli is *good for me*. ⟹	Broccoli is *good for you*.

브로콜리는 몸에 좋다.

How Americans use Good for Me:
미국인들이 "Good for me"를 사용하는 법:

Aunt Trish

Do you have a preference for which day we schedule the get-together next weekend?

Nope, I'm pretty free. Any day is **good for me!**

Gyps 깁스

Meaning in American English:
미국식 영어로 의미:

Doesn't exist

이 단어는 존재하지 않습니다

Say Instead:
미국식 영어로 말할려면:

Cast

Konglish Sentence	American English
She broke her leg, and now she has a *gyps*.	She broke her leg, and now she has a *cast*.
그녀는 다리가 부러졌다. 그래서 기브스를 한다.	

HEALING TIME 힐링타임

Meaning in American English:
미국식 영어로 의미:

The amount of time a specific injury will take to heal

특정 부상이 치유되는 데 걸리는 시간입니다

Say Instead:
미국식 영어로 말할려면:

Self-care, Rest, Relaxation

Konglish Sentence	American English
I like to have a *healing time* at a spa.	I like to *relax* at a spa. It's my *self-care*.

나는 스파를 하며 힐링타임을 가지는 것을 좋아한다.

How Americans use Healing Time:
미국인들이 "Healing Time"을 사용하는 법:

 Niece

How long does it take a broken toe to heal?

The doctor said typical **healing time** is 4-6 weeks

HEALTH 헬스

Meaning in American English:
미국식 영어로 의미:

Your physical and mental wellbeing; never a place
신체 및 정신 건강. 절대 장소를 뜻하지 않습니다.

Say Instead:
미국식 영어로 말할려면:

Gym, Fitness center

Konglish Sentence		American English
He works at a *health*.	⟹	He works at a *gym*.
그 사람은 헬스장에서 일한다.		

How Americans use Health:
미국인들이 "Health"를 사용하는 법:

 Scout

> Why did you decide to stop eating red meat?

Mostly my personal **health** concerns as well as environmental concerns

G **Grace**

> How'd the surgery go?

It went well, and he is in good **health** otherwise, so the doctors think he should recover quickly

HEALTHFUL 헬스풀

Meaning in American English:

미국식 영어로 의미:

Healthful is technically a correct word, but it is rarely used in American English and sounds very awkward and unnatural to most people.

Healthful 은 엄밀히 말하면 틀린 단어는 아니지만, 미국 영어에서 거의 사용되지 않고 대부분의 사람들에게 매우 어색하고 부자연스럽게 들립니다.

Say Instead:

미국식 영어로 말할려면:

Healthy

Konglish Sentence	American English
Spinach is really *healthful*. 	Spinach is really *healthy*.
시금치는 건강한 음식이다.	

HEALTHY MEAL 건강한 식사

Meaning in American English:

미국식 영어로 의미:

A meal that is healthy

건강한 식사

Say Instead:

미국식 영어로 말할려면:

Healthy diet

Konglish Sentence

He has diabetes, so his doctor told him to start eating a *healthy meal*.

⇨

American English

He has diabetes, so his doctor told him to start eating a *healthy diet*.

그는 당뇨가 있어서 의사가 건강한 식사를 하라고 했다.

How Americans use Healthy Meal:

미국인들이 "Healthy Meal"을 사용하는 법:

 Jaeeun

I just found this cooking website with tons of recipes for **healthy meals**! They look really good!

Oh awesome, I'm excited to check it out!

Healthy Meals in Less than 30 Minutes!
www.healthymeals.comm

 Jeff

I think I'm going to cook a **healthy meal** for us tonight. Maybe grilled chicken with vegetables?

That sounds like a great idea!

HOSPITAL 호스피탈

Meaning in American English:
미국식 영어로 의미:

The medical place you go for emergencies or surgeries
응급 상황이나 수술을 받기 위해 가는 의료 장소

Say Instead:
미국식 영어로 말할려면:

The doctor, The doctor's office, (A doctor's) appointment, Appointment, Clinic

Konglish Sentence	American English
Can we reschedule today's lesson? I need to take my son to a *hospital*. – Oh my gosh! Is he OK?! Do you need anything?!	Can we reschedule today's lesson? My son has a *doctor's appointment*. – Sure, no problem. See you next week.

오늘 수업을 다시 예약해도 될까요? 저희 아들이 병원가야 해요.
- *어머! 무슨일 있으셨나요? 뭐 필요한 거 없나요?*

Life & Culture in the USA:
미국의 삶과 문화:

For Americans, going to the *hospital* and going to the doctor are very different things. If you tell an American that you have to skip an event or a class or work to go to the *hospital*, they will react very seriously. "Are you OK?! Do you need anything? Can I bring you anything? What can we do for you?" Usually, going to the hospital is for two main reasons. 1. You go to the *hospital* for surgery or a scheduled operation. 2. You go to the *hospital* for a critical illness or an emergency. The emergency room is usually located in a *hospital*. So if you tell someone that you have to go to the *hospital*, expect that they will react dramatically.

If you are going to a scheduled appointment, whether it's for an annual check-up or because you have a bad cough and a fever, you are likely "going to the doctor."

A few things you can say are, "I'm going to the doctor," or, "I have a doctor's appointment." If you want to mention an appointment that takes place at a *hospital* but is not for an emergency or surgery, you can say, "I have an appointment (at the hospital)."

If your son is sick and you want to take him to see a doctor, please text your friend, "Can we reschedule today? I need to take my son to the doctor." Your friend will likely answer, "Of course. Is he OK? Let me know when you are free next time." If you text your friend, "Can we reschedule today? I need to take my son to the hospital," you will get a much different reaction. Your friend will think your son is dangerously ill, having a serious allergic reaction, a serious injury, or perhaps a sudden surgery.

미국인들에게 going to the hospital 과 going to the doctor 는 매우 다른 것들입니다. 만약 병원에 가기 위해 행사나 수업이나 일을 빠져야한다고 미국인에게 말한다면, 그들은 매우 심각하게 반응할 것입니다. "괜찮아요? 뭐 필요한 거 있어요? 내가 뭘 가져다줄까요? 우리가 무엇을 도와줄까요?". 보통 병원에 가는 것은 두 가지 주요 이유입니다. 1. 수술을 받기 위해 병원에 갑니다. 2. 심각한 질병이나 응급 상황 때문에 병원에 갑니다. 응급실은 보통 병원 안에 위치합니다. 그래서 만약 누군가에게 병원에 가야 한다고 말하면 그들은 심각하게 반응할 수 있습니다.

연간 검진이나 기침이 심하고 열 때문이든 약속한 진료를 받으러 가는 것이라면 "going to the doctor"일 가능성이 높습니다. "I'm going to the doctor," 또는 "I have a doctor's appointment."라고 말을 할 수 있습니다. 병원에서 진료를 받지만 응급이나 수술을 위한 것이 아닌 경우에는 "I have an appointment (at the hospital)."라고 말할 수 있습니다.

아이가 아파서 병원에 데려갈려고 할 때, 친구에게 문자로 "오늘 일정을 변경할 수 있을까? I need to take my son to the doctor." 여러분의 친구는 아마 "물론이지. 괜찮아? 다음에 만나자."라고 걱정하며 답장할 것입니다. 하지만 "오늘 일정을 변경할 수 있을까? I need to take my son to the hospital." 이렇게 친구에게 문자를 보내면 상당히 다른 반응을 보일 것이다. 당신의 아들이 심각한 알레르기 반응을 가지고 있거나, 심각한 부상을 입거나, 아마도 갑작스러운 수술을 받고 있다고 생각할 것입니다.

How Americans use Hospital:
미국인들이 "Hospital"을 사용하는 법:

 Brother	Uncle Josh

Brother:

Do you know who is coming to help grandpa after the surgery?

Aunt Mel said she is going to be here for the actual surgery Uncle J and Aunt S are planning to come stay with him for like a week when he gets home from the **hospital**.

Uncle Josh:

She is still in the **hospital** for a few more days. I am here now and will probably stay until later tonight

My office is super close to the **hospital**. Do you want me to pick up any food for lunch when I come today?

MR 엠알

Meaning in American English:
미국식 영어로 의미:

Doesn't exist in everyday speech, but it is sometimes used in the medical field to mean "MRI" (the same as Konglish). In writing, *Mr.* means "Mister."

일상적으로 쓰이진 않지만 의학 분야에서는 때때로 'MRI'(콩글리쉬와 동일)라는 뜻으로 사용되기도 합니다. Mr.를 글로 쓸땐 남자를 지칭합니다.

Say Instead:
미국식 영어로 말할려면:

MRI

Konglish Sentence	American English
Yun broke her leg really badly and got an *MR*.	Yun broke her leg really badly and got an *MRI*.

윤은 다리가 심하게 부러져서 MR 을 찍었다.

Additional Info:
그 외:

In the medical field in the United States, there are a lot of abbreviations. In fact, people who work in the medical field can take an entire class on medical terminology because there are so many different abbreviations and terms only used in medicine that people outside of the medical field don't use. Because of that, if you tell your friend you have to get an *MR* this week, she may not understand you. Even though MRI is just one letter different, it's important to say MRI. We might think *MR* is just another medical term with a different meaning that we aren't aware of. And who knows, it's even possible someone might think you are saying you need to find mister (abbreviated Mr.) or a man.

미국의 의학 분야에는 약어가 굉장히 많습니다. 사실 의학 분야 이외의 사람들은 사용하지 않는 약어나 용어가 너무 다양해서 의학 분야에서 일하는 사람들은 의학 용어에 대한 수업을 들을 수 있어요. 친구에게 이번 주에 MR 을 받아야 한다고 하면 친구가 이해하지 못할 수도 있습니다. MRI 는 단지 한 글자 차이지만 반드시 MRI 라고 말하는 것이 중요합니다. MR 이 우리가 모르는 다른 의미의 의학 용어라고 생각할 수도 있습니다. 누군가가 남자(약칭 Mr.)를 찾아야 한다고 생각할 수도 있습니다.

How Americans use MRI:
미국인들이 "MRI"를 사용하는 법:

 Meredith

> How'd your appointment go yesterday?

> It went ok. All my **MRIs** came back normal, so that's good. They're going to do a few more tests to see if they can find the cause.

 Adelyne

> I had an **MRI** of my knee this morning. I tore my MCL, but thankfully it will heal without surgery.

> That's good news! Do you have to do PT?

OVEREAT 오바이트

Meaning in American English:
미국식 영어로 의미:

Eat too much
너무 많이 먹음

Say Instead:
미국식 영어로 말할려면:

Vomit, Throw up

Konglish Sentence	American English
I drank too much yesterday, so I *overate*.	I drank too much yesterday, so I *threw up*.

어젯밤에 술을 너무 많이 먹어서 오바이트 했다.

PASS 파스

Meaning in American English:
미국식 영어로 의미:

1. (Verb) To move through, go across, further than, or between things (pass another car on the road)
   (동사) 이동하기, 건너기, 더 멀리 가기, 또는 사물 사이(도로에서 다른 차를 지나가기)

2. (Verb) To get a successful grade on a test or exam; the opposite of fail a test
   (동사) 시험에서 좋은 성적을 얻기 위한 것. 시험에 실패하는 것의 반대.

3. (Verb) To throw/kick a sports ball to another player (in soccer when you kick the ball to your teammate, you pass)
   (동사) 스포츠에서 공을 다른 선수에게 던지거나 차는 것
   (축구에서는 동료에게 공을 차는 것을 패스라고 합니다.)

4. (Noun) A throw/kick to another player (like number 3)
   (명사) 다른 선수에게 던지기/차기 (3 번과 같이)

5. (Noun) A gap between two things (often used with mountains). To go over mountains, you have to drive through a pass.
   (명사) 두 가지 사이의 간격 (산과 함께 자주 사용됨). 산을 넘어가기 위해서는 고갯길을 운전해야 합니다.

6. (Noun) A document of permission needed to enter or go through a place
   (명사) 출입 또는 경유에 필요한 허가서

Say Instead:
미국식 영어로 말할려면:

Pain patch, Heat patch, Cooling patch

Konglish Sentence		American English
I got a bad bruise, so my grandma gave me a *pass*.		I got a bad bruise, so my grandma gave me a *pain patch*.

멍이 심하게 들어서 할머니가 파스를 주셨다.

How Americans use Pass:
미국인들이 "Pass"를 사용하는 법:

---

to: Me <Traveler@TravelLover.com>

subject: Our trip through the foothills of the Himalayas

As we entered the mountainous area, the views were spectacular. We went up and up winding roads until we came to the first mountain **pass**. Traffic was at a standstill. We heard there had been a small avalanche a little earlier and the road ahead was totally blocked! We had some tea on the side of the road and made friends with some locals while the construction crews worked to clear a path on the road. We played card games and **passed** around a soccer ball. Our new friends even kindly offered us a **pass** to visit 4 famous tourist sites in their hometown. We thanked them but told them we'd have to **pass** on the offer since we unfortunately didn't have enough time to visit that city on this particular trip.

4 or 5 hours **passed** before the traffic finally started moving again! After getting over the **pass**, since it was getting late, we found a hotel nearby and stopped for the night before continuing further into the mountains the next day.

Send

PAY DOCTOR 페이닥터

Meaning in American English:
미국식 영어로 의미:

Doesn't exist

이 단어는 존재하지 않습니다

Say Instead:
미국식 영어로 말할려면:

Doctor

Konglish Sentence		American English
He works at the hospital. He is a *pay doctor*.		He works at the hospital. He is a *doctor*.

그는 병원에서 일한다. 그는 페이닥터이다.

Additional Info:
그 외:

There is no English word for this distinction between a doctor who works at a hospital or for a medical group or a doctor who owns his/her own practice. Both are called doctors. If you want to specify that a doctor is a *pay doctor* or does not work for a hospital or another boss, you can say, "He/she has his/her own practice," or, "He/she has his/her own private practice."

병원이나 의료단체에서 일하는 의사나 개업을 한 의사를 구분하는 영어 단어는 없습니다. 둘 다 모두 의사라고 부릅니다. 의사가 'pay doctor' 이거나 병원이나 다른 상사를 위해 일하지 않는다고 말하고 싶다면, "He/she has his/her own practice," or "He/she has his/her own private practice."라고 말할 수 있습니다.

RINGER 링거/링겔

Meaning in American English:
미국식 영어로 의미:

1. Ring sound on a phone
   전화벨 소리
2. A person who looks really similar to someone else
   도플갱어; 다른 사람과 정말 비슷하게 생긴 사람
3. Someone who enters a competition fraudulently acting as someone else
   부정한 방법으로 다른 사람처럼 행동하면서 대회에 참가하는 사람
4. An imposter
   사기꾼
5. Someone on a sports team who is highly skilled
   스포츠팀에서 고도로 숙련된 사람

Say Instead:
미국식 영어로 말할려면:

IV, IV fluids

Konglish Sentence	American English
He got a *ringer* at the hospital. $\Longrightarrow$	He got *IV fluids* at the hospital.
그는 병원에서 수액 맞았다.	

Additional Info:
그 외:

In medical English, there is something called a *lactated ringer's solution* or *Ringer's lactate solutions* that can be given by IV, but this isn't typically called a "ringer."

의학 영어에는 IV 로 줄 수 있는 젖산 링거 용액 또는 링거 젖산 용액이라고 불리는 것이 있지만, 이것은 일반적으로 'a ringer'라고 부르지 않습니다.

SUNCREAM 선크림

Meaning in American English:
미국식 영어로 의미:

Doesn't exist

이 단어는 존재하지 않습니다

Say Instead:
미국식 영어로 말할려면:

Sunscreen, Sunblock, Sunscreen lotion

Konglish Sentence	American English
You should use *suncream* every day.	You should use *sunscreen/sunblock* every day.

썬크림 꼭 발라야한다.

WELL BEING 웰빙

Meaning in American English:

미국식 영어로 의미:

A state of being comfortable, healthy, or happy

편안하거나 건강하거나 행복한 상태

Say Instead:

미국식 영어로 말하려면:

Healthy

Konglish Sentence	American English
This spinach is *well being*.	This spinach is *healthy*.
시금치는 웰빙 푸드이다.	

8

SCHOOL, WORK, &
AROUND THE OFFICE
학교, 일 & 회사 관련

ACADEMIC CLASS 아카데믹 클래스

Meaning in American English:
미국식 영어로 의미:

The most typical meaning of *academic class* is a class related to the main subjects or curriculum of school (math, science, social studies, language arts). There is some variation on how this term is used in American English. It could also mean any class officially offered at a school or any required course at a school. Depending on social context and school district, you may also find other meanings for this term.

'Academic class'의 가장 일반적인 의미는 학교의 주요 과목 또는 교육과정과 관련된 수업(수학, 과학, 사회 과목, 언어 예술)을 의미합니다. 미국 영어에서 이 용어의 사용 방법에는 약간의 차이가 있습니다. 이 용어는 학교에서 공식적으로 제공되는 수업이나 필수 과목을 의미할 수 있습니다. 사회적 맥락과 교육청에 따라 이 용어의 다른 의미를 찾을 수도 있습니다.

Say Instead:
미국식 영어로 말할려면:

Class at an after-school tutoring center

Tutoring

Extra class after school

Konglish Sentence		American English
He has many *academic classes.*		He has many *tutoring sessions.* He has many *extra classes after school at the tutoring center.*
그는 공부하고 있는 아카데믹 클래스가 많다.		

ACADEMY 학원

Meaning in American English:
미국식 영어로 의미:

1. The name of a popular sporting goods store
    인기있는 스포츠용품점의 이름

2. A general word for a school, often used in the name of private schools
    (Natural Science Academy, Wisdom Church Academy, The Village
    Academy) *these are fictional schools listed as examples of similar names*
    학교를 말하는 단어로 쓰이며 특히 사립학교를 뜻함 (예를 들면,
    자연과학 학교, 위즈덤교회 학교, 빌리지 학교 등) *이들은 유사한
    이름의 일예로 나열된 가상의 학교들입니다*

3. A word for a school or specific type of school or training focused on a
    specific goal for studies (for example: a military academy, a police academy,
    a science academy)
    특별한 목적에 초점을 맞춘 학교 또는 훈련을 의미하는 단어 (예:
    사관학교, 경찰학교, 과학학교)

Say Instead:
미국식 영어로 말할려면:

Tutoring center, Korean-style tutoring center, After-school tutoring center

Konglish Sentence	American English
He studies math at an *academy*.	He studies math at an *after-school tutoring center*.

그는 학원에서 수학을 배운다.

How Americans use Academy:
미국인들이 "Academy"를 사용하는 법:

 Alejandra

> Bob gets up at 5am and goes for a 3 mile run every single day – even when he's sick!

Wow! He told me he went to a military **academy,** so he's used to following a crazy schedule and strict rules

 Liston

> Let's bring a frisbee to the park today for the picnic!

Great idea! I don't have one, but I'm sure we can stop at **Academy** and grab one on the way!

---

to: Me <Applicant@Applications.com>

subject: Application for the open Science Teacher Position

To Whom It May Concern:

I am excited to apply for the high school science position and have attached my resume to this email.

I attended high school at the *Academy* of Science and Technology where I was able to complete college-level courses before continuing on to MIT where I graduated with honors and a 4.0. I worked as CTO for 10 years before finding my true passion in teaching. For the past 5 years, most of my time has been spent with the junior high and high school students at the International *Academy* of Scholars, a private school for foreign students, where I have worked as a physics and information technology teacher.

BALL PEN 볼펜

Meaning in American English:
미국식 영어로 의미:

Doesn't exist

이 단어는 존재하지 않습니다

Say Instead:
미국식 영어로 말하려면:

Pen, Ball point pen

Konglish Sentence	American English
Do you have a *ball pen* I can borrow?	Do you have a *pen* I can borrow?

그 볼펜 좀 사용해도 될까요?

BLUE WORKER 블루 워커

Meaning in American English:

미국식 영어로 의미:

Doesn't exist; blue can mean sad, so a blue worker might sound like a sad or depressed worker (though that is not a real phrase).

이 단어는 존재하지 않습니다. 파란색은 슬픔을 의미할 수 있으므로 슬프거나 우울한 근로자처럼 들릴 수 있습니다. (그것이 실제 문구는 아닙니다.)

Say Instead:

미국식 영어로 말할려면:

Blue-collar worker

Konglish Sentence	American English
That city has a lot of *blue workers*.	That city has a lot of *blue-collar workers*.
그 도시는 생산 직종 사람들이 많이 있어.	

BOND 본드

Meaning in American English:
미국식 영어로 의미:

1. (Noun) A relationship or connection
   (명사) 관계 또는 연관성

2. (Verb) To connect with someone
   (동사) 누군가와 연결하는 것

3. (Noun) Two things joined together permanently
   (명사) 영구적으로 결합된 두 가지 (화학에서 화학결합처럼)

4. (Verb) To join two things together like a chemical bond or adhesive
   (동사) 화학결합이나 접착제처럼 두 가지를 결합시키는 것

Say Instead:
미국식 영어로 말할려면:

Glue, Superglue

Konglish Sentence	American English
Where did you get that *bond*?	Where did you get that *(super) glue*?

그 본드 어디에서 샀어요?

How Americans use Bond:
미국인들이 "Bond"를 사용하는 법:

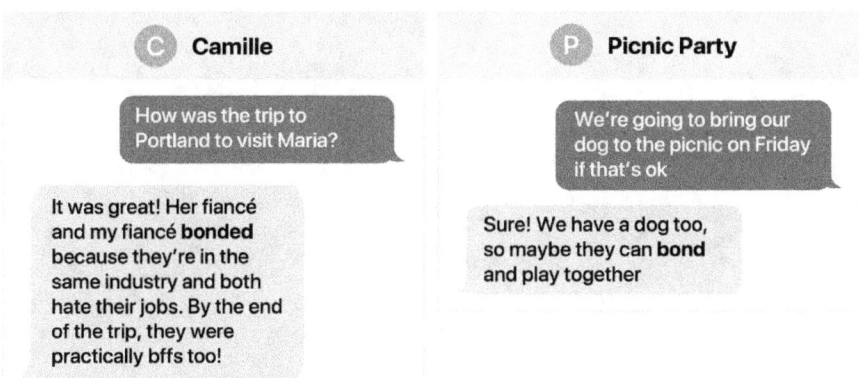

C Camille

How was the trip to Portland to visit Maria?

It was great! Her fiancé and my fiancé **bonded** because they're in the same industry and both hate their jobs. By the end of the trip, they were practically bffs too!

P Picnic Party

We're going to bring our dog to the picnic on Friday if that's ok

Sure! We have a dog too, so maybe they can **bond** and play together

CIRCLE 써클/동아리

Meaning in American English:
미국식 영어로 의미:

1. The shape: circle
   모양: 원

2. Usual group of people that you spend time with or are around in your typical environment
   함께 시간을 보내거나 주변에 있는 사람들

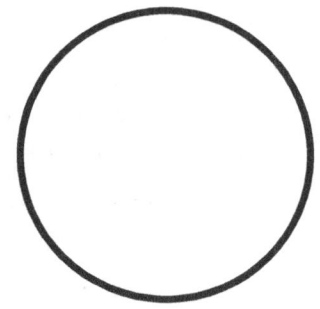

Say Instead:
미국식 영어로 말할려면:

Club, After-school club, (Sports) team

Konglish Sentence	American English
I was in the soccer *circle* when I was in university.	I was in the soccer *club* when I was in college.

나는 대학교 때 축구 써클에 있었다.

CLIP 클립

Meaning in American English:
미국식 영어로 의미:

1. (Noun) A tool to hold things together; press two sides to open and close
   (명사) 오피스 클립, 클립, 헤어클립, 칩클립
2. (Verb) To cut
   (동사) 자르다

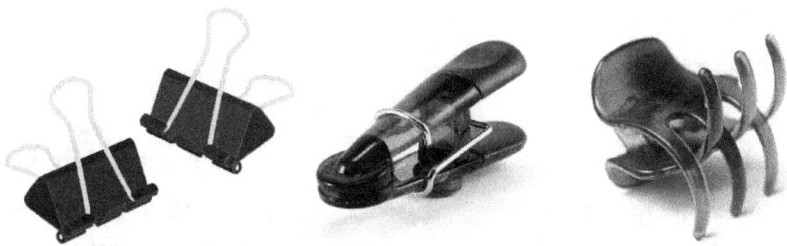

Say Instead:
미국식 영어로 말할려면:

Paperclip

Konglish Sentence	American English
Please use a *clip* to attach your check to your application.	Please use a *paperclip* to attach your check to your application.

체크를 서류에 클립으로 붙여주세요.

How Americans use Clip:
미국인들이 "Clip"을 사용하는 법:

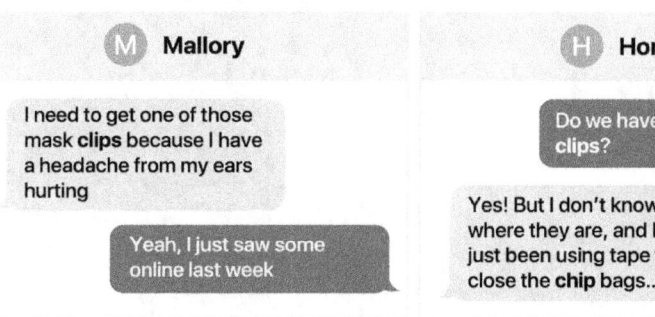

Mallory

I need to get one of those mask **clips** because I have a headache from my ears hurting

Yeah, I just saw some online last week

Honey

Do we have any chip **clips**?

Yes! But I don't know where they are, and I've just been using tape to close the **chip** bags...

COMPANY FOUNDING DAY 개원일

Meaning in American English:
미국식 영어로 의미:

Doesn't exist

이 단어는 존재하지 않습니다

Say Instead:
미국식 영어로 말할려면:

Company's anniversary

Konglish Sentence	American English
We don't have to work tomorrow because it's my *company founding day*.	We don't have to work tomorrow because it's my *company's 5th anniversary*.

내일이 우리 회사 개원일이라 쉰다.

COURSE 코스

Meaning in American English:
미국식 영어로 의미:

1. A class
   수업

2. Part of a meal for example (main course, 1st course)
   식사의 일부 (예: 메인 코스, 첫번째 코스 요리)

Say Instead:
미국식 영어로 말할려면:

Program, Major

Konglish Sentence	American English
I took the English *course* at university.	I *majored in* English in college. *(This is your degree)* I took an English *class* in college. *(This is one class)*

나는 영어 코스를 대학교 때 들었다.

How Americans use Course:
미국인들이 "Course"를 사용하는 법:

to: Me <Student@LearnKorean.com>

subject: Korean 101 *Course*

We wanted to thank you all for joining our 16-week Korean 101 class this fall and hope it's been a great experience! As we are nearing the end of the *course*, I wanted to let you know about options to continue as well as ask for your feedback on the *course*.

We would love to hear any feedback whether positive, negative, or neutral that you are willing to provide in order to help us continually improve our program! This will be shared anonymously with instructor after the *course* is completed, so please feel to leave your honest feedback – good or bad.

Restaurant week is really like restaurant month. For the entire month of August, lots of popular local restaurants, including some top fine dining places, offer 2-*course* lunch menus and 3-*course* dinner menus for really affordable set prices!

It's a huge city-wide fundraiser where most of the money is donated to different food banks around the city that help feed food-insecure Houstonians. It's also a way for restaurants to advertise themselves and for people to try out restaurants they normally might not think to try or maybe not normally be able to afford.

CUNNING 컨닝

Meaning in American English:
미국식 영어로 의미:

Sly, dishonest, able to trick you in a dishonest but smart way

교활하고, 정직하지 않고, 좋지않은 현명한 방법으로 당신을 속일 수 있습니다

Say Instead:
미국식 영어로 말할려면:

Cheating

Konglish Sentence	American English
"Teacher, he's *cunning* me!"	"He's *cheating!*" "He's *cheating off* of me!"
"선생님, 애 컨닝해요!"	

DIARY 다이어리

Meaning in American English:
미국식 영어로 의미:

A secret, private journal where you write your secret thoughts
하루에 대해 비밀스러운 생각이나 사적인 것들을 쓰는 일기

Say Instead:
미국식 영어로 말할려면:

Planner

Konglish Sentence		American English
May 15? That might be good. Let me check my *diary* to see if I have a schedule.		May 15? That might be good. Let me check my *planner/ calendar* to see if I have any plans.
5 월 15 일? 괜찮을 것 같아. 일정이 있는지 내 다이어리 확인해볼께.		

ENGINEER 엔진이어

Meaning in American English:
미국식 영어로 의미:

Someone who has a 4+ year bachelor's degree or higher from a university studying *engineering*. It's considered a high-level and well-paying job. This is not the same as mechanic, technician, or repairman.

엔지니어 또는 공학 전공을 한 4년제 대학에서 학사 학위를 받은 사람. 보통 높은 수준의 보수를 받는 직업으로 여겨집니다. 이것은 정비공, 기술자 또는 수리공과는 다릅니다.

Say Instead:
미국식 영어로 말할려면:

Technician, Repairman, Mechanic

Konglish Sentence		American English
My husband is an *engineer*.		My husband is a *repairman*. My husband is a *technician*.
내남편은기술자예요. / 내남편은엔지니어예요.		

HARD BOARD 하드 보드

Meaning in American English:
미국식 영어로 의미:

Doesn't exist; literally means a board that is hard

이 단어는 존재하지 않으며. 글자 그대로 딱딱한 판을 의미합니다

Say Instead:
미국식 영어로 말하려면:

Poster, Poster board

Konglish Sentence	American English
My son needs some *hard board* for his school project.	My son needs some *poster board* for his school project.
아들이 학교 프로젝트 때문에 하드보드가 필요하다.	

HOTCHKISS 호치키스

Meaning in American English:
미국식 영어로 의미:

Doesn't exist

이 단어는 존재하지 않습니다

Say Instead:
미국식 영어로 말할려면:

Stapler

Konglish Sentence	American English
Wow, I can't believe your *hotchkiss* is made from gold.	Wow, I can't believe your *stapler* is made of gold.

와, 호치키스가 금으로 만들어진 게 믿어지지 않아.

HOUSE WIFE 하우스 와이프

Meaning in American English:
미국식 영어로 의미:

Correct, but now it's more common to say "stay at home mom" instead of "housewife."

바른 표현이지만 오래된 표현으로 들리고 요즘에는 housewife 대신 "Stay at home mom"라고 말하는 것이 더 일반적입니다.

Say Instead:
미국식 영어로 말할려면:

Stay at home mom (SAHM) – (*for a woman with kids* 자녀가 있는 여성)

Stay at home dad (SAHD) – (*for a man with kids* 자녀가 있는 남성)

I stay at home – (*for a woman or man with or without kids* 자녀가 있거나 없는 남성이나 여성)

Konglish Sentence	American English
I'm a *housewife*. 	I'm a *stay at home mom*. I *stay at home*.

나는 하우스 와이프이다.

JUNIOR 후배

Meaning in American English:
미국식 영어로 의미:

1. Someone who is in 11th grade (year 3 of 4) in high school or someone who is in their 3rd year of college/university.
   고등학교 2 학년 또는 대학교 3 학년에 재학 중인 학생

2. Junior can also be part of someone's name if they are named after someone with the same name. For example, a father's name is John and the son's name is John, Jr.
   가족 중 동일한 이름을 가진 사람의 이름을 따르는 경우 주니어도 이름의 일부가 될 수가 있습니다. 예를 들어, 아버지의 이름은 존. 그 아들의 이름은 존 주니어 입니다.

3. Junior can also be used to show a position that's under another position. For example, there can be a salesman, and he might have a junior salesman working with him. That means the junior salesman is not as high of a position as salesman. He probably doesn't have as much experience as the salesman. This is part of the name of a specific position. It doesn't apply to every job or position or company or worker.
   주니어는 또한 낮은 직급을 보여주기 위해 사용될 수 있습니다. 예를 들어, 어떤 판매원은 그와 함께 일하는 주니어 판매원이 있을 수 있습니다. 주니어 판매원이 판매원만큼 높은 직책이 아니라는 것을 의미합니다. 아마도 그 판매원만큼 경험이 많지 않을 것입니다. 이것은 특정한 직책 이름의 일부입니다. 모든 직업, 직책, 회사 또는 근로자에게 적용되지 않습니다.

Say Instead:
미국식 영어로 말할려면:

She is younger than me.

I have worked at this company longer than him.

Konglish Sentence		American English
I met *my junior* at the market.		I ran into a girl I went to high school with at the store. She was *a grade younger than me / a grade behind me.*

일내 주니어를 시장에서 만났다.

Life & Culture in the USA:
미국의 삶과 문화:

In American culture, it is much less common to talk about age than it is in Korean culture. As children, it is normal to talk about age. "How old are you?" "What grade are you in?" are normal questions for kids to ask each other and for adults to ask kids.

But for adults, talking about age is much less common. It is often considered rude to ask someone about their age. Unlike in Korea, it is uncommon for age to determine your position in a job, so asking someone their age in the workplace is considered unprofessional and sometimes even condescending.

With close friends, it's acceptable to ask about age, but still not as common as in Korea. Even as an adult, I have many close friends whose exact age I don't know. Talking about your own age is not considered rude, just asking others, especially those you don't know well.

미국 문화에서는 한국 문화보다 나이에 대해 이야기하는 것은 훨씬 덜 일반적입니다. 어린 시절 나이에 대해 이야기하는 경우는 있습니다. "너 몇 살이야?" "몇 학년이야?"는 아이들이 서로에게 묻고 어른들이 아이들에게 묻는 평범한 질문입니다.

하지만 어른들에게 나이에 대해 이야기하는 것은 훨씬 덜 흔합니다. 누군가에게 나이를 물어보는 것은 종종 무례한 것으로 여겨집니다. 한국과 달리, 나이가 직업에서 당신의 위치를 결정하는 것은 흔하지 않기 때문에, 직장에서 당신의 나이를 묻는 것은 비전문적이고 심지어 가끔은 거들먹거리는 것으로 여겨집니다.

친한 친구들에게 나이를 묻는 것은 괜찮지만, 한국처럼 흔하지는 않습니다. 어른이 되어서도 나는 정확한 나이를 모르는 친한 친구들이 많습니다. 자신의 나이에 대해 말하는 것은 무례한 것은 아니지만, 잘 모르는 사람에게 물어보는 것은 결례가 될 수 있습니다.

Real Life Story:
실화:

There is also an important difference in how Koreans and Americans calculate their ages. When I first visited South Korea, I was 20 years old in American age. My friend introduced me to her cousin, who seemed a lot younger than us and said he was 16. When he told me he was in middle school, I was even more confused. Finally, I asked my friend about this, and she started laughing when she realized the mix-up. He was 16 in KOREAN age and only 14 in American age. She also said I was 22 in Korean age. I was shocked! I had no idea that two different systems for calculating age even existed! Most Koreans already know that Americans and most other countries use a different system for counting age, but it's also important to know that even if you say to an American, "I am 25 in Korean age," they will probably be very confused because most people don't know about Korean age!

Note: The author is calling this "American age" simply because this book is focusing mostly on American English. However, most Western countries count age the same way, and in Korea, this is often called "international age."

**Note: The author would like to note that Korean law has changed in South Korea since this book was written, so this method of age calculation is no longer actively officially used.*

한국인과 미국인이 나이를 계산하는 방법에도 중요한 차이가 있습니다. 제가 한국을 처음 방문했을 때, 저는 미국 나이로 20 살이었습니다. 제 친구는 우리보다 훨씬 어려 보이는 그녀의 사촌을 저에게 소개시켜주었고 그는 16 살이라고 말했습니다. 그가 저에게 중학교에 재학 중이라고 말했을 때, 저는 더 혼란스러웠습니다. 마침내, 저는 이것에 대해 친구에게 물었더니 그녀는 뭔가 잘못된 것을 알고 웃기 시작했습니다. 그는 한국 나이로 16 살이었고, 미국 나이로 겨우

14 살이었습니다. 그녀는 또한 제가 한국 나이로 22 살이라고 말했습니다. 저는 충격을 받았습니다! 나이를 계산하는 두 가지의 다른 방식이 있다는 것을 전혀 몰랐습니다! 대부분의 한국인들은 미국인들과 대부분의 다른 나라들이 나이를 세는 다른 방식을 사용한다는 것을 이미 알고 있지만, 많은 사람들이 한국 나이에 대해 모르기 때문에 여러분이 미국인에게 "저는 한국 나이로 25 살입니다"라고 말을 한다면 아마 매우 혼란스러워 할 것이라는 것을 인지하는 것 또한 중요합니다!

*참고: 저자는 단순히 이 책이 주로 미국 영어에 초점을 맞추고 있기 때문에 이를 "미국 나이"라고 부르고 있습니다. 하지만, 대부분의 서양 국가들은 같은 방식으로 나이를 세고, 한국에서는 이것을 종종 "국제 나이"라고 부릅니다

**참고: 이 책이 쓰인 이후 한국의 법이 바뀌었기 때문에 더 이상 이러한 연령 계산 방식이 공식적으로 사용되지 않습니다.

LETTERING 레터링

Meaning in American English:
미국식 영어로 의미:

Lettering is the style of written and printed letters. It's different than handwriting, which talks about one's own everyday writing style. Lettering is done in a purposeful and artistic way, usually for decorative purposes.

레터링은 글이나 프린트된 글의 스타일을 뜻하며 한 개인이 가지고 있는 필기체와는 다릅니다. 레터링은 데코레이션같이 어떠한 목적이나 예술적으로 표현됩니다.

Say Instead:
미국식 영어로 말할려면:

Handwriting

Konglish Sentence		American English
He has really nice *lettering*.		He has really nice *handwriting*.
그는 멋있는 레터링을 가지고 있다.		

How Americans use Lettering:
미국인들이 "Lettering"을 사용하는 법:

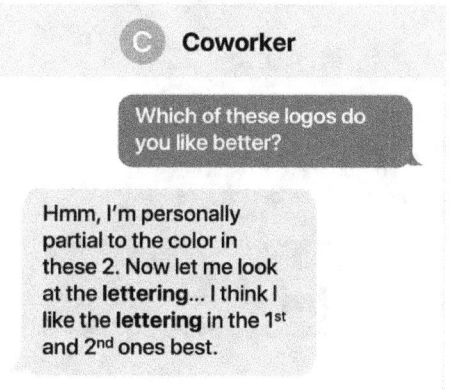

C Coworker

Which of these logos do you like better?

Hmm, I'm personally partial to the color in these 2. Now let me look at the **lettering**... I think I like the **lettering** in the 1st and 2nd ones best.

MAGIC 매직

Meaning in American English:
미국식 영어로 의미:

Magic, like a magician does
마술사가 하는 마술

Say Instead:
미국식 영어로 말할려면:

Magic marker, Sharpie, Permanent
marker

Konglish Sentence	American English
I'd like to write this with a *magic*.	I'd like to write this with a *permanent marker*.

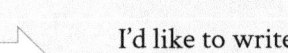

난 이 매직으로 쓰는 게 좋다.

How Americans use Magic:
미국인들이 "Magic"을 사용하는 법:

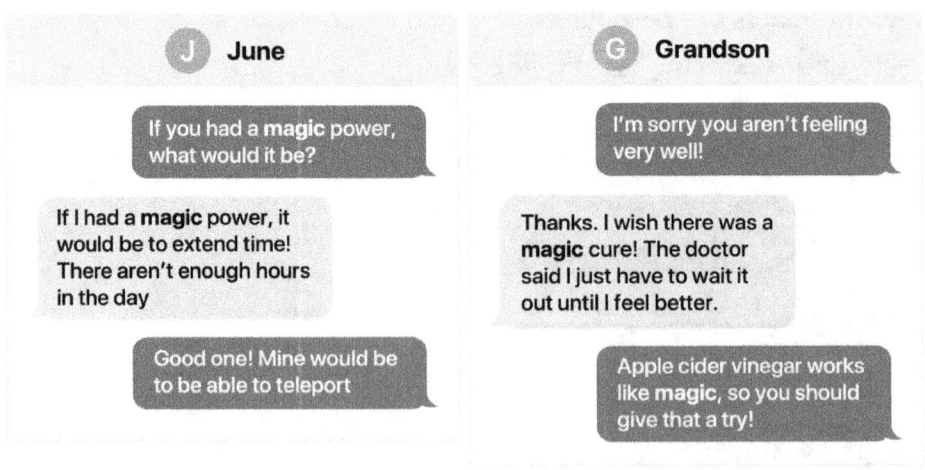

J June

> If you had a **magic** power, what would it be?

If I had a **magic** power, it would be to extend time! There aren't enough hours in the day

> Good one! Mine would be to be able to teleport

G Grandson

> I'm sorry you aren't feeling very well!

Thanks. I wish there was a **magic** cure! The doctor said I just have to wait it out until I feel better.

> Apple cider vinegar works like **magic**, so you should give that a try!

NAME CARD 네임 카드

Meaning in American English:
미국식 영어로 의미:

Doesn't exist

이 단어는 존재하지 않습니다

Say Instead:
미국식 영어로 말할려면:

Business card

Konglish Sentence	American English
It's nice to meet you. Maybe we can do business together in the future. Do you have a *name card*?	It's nice to meet you. Maybe we can do business together in the future. Do you have a *business card*?

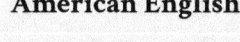

만나서 반가워요. 다음에 우리 같이 협업하면 좋겠어요.
혹시 명함있으세요?

NAME PEN 네임펜

Meaning in American English:
미국식 영어로 의미:

Doesn't exist; maybe a pen with your name engraved on it?

이 단어는 존재하지 않습니다. 아마 이름이 새겨진 펜?

Say Instead:
미국식 영어로 말하려면:

Thin felt-tipped permanent marker, Sharpie

Konglish Sentence	American English
Please put your sign here with your *name pen*.	Please put your signature here with a *thin-tipped Sharpie*.

네임펜으로 여기 이름 싸인 해주세요.

NOTE 노트

Meaning in American English:
미국식 영어로 의미:

1. Short piece of information or message written down somewhere
   짧은 편지, 메모, 주석
2. A music note
   음표

Say Instead:
미국식 영어로 말하려면:

Notebook, Notepad

Konglish Sentence		American English
Let me write this in my *note*.	⇒	Let me write this in my *notebook*.
내 노트에 이 걸 적어야겠어.		

How Americans use Note:
미국인들이 "Note"를 사용하는 법:

 Uncle Steve

> Did you talk to the airline to see about changing his flight?

> They said they might be able to waive the change fee if he submits a doctor's **note** by tomorrow

 Close Friend

> Hi! So I found a stash of TONS of **notes** I kept that we wrote to each other in middle school. I was reading them last night... they are so hilarious! So much dumb middle school girl drama

NOTEBOOK 노트북

Meaning in American English:
미국식 영어로 의미:

A booklet for writing notes,
sometimes with lines

노트

Say Instead:
미국식 영어로 말할려면:

Laptop, Laptop computer, Computer

Konglish Sentence		American English
Let me type this in my *notebook*.		Let me type this in my *computer/laptop*.

내 노트북에 이걸 적어야지.

How Americans use Notebook:
미국인들이 "Notebook"을 사용하는 법:

 Kyle

Do they sell **notebooks** at that grocery store?

Hmmm, I'm not sure. Maybe? I can't remember

Ok, then I might have to go to the office supply store too... I need a small one to write some notes in

 Peggy

Do we need to bring anything to the training?

I'm not sure but I'm bringing a **notebook** and pen to jot down any notes

OFFICER 오피서

Meaning in American English:

미국식 영어로 의미:

Police officer

경찰

Say Instead:

미국식 영어로 말할려면:

Federal worker, Federal employee, Government
worker, Government employee, Government official (for some political
positions), Works for the government

Konglish Sentence		American English
My son is an *officer*.		My son is a *federal worker / works for the government*.

내 아들은 오피서입니다.

Real Life Story:

실화:

I once had a student from Korea who told me her son was an "officer." For
months, I thought her son was a police officer in Korea. At one point, we were
talking about him, and I asked, "Is it dangerous to be an officer in Korea?" She
looked really confused. "Of course not." I later found out he worked for a
government agency in their finance department and that *officer* did not always
mean the same thing to Koreans as it did to me.

예전에 한국에서 온 한 학생이 그녀의 아들이 "officer"라고 말했습니다. 몇
달 동안 저는 그녀의 아들이 한국의 경찰이라고 생각했습니다. 그 아들에
대해 이야기하고 있을때, "한국에서 경찰일이 위험한가요?"라고
물었습니다. 그녀는 매우 혼란스러워 보였습니다. "물론 그렇지
않습니다." 나중에 그가 재무 부서의 정부 기관에서 일했다는 것과 내가
알고 있는 있었던 'officer'가 한국 사람들에게는 같은 의미가 아니라는
것을 알게 되었습니다.

ONE BY ONE 원 바이 원

Meaning in American English:
미국식 영어로 의미:

One at a time, like in a line

한 번에 하나씩, 줄을 서듯이

Say Instead:
미국식 영어로 말할려면:

One on one, Private

Konglish Sentence	American English
I'd like to take a *one by one* lesson.	I'd like to take a *one on one* lesson. I'd like to take a *private* lesson.

1 대 1 레슨을 하고 싶다.

How Americans use One by One:
미국인들이 "One by One"을 사용하는 법:

to: Me <Employee@TheBusiness.com>

subject: Requested Files

Hi John,

I'm attaching the files requested to this email, but I'll probably have to send them **one by one** because of the size. So you can expect probably 4-5 emails from me in the next hour. Please reach out if the files don't send correctly or if you have any problems accessing them!

Thanks,
Laurence

PRINT 프린트

Meaning in American English:
미국식 영어로 의미:

(Verb) To make copies of something like text or pictures on paper

(동사) 종이에 글이나 그림 같은 것을 복사하는 것

Say Instead:
미국식 영어로 말할려면:

Handout, Printout

Konglish Sentence	American English
He brought *prints* for everyone at the meeting.	He brought *handouts/printouts* for everyone at the meeting.

프린트를 미팅 때 모두에게 나눠 주었다.

How Americans use Print:
미국인들이 "Print"를 사용하는 법:

D **Downstairs Neighbor**

Do you by chance have a working printer I could use? I have an interview this afternoon and need to **print** out a copy of my resume, but our printer isn't working

Yes! I can **print** it for you!

READ LOUD 리드아웃

Meaning in American English:
미국식 영어로 의미:

Read aloud with a loud volume

큰 소리로 읽기

Say Instead:
미국식 영어로 말할려면:

Read out loud, Aloud

Konglish Sentence	American English
We're going to read this chapter *loud*.	We're going to read this chapter *aloud / out loud*.

이 단원을 크게 읽을 것이다.

SALARYMAN 샐러리맨

Meaning in American English:
미국식 영어로 의미:

Doesn't exist

이 단어는 존재하지 않습니다

Say Instead:
미국식 영어로 말할려면:

There is not really any way to express this in English. You can say their job or place of work (for example, he works for X company).

영어로 표현되는 단어는 없다. 어떤 사람의 일이나 직장을 말한다. (예를 들면, 그는 X 회사에 다닌다.)

Konglish Sentence	American English
Her dad is a *salaryman*.	Her dad *works at XYZ company*.

우리 아빠는 샐러리맨이다.

SENIOR 선배

Meaning in American English:
미국식 영어로 의미:

1. A person who is in their last year of high school (12th grade) or last year of college/university (usually 4th year)
    고등학교 마지막 학년(고등학교 3 학년) 또는 대학교/대학 마지막 학년(보통 4 학년)에 다니는 학생

2. An elderly person, senior citizen (~older than 65 years old)
    노인, 고령자(65 세 이상)

Say Instead:
미국식 영어로 말할려면:

He is older than me. (*For age only* 나이에 관해 말할 때)

He is my boss/manager/supervisor. (*For position* 직책을 말할 때)

Konglish Sentence	American English
One of *my seniors* in college was very mean.	This guy, who *was a year ahead of me in college*, was very mean. He *was a year ahead of me in college*, and he was very mean.

내 대학교 선배는 아주 나빴다.

Life & Culture in the USA:
미국의 삶과 문화:

School in the USA is divided into grades 1-12. Though there is some variation based on school district, typically Elementary School is 1st through 5th grade. Middle School is 6th through 8th grade. High School is 9th through 12th grade. Americans can always refer to their definitive grade "I'm in 5th grade." "I'm in 8th grade." "I'm in 10th grade." In Korea, it is common to say, "I am in 3rd grade of Middle School," or "I am in 2nd grade of High School." This is very confusing to Americans as the grade-level count does not start over each time you move up. In high school, the last 4 years can be also referred to with special words.

미국의 학교는 1 학년에서 12 학년으로 나뉩니다. 교육구에 따라 약간의 차이가 있지만, 일반적으로 초등학교는 1 학년에서 5 학년입니다. 중학교는 6 학년에서 8 학년입니다. 고등학교는 9 학년에서 12 학년입니다. 미국인들은 보통 학년을 정확히 말합니다. "저는 5 학년입니다." "저는 8 학년입니다." "저는 10 학년입니다." 한국에서는 "저는 중학교 3 학년입니다." 또는 "저는 고등학교 2 학년입니다."라고 말하는 것이 일반적입니다. 이것은 미국인들에게 매우 혼란스러운 것인데, 학년이 올라갈 때마다 시작되지 않기 때문입니다. 고등학교에서 마지막 4 년은 특별한 단어로 지칭하기도 합니다.

9th grade = Freshman = 9 학년

10th grade = Sophomore = 10 학년

11th grade = Junior = 11 학년

12th grade = Senior = 12 학년

So it would be common to say any of the following:
따라서 다음과 같이 말하는 것이 일반적입니다:

저는 9 학년 입니다:

- "I'm in 9th grade."
- "I'm a 9th-grader."
- "I'm a freshman."
- "I'm in my freshman year."

저는 12 학년입니다:

- "I'm in 12th grade."
- "I'm a 12th-grader."
- "I'm a senior."
- "I'm in my senior year."

How Americans use Senior:
미국인들이 "Senior"를 사용하는 법:

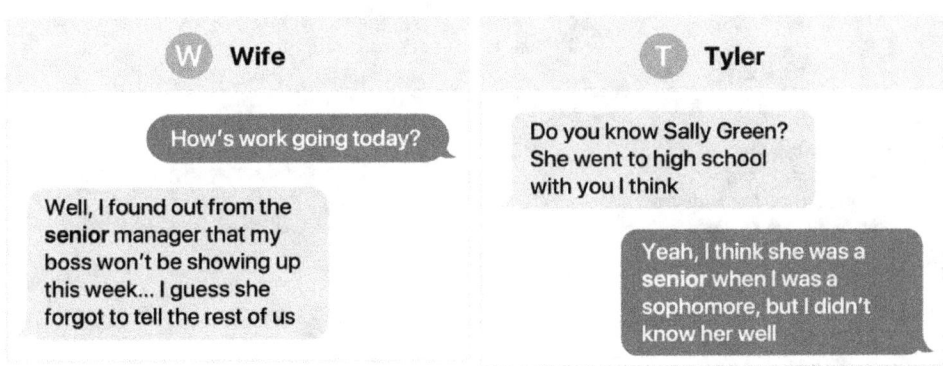

W Wife	T Tyler
How's work going today?	Do you know Sally Green? She went to high school with you I think
Well, I found out from the **senior** manager that my boss won't be showing up this week... I guess she forgot to tell the rest of us	Yeah, I think she was a **senior** when I was a sophomore, but I didn't know her well

SHARP 샤프

Meaning in American English:
미국식 영어로 의미:

(Adjective) Something very pointy; maybe it could cut something easily, like a sharp knife.
(형용사) 아주 뾰족한 것. 아마 날카로운 칼같이 쉽게 자를 수도 있습니다.

Say Instead:
미국식 영어로 말할려면:

Mechanical pencil

Konglish Sentence	American English
Let's write this with a *sharp*. 	Let's write this with a *mechanical pencil.*
이 샤프로 적자.	

How Americans use Sharp:
미국인들이 "Sharp"를 사용하는 법:

 Sister-in-law

> I heard you guys went to the hospital yesterday! What happened? Is everything ok?

> Yeah, we are ok and at home. Around dinner, Aaron said he felt a **sharp** pain in his chest. The doctors thought it might be a heart attack, but after several tests, they said it was just stress.

 Halloween Party

> Pumpkin carving will be at our apartment this evening starting at 7pm. Bring **sharp** knives if you have any!

> Perfect! We'll be there a 7pm **sharp**!

SIGN PEN 싸인펜

Meaning in American English:
미국식 영어로 의미:

Doesn't exist

이 단어는 존재하지 않습니다

Say Instead:
미국식 영어로 말할려면:

Thin felt-tipped permanent marker, Sharpie

Konglish Sentence	American English
Please put your sign here with your *sign pen*.	Please put your signature here with a *felt-tipped pen*.

이 싸인펜으로 싸인해주세요.

SPECS 스펙

Meaning in American English:
미국식 영어로 의미:

1. Glasses: short for "spectacles"
   안경: 'spectacles'의 줄임말
2. Technical specifics (size and weight of a product, memory size of a phone)
   기술적인 세부사항 (예: 제품의 크기와 무게, 전화기의 메모리 크기)

Say Instead:
미국식 영어로 말할려면:

Qualifications, Experience

Konglish Sentence	American English
The candidate for the job has some really good *specs*.	The candidate for the job has some really good *qualifications and experience*.

그 지원자는 스펙이 아주 좋다.

How Americans use Specs:
미국인들이 "Specs"을 사용하는 법:

 Husband

Hey I looked at the **specs** of the battery...

It should be able to power the induction burner for about an hour.

Awesome! That'll be perfect for camping!

TRAINING 트레이닝

Meaning in American English:
미국식 영어로 의미:

Training is usually a course or period of time where you learn a specific set of skills.

When you start a new job, you will have some training or a training period at the beginning for a week or two where you are learning how to do the job.

You might also have a specific training course to complete for specific skills, often job related but for other things as well (for example, you might need to complete a six-hour safety training each year for your job, or you might attend a weekend training course related to your work, or you can complete a CPR and first aid training course to gain CPR and first aid certification).

트레이닝은 일반적으로 특정 기술을 배우는 과정 또는 기간입니다.

새로운 일을 시작할 때, 1-2 주 동안 초기에 일하는 방법을 배우는 훈련 또는 훈련 기간을 가질 것입니다.

특정 기술(종종 직무와 관련된)을 위해 이수해야 하는 교육 과정을 들을 수도 있습니다(예를 들어, 직무를 위해 매년 6 시간의 안전 교육을 이수해야 하거나, 업무와 관련된 주말 교육 과정을 이수해야 하거나, 심폐소생술 및 응급 처치 교육 과정을 이수해야 할 수도 있습니다).

Say Instead:
미국식 영어로 말할려면:

Internship

Konglish Sentence		American English
He's doing a *training* with XYZ company this summer.	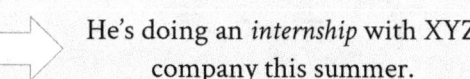	He's doing an *internship* with XYZ company this summer.
그는 XYZ 라는 회사에서 올 여름에 트레이닝을 한다.		

How Americans use Training:
미국인들이 "Training"을 사용하는 법:

---

to: Me <Volunteer@volunteering.com>

subject: Volunteering Application

Thank you for completing your volunteer application! The next step is to complete our Awareness and Abuse Prevention *Training* online. It should take around 2 hours to complete.

When you complete the *training*, please email us a copy your *training* certificate for confirmation, and we will contact you regarding the next steps

---

to: Me <Employee@TheBusiness.com>

subject: MANDATORY Business-Wide *Training*

All employees must attend one of the scheduled *trainings* this week. THIS *TRAINING* IS MANDATORY for all new and current employees. If you cannot attend one of the 4 scheduled *trainings*, please contact your manager ASAP to make the necessary arrangements to get this *training* completed.

Training Options:

Monday 2-6pm	In Person at our Office Location
Wednesday 6-10pm	Virtual, Online via TeemsMeet
Saturday 9am-1pm	In Person at our Office Location
Sunday 9am-1pm	Virtual, Online via TeemsMeet

WHITE 화이트

Meaning in American English:
미국식 영어로 의미:

Only the color white

색상 하얀색

Say Instead:
미국식 영어로 말할려면:

White out

Konglish Sentence	American English
I made a mistake. I need some *white.*	I made a mistake. I need some *white out.*

실수를 해서 화이트가 필요하다.

WHITE WORKER 화이트워커

Meaning in American English:
미국식 영어로 의미:

Doesn't exist

이 단어는 존재하지 않습니다

Say Instead:
미국식 영어로 말할려면:

White-collar worker

Konglish Sentence	American English
He was a *white worker* for 20 years, so he was excited for a change when he retired and started learning to be a mechanic.	He was a *white-collar worker* for 20 years, so he was excited for a change when he retired and started learning to be a mechanic.

그는 20 년동안 사무직 노동을 했다.
그래서 그는 은퇴 후 새로운 기술을 배우는 것을 아주 기대한다.

WORKING LEVEL PEOPLE 직원/사원

Meaning in American English:
미국식 영어로 의미:

Doesn't exist

이 단어는 존재하지 않습니다

Say Instead:
미국식 영어로 말하려면:

Say their specific position, Non-execs

Konglish Sentence	American English
A lot of *working level people* in Korea work at night as well.	A lot of *non-execs* in Korea work late hours at night as well.

한국의 많은 회사 직원들은 야근을 많이 한다.

9

TECHNOLOGY
기술

COMPUTER 컴퓨터

Meaning in American English:
미국식 영어로 의미:

Computer is a very general word for any kind of machine that can do computing operations and includes PCs, desktops, laptops, industrial computers, supercomputers, etc.

컴퓨터는 컴퓨터 작업을 할 수 있는 모든 종류의 기계를 지칭하는 매우 일반적인 단어로 PC, 데스크톱, 노트북, 산업용 컴퓨터, 슈퍼컴퓨터 등을 포함합니다.

Say Instead:
미국식 영어로 말할려면:

Desktop computer

Konglish Sentence	American English
I don't have a *computer*; I only have a notebook.	I don't have a *desktop computer*; I only have a laptop.
나 컴퓨터 없어. 노트북밖에 없어.	

DIKA 디카

Meaning in American English:
미국식 영어로 의미:

Doesn't exist

이 단어는 존재하지 않습니다

Say Instead:
미국식 영어로 말할려면:

Digital camera, Camera

Konglish Sentence	American English
I'm bringing my *dika* on our trip.	I'm bringing my *digital camera* on our trip.

난 디카를 여행갈 때 가져갈꺼야.

FLASH 플래시

Meaning in American English:
미국식 영어로 의미:

A quick bright light - the flash on
your camera for a picture
빠르고 밝은 조명 - 사진을 찍기
위해 카메라에 있는 플래시

Say Instead:
미국식 영어로 말할려면:

Flashlight

Konglish Sentence		American English
When you go camping, you should take a *flash*.		When you go camping, you should take a *flashlight*.
캠핑 갈 땐, 꼭 플래시를 가지고 가야한다.		

How Americans use Flash:
미국인들이 "Flash"를 사용하는 법:

 Haley

Once I took a picture of the
dog and accidentally used
the **flash**

Ohhh that's why every
time I hold up the phone,
she squints like it's gonna
flash

GAME ROOM / PC BAR / PC ROOM
게임방 / 피씨방

Meaning in American English:
미국식 영어로 의미:

Game room - A room in a house used for games, toys, books, etc., for kids

게임방 - 보통 아이들을 위한 게임, 장난감, 책이 있는 방

PC Bar/PC Room – doesn't exist

피씨방 – 이 단어는 존재하지 않습니다

Say Instead:
미국식 영어로 말할려면:

Gaming cafe. The place where you play computer games exclusively doesn't exist at all. You can say "internet cafe" but that's a different meaning.

Konglish Sentence	American English
I loved going to the *game room / PC room* when I was young.	I loved going to the *gaming café to play computer games* with my friends when I was young.

나는 어릴 때 피시방에 가는 걸 좋아했다.

How Americans use Game Room:
미국인들이 "Game Room"을 사용하는 법:

> **D Deirdre**
>
> We have a **game room** upstairs, so we can put the kids in there so the adults can talk downstairs
>
> Sounds great!

GMAP 지맵

Meaning in American English:
미국식 영어로 의미:

Doesn't exist

이 단어는 존재하지 않습니다

Say Instead:
미국식 영어로 말할려면:

Google Maps

Konglish Sentence	American English
I always use *GMap* so I don't get lost.	I always use *Google Maps* so I don't get lost.

난 길을 헤매지 않게 항상 지맵을 사용한다.

HAND PHONE 핸드 폰

Meaning in American English:
미국식 영어로 의미:

Doesn't exist

이 단어는 존재하지 않습니다

Say Instead:
미국식 영어로 말할려면:

Phone, Cell phone

Konglish Sentence	American English
I'm shocked that even kids have *hand phones* nowadays.	I'm shocked that even kids have *phones* nowadays.

요즘에 아이들도 핸드폰이 있는게 놀랍다.

HOMEPI 홈피

Meaning in American English:
미국식 영어로 의미:

Doesn't exist

이 단어는 존재하지 않습니다

Say Instead:
미국식 영어로 말할려면:

Website, Webpage, Blog

Konglish Sentence	American English
I found the information on the *homepi*.	I found the information on the *website*.

그 홈피에서 그 정보를 찾았다.

ID / MEMBER ID 아이디

Meaning in American English:
미국식 영어로 의미:

Membership number to an exclusive club or organization (e.g., Costco member ID number)

전용 단체 또는 조직의 회원번호 (예: 코스트코 회원번호)

Say Instead:
미국식 영어로 말할려면:

Username, Login

Konglish Sentence	American English
What's your *member ID* for the new SNS?	What's your *username/login* for the new social media?

네 페북 아이디가 뭐야?

MULTI-PLAYER 멀티플레이어

Meaning in American English:
미국식 영어로 의미:

More than one person can play the game
(video games)
한 명 이상이 게임 할 수 있는
(비디오 게임)

Say Instead:
미국식 영어로 말할려면:

Multi-tasker (person/noun), Multi-task (verb)

Konglish Sentence	American English
She's a *multi-player*.	She's good at *multi-tasking*.

그녀는 멀티플레이어이다.

How Americans use Multi-player:
미국인들이 "Multi-player"를 사용하는 법:

 Brent

I've got a few **multi-player** games in my car that I can bring to the going away party tomorrow

Sounds great!

 Girlfriend

Can both of us play the game together?

It's not a **multi-player** game, but we can take turns with the controller

NAVI (NAVIGATION) 네비 (네비게이션)

Meaning in American English:
미국식 영어로 의미:

Navi doesn't exist

Navi 라는 단어는 존재하지 않습니다

Navigation - the process or system of finding the right way to go

내비게이션 - 올바른 길을 찾는 프로세스 또는 시스템.

Say Instead:
미국식 영어로 말할려면:

GPS, Navigation system

Konglish Sentence	American English
Does your car have *navi*?	Does your car have a *GPS*?
니 자동차에 네비 있어?	

PC 피씨

Meaning in American English:
미국식 영어로 의미:

PC means personal computer and can be any type of personal computer including desktops and laptops, but many people use PC to mean desktop, or a type of computer that is not easily moved around. In this, they are using PC to mean desktop.

PC 는 개인용 컴퓨터를 의미하고 데스크톱과 노트북을 포함한 모든 종류의 개인용 컴퓨터가 될 수 있지만, 많은 사람들은 PC 를 데스크톱 또는 쉽게 옮겨 다니지 않는 컴퓨터를 의미하기 위해 사용합니다. 이런 경우엔, PC 는 데스크탑을 뜻합니다.

Say Instead:
미국식 영어로 말할려면:

Desktop computer, Computer

Konglish Sentence	American English
My *PC* is pretty old, so it doesn't work well.	My *(desktop) computer* is pretty old, so it doesn't work well.

내 피씨는 오래되서 성능이 안좋다.

How Americans use PC:
미국인들이 "PC"를 사용하는 법:

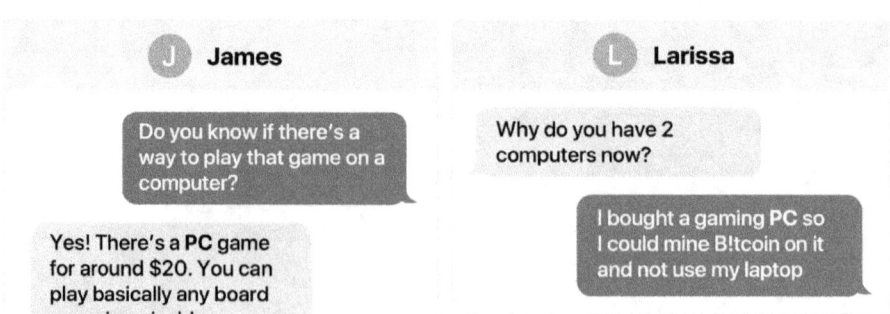

J James

> Do you know if there's a way to play that game on a computer?

Yes! There's a **PC** game for around $20. You can play basically any board game imaginable.

L Larissa

> Why do you have 2 computers now?

I bought a gaming **PC** so I could mine B!tcoin on it and not use my laptop

SECRET NUMBER 비밀번호

Meaning in American English:
미국식 영어로 의미:

Any number that is secret

비밀인 번호

Say Instead:
미국식 영어로 말할려면:

Password, PIN number

Konglish Sentence	American English
You should never share your *secret number.*	You should never share your *password / pin number.*

비밀번호는 절대 공유하면 안된다.

SELCA 셀카

Meaning in American English:
미국식 영어로 의미:

Doesn't exist

이 단어는 존재하지 않습니다

Say Instead:
미국식 영어로 말할려면:

Selfie

Konglish Sentence		American English
Let's take a selca!	⟹	Let's take a selfie!
셀카 찍자!		

SELF-CAM 셀프캠

Meaning in American English:
미국식 영어로 의미:

Doesn't exist

이 단어는 존재하지 않습니다

Say Instead:
미국식 영어로 말할려면:

(Taking) a video of yourself, A video

Phone stand, phone holder

Konglish Sentence	American English
Self-cams are really popular for teenagers on social media.	It's really popular for teenagers to *take and post videos of themselves* on social media.

셀프캠을 청소년들이 많이 쓴다.

10

MONEY
돈

▶ Scan for Audio!

BIG MONEY 빅머니

Meaning in American English:
미국식 영어로 의미:

Typically only used in casual conversation, in jokes, on a game show, or as a tagline. It is less common to use this in serious discussions of money or in professional settings. It may sometimes be appropriate even in serious discussions, but it has the risk of making it sound like you aren't taking the discussion seriously and are making jokes instead.

일반적으로 일상적인 대화, 농담, 게임쇼에서 핵심이 되는 구절로만 사용됩니다. 돈에 대한 진지한 토론이나 전문적인 환경에서 이 용어를 사용하는 경우는 적습니다. 때로는 진지한 토론에서도 적절할 수 있지만, 토론을 진지하게 받아들이지 않고 농담을 하는 것처럼 들릴 위험이 있습니다.

Say Instead:
미국식 영어로 말할려면:

A lot of money

Konglish Sentence	American English
The boss makes *big money*.	The boss makes *a lot of money*.
보스는 빅머니를 벌어.	

FUND 펀드

Meaning in American English:
미국식 영어로 의미:

Money saved and used to pay for a specific event or use or cause
특정 이벤트, 사용 또는 원인에 대한 지불을 위해 저축되고 사용되는 돈

Say Instead:
미국식 영어로 말하려면:

Fundraiser

Konglish Sentence	American English
They have a *fund* for the school every year.	They have a *fundraiser* for the school every year.

그들은 학교를 위해 매 해 펀드를 모은다.

How Americans use Fund(s):
미국인들이 "Fund"를 사용하는 법:

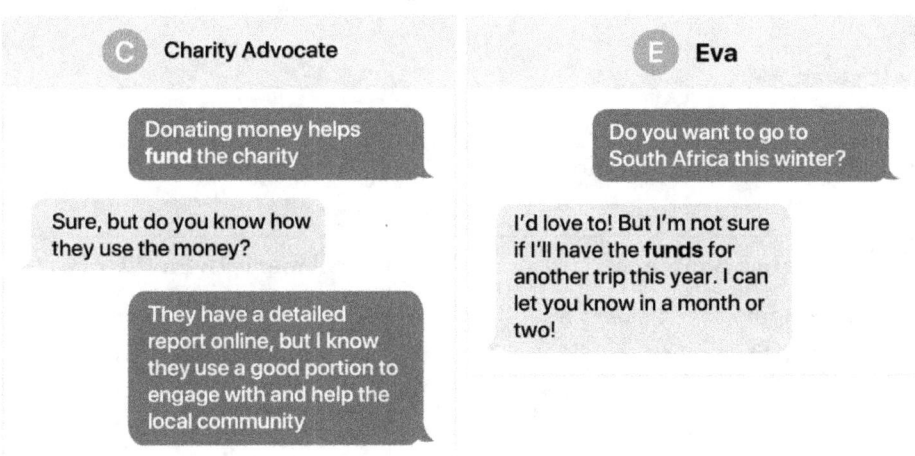

C Charity Advocate

> Donating money helps **fund** the charity

Sure, but do you know how they use the money?

> They have a detailed report online, but I know they use a good portion to engage with and help the local community

E Eva

> Do you want to go to South Africa this winter?

I'd love to! But I'm not sure if I'll have the **funds** for another trip this year. I can let you know in a month or two!

POCKET MONEY 포켓 머니

Meaning in American English:
미국식 영어로 의미:

Extra money in your "pocket", usually used for buying small things, like loose change or left over money after you spent your money on something else. To a small number of people, this can also mean an allowance given to kids. Usage of this phrase seems to vary throughout the United States, so you may find people who use this term regularly, but you also may find many people who find this term outdated or awkward-sounding.

'주머니'에 있는 여분의 돈. 무엇인가 사고 남은 잔돈으로 작은 것들을 살 때 사용됩니다. 몇몇 사람들에게 이것은 아이들에게 주어지는 용돈을 의미할 수 있습니다. 이 문구의 사용은 미국 전역에서 다양하므로 이 용어를 정기적으로 사용하는 사람들을 볼 수도 있고, 이 용어가 구식이거나 어색하게 생각하는 사람들을 볼 수도 있습니다.

Say Instead:
미국식 영어로 말할려면:

Extra money, A little extra money

Konglish Sentence		American English
He earned some *pocket money* by selling his old books.		He earned some *extra money* by selling his old books.
그는 중고책을 팔아서 용돈을 모았다.		

POOR 포어

Meaning in American English:
미국식 영어로 의미:

Only money. "He is *poor*," means he doesn't have a lot of money or belongings.
오직 돈/부. "그는 가난하다"는 것은 그가 많은 돈이나 소유물을 가지고 있지 않다는 것을 의미합니다.

Say Instead:
미국식 영어로 말할려면:

He/she is bad at something.
I feel bad for them.

Konglish Sentence	American English
He is *so poor* at basketball. 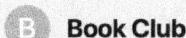	He is *so bad at* basketball.

그는 농구를 못한다.

Konglish Sentence	American English
She broke his heart. *He is so poor.*	She broke his heart. *He is so sad. / I feel so bad for him.*

그 여자는 그 남자의 마음을 아프게했다. 그가 불쌍하다.

How Americans use Poor:
미국인들이 "Poor"를 사용하는 법:

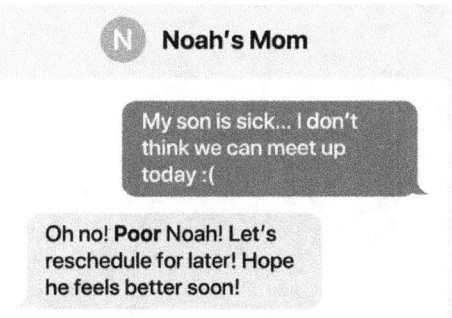

N Noah's Mom	B Book Club
My son is sick... I don't think we can meet up today :(	What's the book about?
Oh no! **Poor** Noah! Let's reschedule for later! Hope he feels better soon!	It's based on a true story of the author's life growing up in a super **poor** village and school in Indonesia on one of the wealthiest islands.

RENTAL FEE 렌트비

Meaning in American English:
미국식 영어로 의미:

An additional fee you may need to pay when renting a place (like an event venue or a storage unit) or a thing (like a kind of equipment); not the same as the price of rent

장소(행사장, 보관소 등) 또는 물건(장비 등)을 임대할 때 추가로 지불해야 할 비용. 렌트비를 뜻하지 않습니다.

Say Instead:
미국식 영어로 말할려면:

Rent, Rent money

Konglish Sentence	American English
In the United States, you pay your *rental fee* for your apart each month.	In the United States, you pay your *rent* for your apartment each month.
미국에선, 렌트비를 매 달 내야한다.	

SMALL MONEY 스몰 머니

Meaning in American English:
미국식 영어로 의미:

Literally physically small money;

money that is small in size (not quantity)

말 그대로 물리적으로 작은 돈. (양이

아닌) 크기가 작은 돈

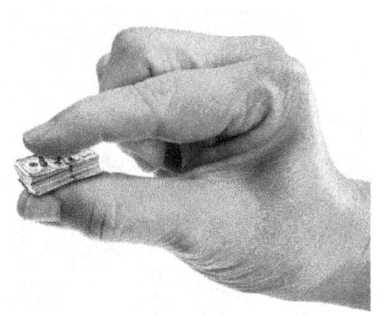

Say Instead:
미국식 영어로 말할려면:

A little money, Not enough money, Less money

Konglish Sentence	American English
My son wants to become a gagman. That's OK, but will he be comfortable making *small money?*	My son wants to become a comedian. That's OK, but will he be comfortable making such *little money?*

내 아들은 개그맨이 되고 싶어한다.
좋지만, 적은 돈으로 편하게 살 수 있을까?

11

SHOPPING
쇼핑

Scan for Audio!

Bargain 바겐

Meaning in American English:

미국식 영어로 의미:

1. (Verb) To negotiate

   (동사) 흥정하다/협상하다

2. (Noun) Something that is cheaper / a better deal than usual

   평소보다 싸게 파는 물건

Say Instead:

미국식 영어로 말할려면:

Sale

Konglish Sentence		American English
That store is having a *bargain* this weekend.		That store is having a *sale* this weekend.
그 가게는 이번 주말에 세일을 한다.		

CORNER 코너

Meaning in American English:
미국식 영어로 의미:

A place where two or more sides meet
모서리, 둘 이상의 면이 만나는 곳

Say Instead:
미국식 영어로 말할려면:

Department

Konglish Sentence	American English
I went to the fish *corner* to buy some fish.	I went to the seafood *department* to buy some fish.

생선코너에 가서 생선 샀다.

DEPART/DEPARTMENT 디파트/디파트먼드

Meaning in American English:
미국식 영어로 의미:

> *Department:* (Noun) A section or area of a store or business (e.g., electronics department, accounting department)
> (명사) 매장의 한 구역 또는 구역 (예. 가전제품 부서)

> *Depart:* (Verb) To leave
> (동사) 출발하다

Say Instead:
미국식 영어로 말할려면:

> Mall, Korean department store

Konglish Sentence	American English
In Korea, you an spend all day at a *depart*! They're so big and have everything!	In Korea, you can spend all day at a *department store*! They're so big and have everything!

한국에서는 하루 종일 백화점에서 놀 수 있어! 모든 게 크고 다 있어!

How Americans use Depart and Department:
미국인들이 "Depart and Department"를 사용하는 법:

 Greg

> They basically laid off my entire **department** including my boss and boss's boss. They only kept the people at the very bottom who can be moved around easily

> Wow! That's terrible! I'm so sorry to hear that. I'm sure you'll find something else soon though!

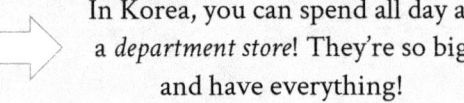 **LY Airlines**

> LY Airlines Alert: Your flight now **departs** at 9:50 AM from gate C15.

Doz 다스

Meaning in American English:
미국식 영어로 의미:

Doesn't exist. Sounds like "does"

이 단어는 존재하지 않습니다. 'Does' 처럼 들립니다.

Say Instead:
미국식 영어로 말할려면:

Dozen

Konglish Sentence	American English
How many donuts do you want?	How many donuts do you want?
A *doz*.	A *dozen*.

도넛츠 얼마나 드릴까요? 다스요.

EYE SHOPPING 아이 쇼핑

Meaning in American English:
미국식 영어로 의미:

Doesn't exist; Sounds like you're shopping to buy a new eye.

이 단어는 존재하지 않습니다. 새로운 눈을 사기 위해 쇼핑하는 것처럼 들립니다.

Say Instead:
미국식 영어로 말할려면:

Window shopping

Konglish Sentence	American English
I'm not planning to buy anything today, just *eye shopping*. 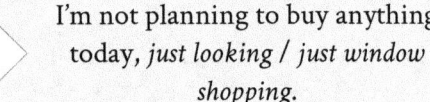	I'm not planning to buy anything today, *just looking / just window shopping*.

뭐 사고 싶지는 않고 아이 쇼핑을 할 것이다.

GROCERY 그로셔리

Meaning in American English:
미국식 영어로 의미:

Food and items you buy at the grocery store
식료품점에서 구매하는 것들

Say Instead:
미국식 영어로 말할려면:

Grocery store

Konglish Sentence	American English
I went to the *grocery* on Sunday.	I went to the *grocery store* on Sunday.

토요일에 그로셔리 갔다.

How Americans use Grocery:
미국인들이 "Grocery"를 사용하는 법:

S Significant Other

Can you think of anything we need from the **grocery** store?

Definitely milk, eggs, bread, mustard, oatmeal, and broccoli

Awesome – I'm making a list so I can stop and get **groceries** on the way home from work later

HANDMADE 핸드메이드

Meaning in American English:
미국식 영어로 의미:

Handmade is usually for crafted items (e.g., handmade jewelry)
핸드메이드는 일반적으로 세공품을 위한 것입니다. (예: 핸드메이드 주얼리)

Say Instead:
미국식 영어로 말할려면:

Handmade *(for crafted items, e.g., handmade jewelry)*
Homemade *(for any item made at home, e.g., homemade pie/candles)*
Made from scratch *(for food that is made from fresh ingredients)*

Konglish Sentence	American English
Our bread is *handmade*. 	Our bread is *made from scratch*.
우리 빵은 핸드매이드이다.	

Additional Info:
그 외:

Handmade is usually for crafted items. For example, handmade jewelry, handmade furniture, handmade knives, handmade shoes. This typically means the maker has a superior skill, and items are often made by artisans who sell their goods for an expensive price. Because they are not mass-produced, the items are generally worth more and cost more. You can find many handmade goods for sale on Etsy or at unique artisan stores or festivals across the United States.

Homemade is usually for any item made at home. For example, homemade pie, potholders, or playdough. Many children make a homemade gift for their parents on Christmas. For example, they learn to sew something that says, "Mom" written on it. Homemade food is usually another common use. Typically, homemade food is made at home from scratch. It usually isn't sold for money unless it is for a fundraiser like a bake sale to raise money for a cause or school.

Made from scratch is for food that is made from fresh ingredients, and nothing is pre-prepared. Made from scratch can be used for homemade food that is made from completely fresh ingredients and nothing pre-made or frozen. It can also be used at a restaurant where they want to show that the food has been made fresh that day from fresh ingredients. A popular grocery store in Houston is proud to advertise their "made from scratch tortillas."

Handmade 는 어떤 물건을 만들 때 쓰입니다. 예를 들면, 손으로 만든 악세사리, 가구, 칼, 신발등이 있습니다. 보통 그것을 만드는 사람은 장인이고 아주 비싼 가격에 물건이 판매됩니다. 대량 생산하지 않으며 더 많은 가치가 있고 가격이 더 비쌉니다. 미국에선 Etsy 나 특별한 장인 가게나 행사에서 핸드매이드 물건을 살 수 있습니다.

Homemade 는 보통 집에서 만들어집니다. 예를 들면, 직접 만든 파이, 냄비 받침대, 찰흙등이 있습니다. 많은 아이들이 부모님크리스마스 선물을 직접 만듭니다. 예를 들면, "엄마에게"라고 새겨진 뜨게질 한 물건이 있습니다. 집에서 만든 음식은 보통 또 다른 용도로 사용 될 수 있습니다. 집에서 직접 처음부터 만들어집니다. 보통 돈을 벌기위해 만들지 않고 학교를 위한 베이크 세일이니 모금 행사를 위한 경우가 많습니다.

Made from scratch 는 신선한 재료로 만들어지고 아무것도 미리 준비되지 않은 것입니다. 집에서 만든 음식을 Made from scratch 로 만들었다는 것은 신선한 재료나 미리 준비하지 않고 냉동안 된것으로 만든것을 뜻합니다. 신선한 재료로 음식이 만들어졌다는 것을 보여주고 싶은 식당에서 사용될 수 있습니다. 휴스턴에 한 유명한 마트에선 '직접 만든 토티아'라고 자랑스럽게 광고합니다.

How Americans use Handmade:
미국인들이 "Handmade"를 사용하는 법:

MAKER 메이커

Meaning in American English:
미국식 영어로 의미:

Someone or something who makes something (e.g., ship-maker, coffee maker, filmmaker); a creator, often used to refer to God

무언가를 만드는 사람 또는 기계 (예: 선박 제조업자, 커피 메이커, 영화 제작자); 종종 신을 언급하는 창조자

Say Instead:
미국식 영어로 말할려면:

Brand

Konglish Sentence	American English
What's the *maker* of these sunglasses?	What *brand* are these sunglasses?

이 썬글라스는 무슨 브랜드인가요?

How Americans use Maker:
미국인들이 "Maker"를 사용하는 법:

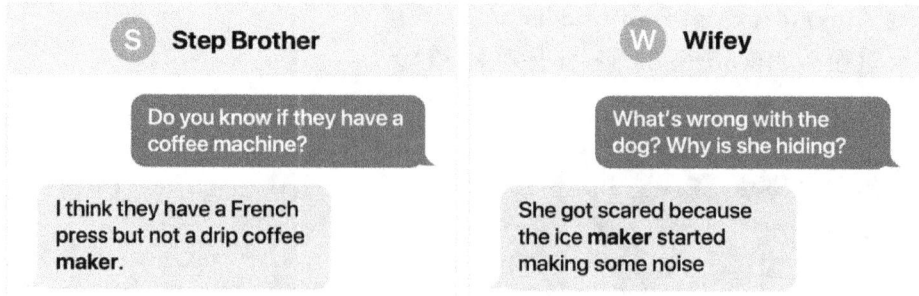

S Step Brother

> Do you know if they have a coffee machine?

I think they have a French press but not a drip coffee **maker**.

W Wifey

> What's wrong with the dog? Why is she hiding?

She got scared because the ice **maker** started making some noise

MART 마트

Meaning in American English:
미국식 영어로 의미:

Not used as a word by itself, usually used as part of the name of a store
(e.g., Mini Mart, H Mart, Malaysian Food Mart, etc.)
자체적인 단어로 사용되지 않으며, 보통 매장명칭의 일부로 사용됩니다
(예: 미니마트, H 마트, 말레이시아 푸드마트 등)

Say Instead:
미국식 영어로 말할려면:

Store, Grocery store

Konglish Sentence	American English
I went to the *mart* this weekend.	I went to the *grocery store / supermarket* this weekend.

이번 주말에 마트 갔었다.

ONE PLUS ONE 원플러스원

Meaning in American English:
미국식 영어로 의미:

Math (1+1)

수학(1+1)

Say Instead:
미국식 영어로 말할려면:

Buy one, get one free

Konglish Sentence	American English
The store is having a *one plus one*.	The store is having a *buy one, get one free sale*.

가게에서 1 플러스 1 세일을 하고 있다.

How Americans use One Plus One:
미국인들이 "One Plus One"을 사용하는 법:

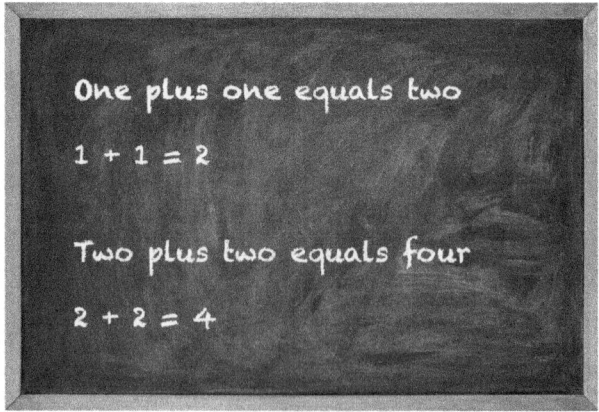

246

PART 파트

Meaning in American English:
미국식 영어로 의미:

A piece of a whole or a section or portion of something bigger
전체나 큰 부분의 작은 부분이나 조각

Say Instead:
미국식 영어로 말할려면:

Department

Konglish Sentence	American English
She works in the accounting *part*.	She works in the accounting *department*.

그녀는 회계 부서에서 일한다.

Konglish Sentence	American English
I didn't like working in the produce *part* at the mart.	I didn't like working in the produce *department* at the grocery store.

나는 마트에서 농산물 파트 일을 하는 게 싫었다.

Real Life Story:
실화:

Recently, I was shopping at our local HMart and needed to buy some sweet potatoes. I didn't see any, so as we walked around the store away from the produce department, I kept my eyes opened for any other employees I could ask about it. Finally, we got to the seafood area, and I saw a nice and knowledgeable-looking lady.

"Excuse me, do you have any fresh sweet potatoes today?" I asked.

"I'm sorry, I don't know. This is the fish part," she responded.

"Gam-sa-hab-ni-da," I said in my really bad American accent to thank her for her time before moving on. My husband looked slightly confused, but thankfully because my Korean friends and students have taught me tons of Konglish, I understood. This was the fish department, and if we wanted to know about the sweet potatoes, we had to ask someone else.

최근에 집 근처에 있는 H 마트에서 쇼핑하고 있었고 고구마를 사고 싶었습니다. 그런데 잘 찾지 못했고 야채와 과일 코너 주위를 빙빙 돌며 직원에게 물어보려고 살펴보았습니다. 해산물 코너에서 친절하게 생긴 마트를 잘 알 것 같은 아주머니에게 물어봤습니다.

"죄송한데요, 오늘 신선한 고구마가 있나요?"

그 분은 "죄송합니다, 잘 모르겠네요. 여기는 생선 코너입니다."라고 대답하셨다.

그래서 난 "감사합니다"라고 서툴게 미국 억양으로 말하고 다시 찾기 시작했습니다. 남편은 그 표현을 이해하지 못했지만 감사하게도 난 한국 친구들과 학생들이 가르쳐준 많은 콩글리시들 때문에 무슨 말인지 이해할 수 있었습니다. 그 부서는 생선 부서였고 고구마를 찾고 싶다면 다른 분에게 물어보아야 했습니다.

SELF 셀프 (서비스)

Meaning in American English:
미국식 영어로 의미:

Doesn't usually exist alone; only as myself, yourself, himself, herself, itself, oneself, themselves, ourselves.

보통 단어 자체로만 사용되지 않습니다. Myself, yourself, himself, herself, itself, oneself, themselves, ourselves 같이 사용됩니다.

Say Instead:
미국식 영어로 말할려면:

Self-service, Self-serve
BYO, Bring your own

Konglish Sentence	American English
The water is *self*.	The water is *self-serve*.
물은 셀프이다.	

Konglish Sentence	American English
The water is *self*.	*Bring your own (BYO)* water.
물은 셀프로 가져온다.	

SERVICE 서비스

Meaning in American English:
미국식 영어로 의미:

1. (Noun) The act of helping, serving, or assisting someone (e.g., community service = doing free work to help your community or those in need)
    (명사) 누군가를 돕고, 섬기거나 돕는 행위 (예: 사회봉사 = 지역사회 또는 도움이 필요한 사람들을 돕기 위해 무료로 봉사하는 행위)

2. (Noun) Work, help, or assistance provided for a customer (versus a good) (e.g., customer service = helping customers with needs, questions, complaint)
    (명사) 고객을 위해 제공하는 일, 도움 또는지원 (예: 고객 서비스 = 고객의 요구, 질문, 불만, 문제 해결등을 돕는 일)

3. (Noun) Jobs that provide a skill (rather than a good) (e.g., accountant or lawyer provides a service (or help with taxes or information and advice), a language school provides a service (of providing lessons in a language)
    (명사) 물품이 아닌 기술을 제공하는 직업 (예: 회계사 또는 변호사가 제공하는 서비스 (세금 또는 정보와 조언의 도움), 어학원이 제공하는 서비스 (언어 수업을 제공)

Say Instead:
미국식 영어로 말할려면:

On the house, Complementary, Free

Konglish Sentence	American English
The manager was so nice and gave us a free dessert for *service*.	The manager was so nice and gave us a *complementary* dessert.
매니저가 친절해서 무료로 디저트를 서비스로 주셨다.	

How Americans use Service:
미국인들이 "Service"를 사용하는 법:

SUPER 슈퍼

Meaning in American English:
미국식 영어로 의미:

1. Never a place. It means excellent, great, wonderful, very, super...
   절대로 장소를 뜻하는 것이 아닙니다. 훌륭하고, 멋지고, 아주 좋다.
2. Super can also be short for "superintendent" (manager of a building)
   Super 는 'superintendent'(건물의 관리자)의 줄임말일 수도 있습니다.

Say Instead:
미국식 영어로 말할려면:

Supermarket, Grocery store

Konglish Sentence	American English
I went to the *super* this weekend.	I went to the *supermarket* this weekend.
이번 주말에 수퍼에 갔었다.	

How Americans use Super:
미국인들이 "Super"를 사용하는 법:

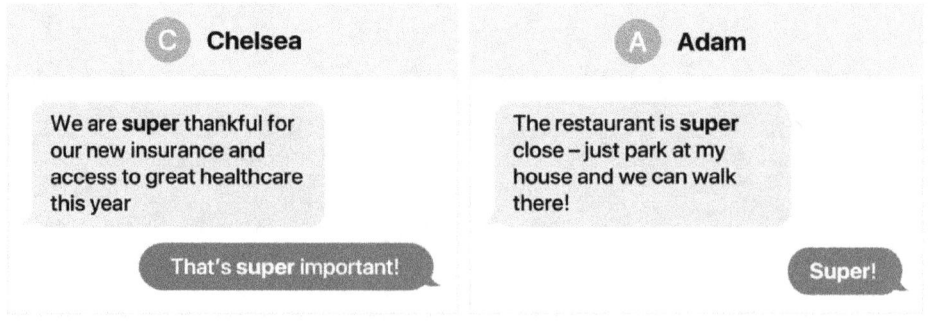

C Chelsea

We are **super** thankful for our new insurance and access to great healthcare this year

That's **super** important!

A Adam

The restaurant is **super** close – just park at my house and we can walk there!

Super!

HOUSES, HOMES, & LIVING
거주지, 집과 삶

12

AIR CON 에어컨

Meaning in American English:
미국식 영어로 의미:

Doesn't exist

이 단어는 존재하지 않습니다

Say Instead:
미국식 영어로 말할려면:

Air Conditioner, A/C

Konglish Sentence	American English
It's hot. Can we please use *air con*?	It's hot. Can we please use the *air conditioner*?

여기 덥다. 에어컨 틀어도 될까?

APART (APT) 아파트

Meaning in American English:
미국식 영어로 의미:

Separated, not together. Apt. is often used to abbreviate "apartment" but only when writing an address, never in spoken English.
함께가 아니라 분리되어 있습니다. Apt 는 보통 'apartment'의 줄임말로 사용되며 주소를 쓸 때만 사용되며 영어로는 절대 사용되지 않습니다.

Say Instead:
미국식 영어로 말할려면:

Apartment

Konglish Sentence		American English
My *apart/APT* is really old.		My *apartment* is really old.
우리 아파트는 오래되었다.		

Konglish Sentence		American English
You can come to my *apart*.		You can come to my *apartment*.
우리 아파트에 놀러와.		

How Americans use Apart:
미국인들이 "Apart"를 사용하는 법:

 Kurt

> How was the birthday party this weekend?

It was great and so good to see people! The party was at the park, so most people didn't wear masks because it was outside. But we all stood 6 feet **apart**

 Daniel

> I can't figure out what's wrong with the vacuum cleaner

Ok, we may have to take it **apart** later to see if we can figure it out

CARPET 카펫

Meaning in American English:
미국식 영어로 의미:

Carpet is typically attached to the floor and usually covers the entire room. It is not moveable like a rug.

카펫은 보통 바닥에 고정되 있고 보통 방 전체에 깔려 있습니다. 카펫은 양탄자처럼 움직이지 않습니다.

Say Instead:
미국식 영어로 말할려면:

Rug

Konglish Sentence	American English
My friend just bought beautiful new *carpet* for her dining room.	My friend just bought a beautiful new *rug* for her dining room.

내 친구는 거실에 놓을 새로운 이쁜 카펫을 샀다.

How Americans use Carpet:
미국인들이 "Carpet"을 사용하는 법:

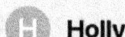 **Holly**

> How are the house renovations going?

Good! Last week they ripped out all the **carpet** and the old wallpaper. They put in wood floors and repainted the walls. It looks so much better now!

 My Fam

> When are they coming to clean the **carpet** this week?

They're coming on Tuesday. So we need to keep the pets downstairs (on the tile floor) while they clean the **carpets** during the day.

CLOSET 클로젯

Meaning in American English:

미국식 영어로 의미:

A walk-in closet or a small room for storing things like clothes or boxes or coats; usually part of the house/building rather than a piece of furniture

일반적으로 옷장, 옷이나 상자 또는 코트와 같은 물건을 보관할 수 있는 작은 방, 가구가 아닌 집/건물의 일부

Say Instead:

미국식 영어로 말할려면:

Wardrobe, Armoire

Konglish Sentence	American English
I need to buy some new furniture. My wife and I are looking for a new *closet*.	I need to buy some new furniture. My wife and I are looking for a new *wardrobe/armoire*.

새 가구를 사야한다. 우리 아내와 함께 새로운 클로젯을 찾고있다.

How Americans use Closet:

미국인들이 "Closet"을 사용하는 법:

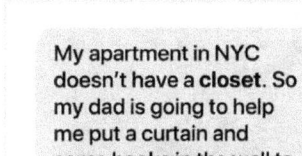

J Jean

R Room for Rent

Jean: My apartment in NYC doesn't have a **closet**. So my dad is going to help me put a curtain and some hooks in the wall to work like a **closet**.

Room for Rent: Hi, I'm interested in the room for rent. Could you give me more details?

Room for Rent: The room for rent has its own bathroom and a decent sized **closet** too...

Jean: That sounds great! Send me some pictures of it when it's finished!

CONSENT 콘센트

Meaning in American English:
미국식 영어로 의미:

To give permission or agree
허락하거나 동의하는 것

Say Instead:
미국식 영어로 말할려면:

(Electrical) outlet, Socket

Konglish Sentence	American English
Where is the *consent*?	Where is the (*electrical*) *outlet*?

콘센트가 어디에 있나요?

How Americans use Consent:
미국인들이 "Consent"를 사용하는 법:

 Doctor's Office

Text Y to agree to **consent** to receive alerts and agree to our terms and conditions. Msg & data rates may apply. Text STOP to opt-out. Text HELP for Help.

Your appointment on Monday at 8:00pm has been confirmed. You may fill out our confidentiality and **consent** forms online to save time in the office.

 Jonathan

I really want to record the phone call next time she calls and threatens us. It would be good evidence if I need to get a lawyer

What are your state's laws about recording **consent**? Do both parties have to **consent** to being recorded or just one?

CORRIDOR 코리도

Meaning in American English:
미국식 영어로 의미:

A long narrow passage-way, often in big hotels or office buildings. It is not usually used to talk about smaller passages like those in houses. *Corridor* can also describe a long, narrow strip of land or a path outdoors.

길고 좁은 통로. 큰 호텔이나 사무실 건물에 볼 수 있습니다. 집처럼 작은 통로에 사용되지 않습니다. 길고 좁은 땅 조각이나 야외의 길을 묘사할 수도 있습니다.

Say Instead:
미국식 영어로 말할려면:

Hallway

Konglish Sentence	American English
When I lived in Texas, I learned that if there is a tornado, you should go to the first floor of your house. It's best to go into a small room with no windows, like a closet or bathroom, or you can also go into a *corridor* in the middle of your house.	When I lived in Texas, I learned that if there is a tornado, you should go to the first floor of your house. It's best to go into a small room with no windows, like a closet or bathroom, or you can also go into a *hallway* in the middle of your house.

내가 텍사스에 살았을 때, 토네이도가 발생하면, 1층으로 가야 한다는 것을 배웠다. 옷장이나 욕실처럼 창문이 없는 작은 방으로 들어가는 것이 가장 좋으며, 집 한가운데에 있는 복도로 들어가도 된다.

DRESS ROOM 드레스 룸

Meaning in American English:
미국식 영어로 의미:

A dressing room is for changing into costumes or makeup for theater or acting
연극이나 연기를 위한 의상이나 분장으로 갈아입기 위한 분장실입니다

Say Instead:
미국식 영어로 말할려면:

Closet, Walk-in closet

Konglish Sentence	American English
I need to clean up my *dress room.*	I need to clean up my *closet.*

드레스룸 정리를 해야겠다.

INTERPHONE 인터폰

Meaning in American English:
미국식 영어로 의미:

Doesn't exist

이 단어는 존재하지 않습니다

Say Instead:
미국식 영어로 말할려면:

Intercom

Konglish Sentence	American English
Call me on the *interphone* when you arrive.	Call me on the *intercom* when you arrive. / *Call me when you arrive, and I'll buzz you up.*

떠나기 전에 인터폰으로 연락해.

My Room 마이룸

Meaning in American English:
미국식 영어로 의미:

My bedroom
침실

Say Instead:
미국식 영어로 말할려면:

Say the name of the specific place: "My office," "My house," "My apartment"
정확한 장소를 말해야한다.

Konglish Sentence		American English
Please come to *my room* to discuss this issue.		Please come to my *office* to discuss the issue.

우리 집에가서 이야기 해보자.

Konglish Sentence		American English
Let's meet at *my room*; we can go to the restaurant together.		Let's meet at my *apartment*; we can go to the restaurant together.

우리 집에서 만난 다음에 음식점으로 가자.

How Americans use My Room:
미국인들이 "My Room"을 사용하는 법:

 Roommate

Do you think the dog will be a problem if you give the cooking class at our house?

I can shut her in **my room** while we're cooking so she doesn't try to steal food from the counter

 Step-Sister

Did you leave your sunglasses at my house? I just found these in **my room** on the dresser next to my bed.

Omg yes! THAT's where they are! I couldn't remember where I left them!

OFFICETEL 오피스텔

Meaning in American English:
미국식 영어로 의미:

Doesn't exist

이 단어는 존재하지 않습니다

Say Instead:
미국식 영어로 말할려면:

Studio apartment

Konglish Sentence	American English
I rented a cheap *officetel*.	I rented a cheap *studio apartment that I also use as my office.*
싼 오피스텔을 얻었다.	

ONE ROOM 원룸

Meaning in American English:
미국식 영어로 의미:

Literally one room

말 그대로 하나의 방

Say Instead:
미국식 영어로 말할려면:

Furnished studio apartment, Studio apartment

Konglish Sentence	American English
A lot of my friends live in *one rooms*.	A lot of my friends live in *studio apartments*.

내 친구들은 원룸 아파트에 많이 산다.

How Americans use One Room:
미국인들이 "One Room"을 사용하는 법:

 Kelly

Are you guys planning to get **one** hotel **room** or two for the weekend?

I think we just need **one room**, not two

OUTSIDE 밖에/외부에서

Meaning in American English:
미국식 영어로 의미:

Not in a building; out in nature, outdoors
건물 밖에서, 자연 밖에서, 야외에서

Say Instead:
미국식 영어로 말할려면:

Out, At a restaurant, Eat out, Go out

Konglish Sentence	American English
We ate *outside* on Friday.	We ate *out* on Friday. We ate *at a restaurant* on Friday.

우리 금요일에 외식했다.

How Americans use Outside:
미국인들이 "Outside"를 사용하는 법:

 Kids

We're finished shopping. We'll be sitting on the bench **outside** waiting

Ok, I'll be there in about 10 minutes to pick you up.

 Alexa

It's a beautiful day with perfect weather! We should do something **outside**!

I agree! Maybe we can have a picnic and eat **outside** this afternoon

Rox/Lox 락스

Meaning in American English:
미국식 영어로 의미:

Sounds like rocks

돌멩이처럼 들립니다

Say Instead:
미국식 영어로 말할려면:

Clorox, Bleach

Konglish Sentence		American English
My toilet overflowed, so I had to use *rox* in the bathroom.		My toilet overflowed, so I had to use *bleach/Clorox* in the bathroom.

변기가 막혀서 락스를 사용해야 했다.

Life and Culture in the USA:
미국의 삶과 문화:

One of my Korean students in the USA told me she usually cleans her bathroom with Rox. I was really confused at first. How can someone clean something using *rocks?* As we discussed it, I realized she meant 'Clorox spray' because she needed to use some kind of cleaner that can easily be wiped up since bathrooms in the USA don't have a central drain like they usually do in Korea. Because of this, you cannot just spray water everywhere, and it is considered important to keep water within the bathtub, shower, and sink. Getting water outside of these areas, including on the floor, is considered a big no-no. Water on the floor, the counter, sink area, the walls, even the toilet seat, etc., should be wiped up with a towel immediately.

Growing up, one of the biggest fights I used to have with my younger brother when we were teenagers was related to water in the bathroom. If he took a shower first, there would be water on the floor, water on the counters around the sink, water on the mirror, on the toilet, everywhere! "Mom!" I'm sure I complained annoyingly tons of times since we were expected to clean up our own messes in the bathroom, "He left water all over the bathroom again! Ewwww! Everything is wet! Make him clean it up!" In most cases, if you visit an American household with typical American style bathrooms, make sure you take advantage of the shower curtain to keep any water inside the bathtub or shower, and if necessary, use a nearby towel to wipe up whatever mess of water you have left outside of those areas. A clean bathroom is also a dry bathroom. Otherwise, it could be very shocking to your host and even considered rude to leave such a watery mess!

미국에 있는 한국 학생이 미국에서는 Rox 로 화장실을 자주 청소한다고 말했습니다. 처음에 정말 혼란스러웠습니다. 어떻게 돌을 이용해서 청소를 할 수 있나요? 이야기를 나누면서, 그녀가 Clorox 스프레이를 의미한다는 것을 깨달았습니다. 왜냐하면 미국의 화장실에는 한국처럼 중앙 배수구가 없기 때문에 쉽게 닦을 수 있는 일종의 청소제가 필요하기 때문입니다. 이로 인해 물을 어디서나 뿌릴 수 없으며, 욕조, 샤워실, 세면대를 제외한 곳에 물을 흘리지 않는 것이 중요하며 흘린 물은 즉시 수건으로 닦아야 합니다.

우리가 10 대였을 때 제가 남동생과 자주 했던 가장 큰 싸움 중 하나는 욕실 물 사용과 관련된 것이었습니다. 남동생이 먼저 샤워를 했다면 바닥, 세면대 주변의 카운터, 거울, 화장실 모든 곳에 물이 있을 거예요! "엄마!" 욕실의 엉망진창인 것들을 청소해야 했기 때문에 분명히 큰 소리로 불평을 많이 했을 거예요, "물을 다 흘려서 모든 것이 다 젖었어! 깨끗이 청소하세요!" 보통 전형적인 미국 스타일의 욕실이 있는 미국 가정을 방문한다면, 반드시 샤워 커튼을 이용해서 욕조나 샤워실 밖으로 물이 안가도록 하고, 필요하다면 가까운 수건을 사용해서 남아있는 물기를 닦아내세요. 깨끗한 화장실은 건조한 화장실이기도 합니다. 그렇지 않으면, 주인에게 매우 충격적일 수 있고, 심지어 물이 많이 흘러있는 상태로 방치하는 것은 무례한 일로 여겨질 수도 있습니다!

Real Life Story:
실화:

My first time in Korea, I was around 20 years old and had no idea there were such different expectations for the bathroom. The first night, my friend pointed me to the bathroom at her aunt's house and politely told me I could shower first. When I entered, I noticed there was water scattered around including splashed on the toilet seat, the sink, and the mirror. I didn't think too much of it, but just assumed maybe my friend's teenage boy cousin had previously showered messily.

As I started to get into the bathtub, I noticed there was no shower head to stand under, only a handheld one at waist-height. I turned on the water and went to close the shower curtain but realized there wasn't one. I paused, confused. What should I do?! How am I supposed to shower without a shower curtain?! The water will go EVERYWHERE! It will be a huge rude mess! I turned off the water for a minute and just sat there thinking. I was too embarrassed to ask my friend – I couldn't imagine we had different culture about how to properly take a shower! In the end, I couldn't figure out what to do, so I squatted down in the bathtub and showered best I could that way to avoid getting water outside of the basin.

When I finally got the courage to bring it up to my friend, we both had a good laugh because neither of us had ever expected that how to take a shower could be a cultural difference.

스무살 정도에 한국에 처음 왔을 때 화장실에 많은 차이가 있다는 것을 전혀 몰랐습니다. 첫날 밤, 친구는 이모 집의 욕실을 가리키며 먼저 샤워를 해도 된다고 정중하게 말했습니다. 제가 들어갔을 때 변기, 세면대, 거울 주변에 물이 젖어 있는 것을 발견했습니다. 그것에 대해 너무 많이 생각하지는 않았지만, 아마 제 친구의 10대 사촌이 전에 (제 남동생처럼) 엉망진창으로 샤워를 한 것 같은 거라고 생각했습니다.

욕조에 안에 들어가보니 밑에 샤워 헤드가 없고 오직 허리 높이의 샤워 손잡이만 있었습니다. 물을 틀고 샤워 커튼을 닫으려고 했지만 샤워 커튼이 없다는 것을 깨달았습니다. 저는 혼란스러워서 멈추었습니다. 어떻게 해야 할까요?! 샤워 커튼 없이 어떻게 샤워를 해야 하나요?! 물이 사방으로 흘러갈 거에요! 정말 무례한 일이에요! 잠깐 동안 물을 잠그로 거기에 앉아서 생각을 했습니다. 내 친구에게 물어보기는 부끄러웠습니다. 샤워하는 방법에 대한 문화적 차이가 있을 거라고 상상할 수 없었습니다!. 결국 저는 어떻게 해야 할지 몰랐습니다. 욕조에 쪼그려 앉아 욕조 밖으로 물이 나가지 않도록 최선을 다해 샤워를 했습니다.

마침내 용기를 내어 친구에게 이 이야기를 꺼냈을 때, 우리 둘 다 샤워하는 방법에 문화적인 차이가 있을 수 있다는 것을 전혀 예상하지 못했기 때문에 웃음을 터뜨렸습니다.

SENIOR TOWN 시니어 타운

Meaning in American English:

미국식 영어로 의미:

Doesn't exist

이 단어는 존재하지 않습니다

Say Instead:

미국식 영어로 말할려면:

Retirement home, Retirement community, Assisted living home, Nursing home, Assisted living facility

Konglish Sentence	American English
Her grandmother lives in a *senior town*.	Her grandmother lives in a *retirement home*.

그녀의 할머니는 시니어 타운에 사신다.

SILVER TOWN 실버타운

Meaning in American English:
미국식 영어로 의미:

Doesn't exist

이 단어는 존재하지 않습니다

Say Instead:
미국식 영어로 말할려면:

Retirement home, Retirement community, Assisted living home, Nursing home, Assisted living facility

Konglish Sentence	American English
Her grandmother lives in a *silver town.*	Her grandmother lives in a *retirement home.*

그녀의 할머니는 실버타운에 사신다.

SHOWER BATH 샤워 목욕

Meaning in American English:
미국식 영어로 의미:

Doesn't exist

이 단어는 존재하지 않습니다

Say Instead:
미국식 영어로 말할려면:

Bath, Bathtub, Shower

Tub/shower combo, Shower/tub combo (when talking about this design)

Konglish Sentence	American English
He is in the *shower bath*.	He is in the *shower*.
	He is in the *bath(tub)*.
그는 샤워를 한다.	

Konglish Sentence	American English
Most American houses have *shower baths*.	Most American houses have *bathtub/shower combos*.
거의 모든 미국 집에는 샤워 배스가 있다.	

SHOWER BOOTH 샤워 부스

Meaning in American English:
미국식 영어로 의미:

Doesn't exist

이 단어는 존재하지 않습니다

Say Instead:
미국식 영어로 말할려면:

Shower

Konglish Sentence	American English
He is in the *shower booth*.	He is in the *shower*.

그는 샤워 부스에 있다.

SINGLE HOUSE OR SINGLE HOME 싱글홈

Meaning in American English:
미국식 영어로 의미:

One house

집 한 채

Say Instead:
미국식 영어로 말할려면:

House

Konglish Sentence	American English
I live in a *single house*. It's not an apart; it's a *single house*.	I live in a *house*. It's not an apartment; it's a *single family home*.

나는 싱글홈에 산다. 아파트가 아니라 싱글홈이다.

Life and Culture in the USA:
미국의 삶과 문화:

House and single family home can be slightly different. House is a pretty general word. If you live in a place that isn't an apartment, you would usually just talk about your house. However, if you are in the process of buying a house, you might hear and use the word single family home quite often.

Single family home has a very specific meaning. There are many different types of homes. There are condominiums (condos) or townhouses or multi-family homes or single family homes. A real estate agent could tell you all of the legal definitions, but the basics are that a single family home is a stand-alone house. It doesn't share any walls or roofs with other houses (like a townhouse would), and it typically has its own land that isn't shared with any other owners or properties, even if it's just a small area.

If you live in the suburbs around a big city in the United States, where the houses are bigger and more affordable than in the city and have a yard around your house, chances are, you are living in a single family home.

But when we talk about it, we will probably say "house" unless you are trying to buy or sell a house. I have never heard any American say, "We are going to my friend's single family house tonight."

하우스와 싱글 패밀리 하우스는 약간 다를 수 있습니다. 집은 아주 일반적인 단어입니다. 만약 아파트가 아닌 곳에 산다면, 여러분은 보통 여러분의 집에 대해 이야기 할 것입니다. 하지만 집을 구입하는 과정에 있다면 싱글 패밀리 하우스라는 단어를 자주 듣고 사용할 것입니다.

싱글 패밀리 하우스는 매우 구체적인 의미를 가지고 있습니다. 집에는 다양한 유형이 있습니다. 콘도나 타운하우스, 다세대 주택 또는 단독 주택이 있습니다. 부동산 중개인이 집 종류에 대해 자세히 알려줄 수 있지만 기본적으로 단독 주택을 말합니다. 타운하우스처럼 다른 집과 벽이나 지붕을 공유하지 않으며, 일반적으로 작은 면적일지라도 다른 소유자나 부동산과 공유되지 않는 자신만의 땅을 가지고 있습니다.

만약 미국의 큰 도시 주변 교외에 살고 있고, 도시보다 집이 더 크고 더 저렴하며 주변에 마당이 있다면, 싱글 패밀리 하우스에서 살고 있을 가능성이 높습니다.

집을 사거나 팔려고 하지 않는 한 우리는 아마 "하우스"라고 말할 것입니다. "우리는 오늘 밤 제 친구의 싱글 가족 하우스에 갈 거예요."라는 미국인의 말을 들어본 적이 없습니다.

STAND 스탠드

Meaning in American English:
미국식 영어로 의미:

1. (Verb) The opposite of sitting
   (동사) 앉는 것의 반대
2. (Noun) Something that is used to put something else on top of or make it higher (e.g., a TV stand, music stand)
   (명사) 어떤것을 올리거나 높이는 데 사용되는 것, 예를 들어 TV 스탠드, 음악 스탠드

Say Instead:
미국식 영어로 말할려면:

Floor lamp

Konglish Sentence	American English
The room is dark. We should buy a *stand* to put in the corner.	The room is dark. We should buy a *floor lamp* to put in the corner.

이 방이 어둡다. 구석에 스탠드를 사서 놓는 건 어떨까?

How Americans use Stand:
미국인들이 "Stand"를 사용하는 법:

 Donation Pick Up

Do you know how much furniture we need to fit in the truck? Do we need a 2ⁿᵈ truck?

They are donating a night **stand**, a TV **stand**, and 2 bookshelves. I think 1 should be enough

 Martha

My feet are so tired! I have to **stand** most of the day at work. I need to get some more comfortable shoes

I need to get some new shoes too. Want to go shoe shopping on Saturday afternoon?

VERANDA 베란다

Meaning in American English:
미국식 영어로 의미:

A covered patio on the ground floor, but this
word is not so commonly used
1 층에 지붕으로 가려진 공간이지만, 이
단어는 일반적으로 사용되지 않습니다

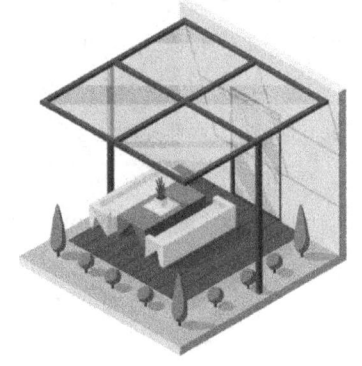

Say Instead:
미국식 영어로 말할려면:

Balcony

Konglish Sentence	American English
I have many plants on my *veranda*.	I have many plants on my *balcony*.
내 베란다에는 식물들이 많다.	

How Americans use Veranda:
미국인들이 "Veranda"를 사용하는 법:

 Amani

> How was your vacation?
> What did you think of the
> view on the mountain?

It was great! We had
breakfast on the **veranda** of
the restaurant on the top of
the mountain one morning.
The view was incredible!

R **Renee**

> Should we eat inside or
> outside this evening?

The weather is perfect
right now, but it might rain
later... I'll set up some
tables under the **veranda**,
but if the weather gets
bad, we can move inside

13

APPLIANCES
가전제품

Scan for Audio!

COOKER 쿠커

Meaning in American English:
미국식 영어로 의미:

A machine that cooks something, but it is usually not used as a word alone. For example, a rice cooker, a slow cooker, or a pressure cooker
요리할 때 사용하는 기계로 보통 단독으로 단어로 사용되지는 않습니다. 예를 들어, 밥솥, 전기 찜솥 또는 압력밥솥이 있습니다.

Say Instead:
미국식 영어로 말할려면:

Cook, Chef

Konglish Sentence	American English
He's a *cooker*.	He's a *chef*.
그는 요리사야.	

Additional Info:
그 외:

Types of cookers: Rice cooker, Pressure cooker, Slow cooker (Crockpot)
밥솥의 종류: 밥솥, 압력밥솥, 전기 찜솥 (크록팟이라고도 함)

Life & Culture in the USA:
미국의 삶과 문화:

Rice cookers are somewhat common in the United States, but not nearly as common as in South Korea or other Asian countries. In some areas, especially South Louisiana where you can find many rice fields, people eat rice as a side with almost every meal, similar to Koreans. For example, my parents are originally from south Louisiana. My grandma always had a rice cooker filled with fresh rice for every meal and occasion. Many of the adults mixed gravy and other sauces from the other main or side dishes into their rice, and the kids sometimes ate rice as a side with salt and butter (but rarely 100% plain). For me, a rice cooker was always seen as a necessary item in the kitchen. However, in other parts of the country, eating rice is much less common. Over time, I have met several people who weren't familiar with a rice cooker or didn't eat rice often enough to have a need for one. I have a couple of friends who don't understand the need for a rice cooker and prefer to cook rice in a pot on the stove.

밥솥은 미국에서는 어느 정도 흔하지만, 한국이나 다른 아시아 국가들처럼 그렇게 흔하지는 않습니다. 논밭이 많은 사우스 루이지애나 주에서는 한국처럼 거의 모든 식사에 밥을 곁들여 먹습니다. 예를 들어, 저희 부모님은 원래 사우스 루이지애나 주 출신입니다. 할머니는 항상 매 끼니마다 신선한 밥을 가득 채운 밥솥을 가지고 계셨습니다. 어른들 중에는 메인 요리나 반찬에서 나온 소스와 그래비 고기 육즙을 밥에 섞어서 먹고, 아이들은 가끔 소금과 버터를 곁들여 밥을 먹기도 했습니다 (그러나 거의 100% 밥만 먹은 적은 없다). 나에게 밥솥은 항상 부엌에서 필수적인 물건이었습니다. 하지만, 미국 다른 지역에서 밥을 먹는 일은 흔하지 않습니다. 시간이 지나면서, 밥솥에 익숙하지 않거나 밥솥이 필요할 정도로 밥을 자주 먹지 않는 사람들을 여럿 만났습니다. 내 친구들 중에는 밥솥의 필요성을 이해하지 못하고, 스토브에 냄비로 밥을 짓는 것을 선호하는 사람들이 몇 명 있습니다.

How Americans use Cooker:
미국인들이 "Cooker"를 사용하는 법:

A Alison

You have a rice **cooker**, right?

Yes, but it's a super small 3-cup one

How about a pressure **cooker**?

I'm kind of afraid of pressure **cookers**, aren't they dangerous?

The old ones were a little dangerous, but most of the new ones are totally safe.

DRYER 드라이어

Meaning in American English:
미국식 영어로 의미:

A machine that dries things; usually a
dryer for clothes
건조기

Say Instead:
미국식 영어로 말할려면:

Hair dryer, Blow dryer

Konglish Sentence	American English
I need to use the *dryer* to make my hair look pretty.	I need to use the *hair dryer* to make my hair look good.

드라이어해야 머리가 이뻐보인다.

How Americans use Dryer:
미국인들이 "Dryer"를 사용하는 법:

 Anna

> You left some clothes in the **dryer** btw in case you are looking for them. I placed them on top of the dryer for now because I needed to dry some stuff.

> Sorry, I forgot about it. Thanks for letting me know!

 Jen

> Just double checking, do you have a **hair dryer** I can use?

> Absolutely!

GAS RANGE 가스렌지

Meaning in American English:
미국식 영어로 의미:

This is a correct word in English but is not commonly used in everyday speech.
이것은 영어에서는 맞는 단어이지만 일반적으로 사용되지 않습니다.

Say Instead:
미국식 영어로 말할려면:

Stove (*when speaking generally* 일반적으로 말할때)

Gas stove *or less commonly,* Gas range (*if you need to specify which type of stove for the conversation* 가스레인지 또는 덜 일반적으로 가스스토브, 정확한 표현을 위해 어떤 종류의 스토브를 말해야한다면)

Konglish Sentence	American English
Please turn off the *gas range* before going out.	Please turn off the *stove* before going out.

가스렌지를 끄고 나가야한다.

Additional Info:
그 외:

While *gas range* is absolutely a correct word in English, most people just talk about the stove, regardless of what kind it is unless they want to specify which kind they have or would like to buy or discuss. But you can certainly find the word *gas range* when shopping for or reading about these specific appliances. As an example, I recently read an article discussing why "gas ranges" are perhaps not very eco-friendly and perhaps more people should consider switching to "induction cooktops" or "electric ranges." But it might be a bit strange sounding to many people to say it that way in regular speech, especially for younger people. So if a friend asks me how I cooked a delicious chicken recipe, I would answer simply, "On the stove," regardless of my appliance type.

가스레인지가 영어에서 올바른 표현인 반면, 대부분의 사람들은 어떤 종류의 제품을 가지고 있거나 구입하고 싶거나 논의하고 싶은지 특별히 지정하지 않는 한, 어떤 종류의 제품인지에 관계없이 그냥 스토브라고 말한다. 그러나 특정한 가전제품을 쇼핑하거나 읽을 때 '가스레인지'라는 단어를 확실히 찾을 볼수 있습니다. 예를 들어, 최근에 "가스레인지"가 그다지 친환경적이지 아니여서 더 많은 사람들이 "인덕션 쿡탑 또는 전기레인지"로 바꾸는 것을 고려해야 한다는 기사를 읽은적이 있습니다. 그러나 많은 사람들 특히 젊은 사람들에게 그것을 그렇게 말하는 것은 약간 이상하게 들릴 수 있습니다. 만약 친구가 제게 맛있는 치킨 요리 레시피를 어떻게 요리 했냐고 묻는다면, 저는 제 가전제품 종류에 상관없이 간단하게 "스토브 위에서"라고 대답할 것입니다.

How Americans use Gas Range and Gas Stove:
미국인들이 "Gas Range and Gas Stove"를 사용하는 법:

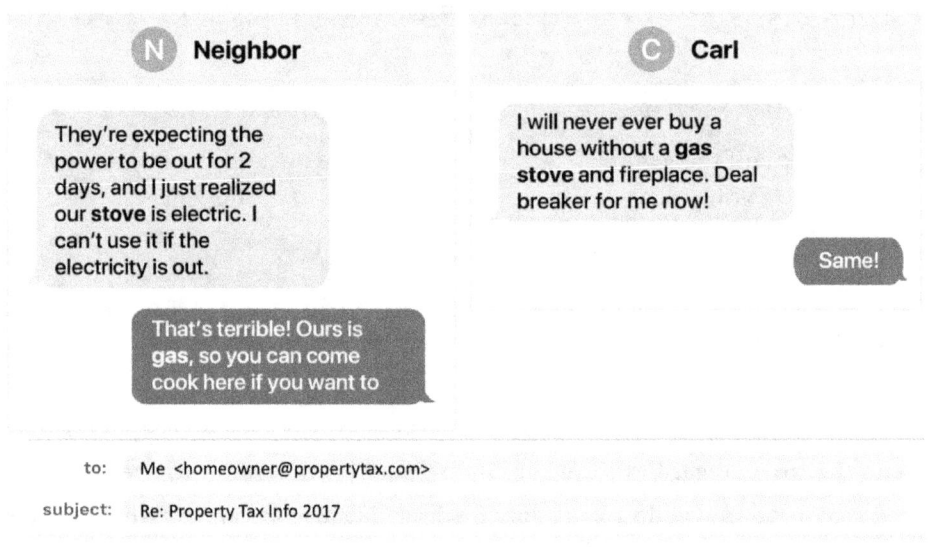

INDUCTION 인덕션

Meaning in American English:
미국식 영어로 의미:

1. A formal ceremony to enter a club or organization or position
   클럽, 조직 또는 직책에 가입할 때의 공식적인 의식
2. The process of making a woman go into labor (usually with medicine) if it isn't happening naturally
   여성에게 약을 써서 아이 분만을 유도하는 과정
3. A specific way to make electricity using magnetic fields
   유도 에너지를 이용해 전기를 만드는 구체적인 과학적 방법;
   유도 전기; 전자기 유도

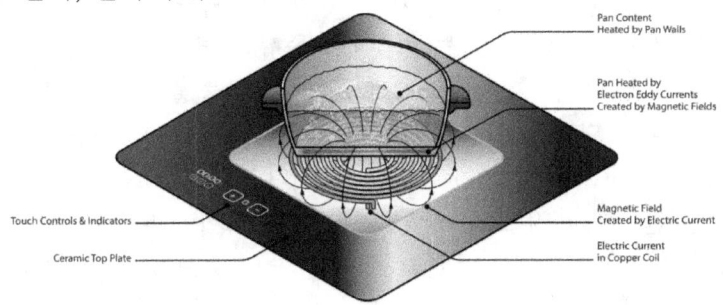

Say Instead:
미국식 영어로 말할려면:

Stove (*when speaking generally* 일반적으로 말할때)

Induction cooktop, Electric range, Electric stove (*if you need to specify which type of stove for the conversation* 인덕션이나 전기레인지나 전기스토브, 정확한 표현을 위해 어떤 종류의 스토브를 말해야한다면)

Konglish Sentence	American English
Please turn off the *induction* before going out.	Please turn off the *stove* before going out.

인덕션 *끄고* 외출하세요.

Additional Info:
그 외:

It is correct to talk about an *induction cooktop* in English. However, like *gas range*, most people just talk about their stove, regardless of what kind it is unless they want to specify which kind they have or would like to buy or discuss. But you can certainly find the word *induction* when shopping for or reading about these specific appliances. As an example, I recently read an article discussing why "gas ranges" are perhaps not very eco-friendly and perhaps more people should consider switching to "induction cooktops" or "electric ranges." But many Americans aren't familiar with their specific type of stove, nor do they often discuss it by type. So if a friend asks me how I cooked a delicious chicken recipe, I would answer simply, "On the stove," regardless of my appliance type.

가스레인지처럼 인덕션 쿡탑이 영어에서 올바른 표현인 반면, 대부분의 사람들은 어떤 종류의 제품을 가지고 있거나 구입하고 싶거나 논의하고 싶은지 특별히 지정하지 않는 한, 어떤 종류의 제품인지에 관계없이 그냥 스토브라고 말한다. 그러나 특정한 가전제품을 쇼핑하거나 읽을 때 '인덕션'이라는 단어를 확실히 찾을 볼수 있습니다. 예를 들어, 최근에 "가스레인지"가 그다지 친환경적이지 아니여서 더 많은 사람들이 "인덕션 쿡탑 또는 전기레인지"로 바꾸는 것을 고려해야 한다는 기사를 읽은적이 있습니다. 하지만 많은 미국인들은 특정한 스토브 종류에 익숙하지 않고, 종종 종류에 대해 논의하지 않습니다. 만약 친구가 제게 맛있는 치킨 요리 레시피를 어떻게 요리 했냐고 묻는다면, 저는 제 가전제품 종류에 상관없이 간단하게 "스토브 위에서"라고 대답할 것입니다.

How Americans use Induction:
미국인들이 "Induction"을 사용하는 법:

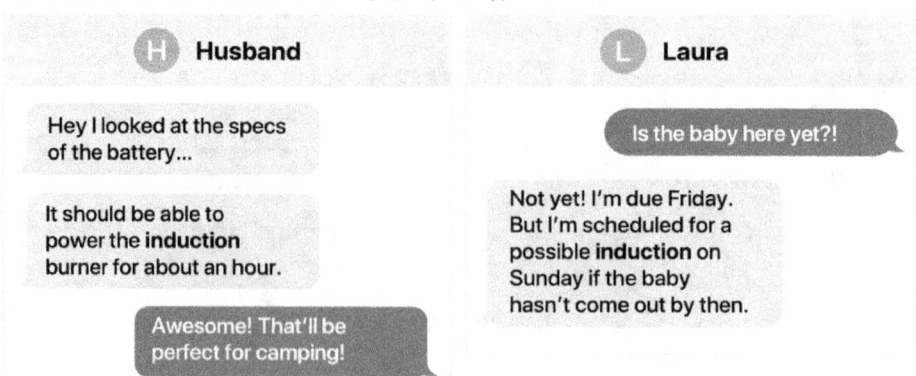

Husband

Hey I looked at the specs of the battery...

It should be able to power the **induction** burner for about an hour.

Awesome! That'll be perfect for camping!

Laura

Is the baby here yet?!

Not yet! I'm due Friday. But I'm scheduled for a possible **induction** on Sunday if the baby hasn't come out by then.

MIXER 믹서

Meaning in American English:
미국식 영어로 의미:

A machine that mixes food, usually in baking like a stand mixer or hand mixer
음식을 섞는 기계로, 보통 스탠드 믹서나 핸드 믹서와 같이 베이킹에
사용됩니다

Say Instead:
미국식 영어로 말할려면:

Blender

Konglish Sentence		American English
Put fruit and vegetables in the *mixer* to make a smoothie.		Put fruit and vegetables in the *blender* to make a smoothie.
스무디를 만들려면 믹서기에 과일하고 채소를 넣으세요.		

Additional Info:

Confusing a blender and a mixer probably won't be much of a problem for you unless you are into cooking. But if you ask someone to make a smoothie in a mixer or ask someone to make a cake batter in a blender, there might be some confusion.

요리에 관심이 없다면 블렌더와 믹서기를 혼동하는 것은 아마도 큰 문제가 되지 않을 것입니다. 하지만 믹서기로 스무디를 만들어 달라고 하거나 블렌더로 케이크 반죽을 만들어 달라고 하면 약간의 혼란이 있을 수 있습니다.

REFRIDGE 냉장고

Meaning in American English:

미국식 영어로 의미:

Doesn't exist

이 단어는 존재하지 않습니다

Say Instead:

미국식 영어로 말할려면:

Refrigerator, Fridge

Konglish Sentence	American English
The milk is in the *refridge*.	The milk is in the *fridge*. The milk is in the *refrigerator*.

우유는 냉장고에 있어요.

Additional Info:

그 외:

This is one Konglish word that people will still understand. It just sounds awkward and unnatural because most Americans say "fridge" as the shortened form of "refrigerator." You can also find a small number of people (typically older populations) who call the refrigerator the "ice box," but this is becoming less common.

이 단어는 사람들이 여전히 이해할 수 있는 콩글리쉬 단어 중 하나입니다. 대부분의 미국인들이 냉장고 "refrigerator"를 줄여서 "fridge"라고 말하기 때문에 이것은 단지 어색하고 부자연스럽게 들릴 뿐입니다. 또한 냉장고를 소수의 나이든 분들은 "ice box"라고 부르기도 하지만 이는 흔하지 않습니다.

REMO CON 리모콘

Meaning in American English:
미국식 영어로 의미:

Doesn't exist
이 단어는 존재하지 않습니다

Say Instead:
미국식 영어로 말하려면:

Remote, Remote control

Konglish Sentence	American English
Can you pass me the *remo con*?	Can you pass me the *remote*?

리모컨 좀 줄래?

Life & Culture in the USA:
미국의 삶과 문화:

In American English, there are numerous ways people refer to the remote control. Here are a few of the most common:

미국 영어에는 사람들이 리모콘을 언급하는 방법들이 많이 있습니다. 여기에 가장 흔한 몇 가지가 있습니다:

Clicker
The Remote
Remote Control
Channel Changer
Volume Control
The Switcher
Flipper
Zapper

STAINLESS 스테인리스

Meaning in American English:
미국식 영어로 의미:

Something that isn't stained or can't be stained
얼룩이 지지 않거나 얼룩질 수 없는 것

Say Instead:
미국식 영어로 말할려면:

Stainless steel

Konglish Sentence	American English
I want *stainless* bowls because they won't break.	I want *stainless steel* bowls because they won't break.

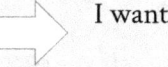

스테인레스 그릇을 갖길원해요 그래서 깨지지 않도록요.

Additional Info:
그 외:

Stainless is a correct word, but it's usually used as an adjective in American English rather than a noun. By itself, *stainless* means "free from stain or pure or stain-free." So when you use *stainless* as a noun alone, while technically correct, it feels like you've forgotten to finish your sentence. A stainless what? While there are certainly some Americans who use this the same way as in Konglish (stainless bowls), many Americans do not just use the word *stainless* alone. Instead, they use the whole phrase *stainless steel*.

'스테인리스'는 바른 단어이지만, 미국 영어에서 보통 명사보다는 형용사로 사용됩니다. 그 자체로, '스테인리스'는 '때 묻지 않거나 순수하거나 얼룩이 없는' 의미입니다. 스테인리스를 명사로 단독으로 사용할 때, 기술적으로는 정확하지만, 마치 여러분이 문장을 끝내는 것을 잊어버린 것처럼 느껴집니다. 스테인리스 뭐라고요? 콩글리쉬 '스테인리스 그릇'과 같은 단어를 사용하는 미국인들도 분명히 있지만,

많은 미국인들은 '스테인리스'라는 단어를 단독으로 사용하지 않습니다. 대신 그들은 '스테인리스-스틸' 또는 '스테인리스-스틸 그릇'이라는 전체 문구를 사용합니다.

How Americans use Stainless:
미국인들이 "Stainless"를 사용하는 법:

M **Mom**

What kind of fridge do you have?

Not sure what brand, but it's a **stainless steel** French door style

to: Me <Tenant@apartments.com>

subject: Apartment Unit Upgrades

All apartment units will be updated in the coming months. Upgrades include: all new *stainless steel* appliances and new washer/dryer, resurfaced kitchen and bathroom cabinets, and all new brushed nickel faucets, ceiling fans, light fixtures, door knobs and locks, curved shower curtain rods, and 2 inch faux-wood blinds.

You will be notified at least 24 hours before work in your apartment unit begins. Please contact the front office if you have any questions about this project.

14

SOCIAL LIFE
사회 생활

Scan for Audio!

EVENT 이벤트

Meaning in American English:
미국식 영어로 의미:

Event is typically only used for bigger events that require a lot of planning and organization before hand and usually include a lot of people. This can't be used for small things like a birthday party or dinner, unless it is a large, extravagant event. Some examples of events are a wedding, a party, a festival, a service. Most people will use the specific name of the event, "I went to a wedding this weekend." "The school had a festival." If you don't know what kind of event it is or it isn't relevant, then you can call it an event. For example, "The hotel was really crowded this weekend because they had a special event." "I'm sorry, the restaurant isn't taking any reservations this weekend because they are booked for an event."

일반적으로 사용되는 단어이지만 보편적으로 계획을 세우고 사람들이 많이 오는 아주 큰 행사를 뜻할 때 사용됩니다. 규모가 크고 사치스러운 행사가 아닌 이상 생일 파티나 저녁 식사같이 작은 일에 사용되지 않습니다. 보통 결혼시, 파티, 페스티벌이나 서비스 같은 곳에 쓰이는 단어입니다. 보통 사람들은 특정 행사에 맞쳐 이 단어를 사용합니다. 예를 들면, "결혼식에 갔습니다. 학교에서 페스티벌이 있었습니다"라고 말합니다 어떤 종류의 행사인지 모르면 "event"라는 단어를 사용합니다. 예를 들면, "죄송합니다. 저희 레스토랑에서 이벤트가 있어서 주말 예약을 받지 않습니다."

Say Instead:
미국식 영어로 말할려면:

Sale

Name of event (*unless speaking generically* 어떤 이벤트의 이름)

Konglish Sentence		American English
The store is having an *event*.		The store is having a *sale*.
가게에 이벤트가 있다.		

Real Life Story:

실화:

One of my students went to a popular restaurant for her 7-year-old son's birthday. "The restaurant had an event for his birthday," she told me. I thought maybe she meant they had a big birthday party there with activities, food, and fun for a big group of her son's friends. Actually, she meant that they served him a free piece of cake and sang happy birthday. (That's very common in American restaurants if you tell them it's someone's birthday). For Americans, though, this is not an event. An event involves a lot of people and a lot of planning and resources.

제 학생이 7 살짜리 아들의 생일을 맞아 유명한 식당에 갔습니다. "그 식당에서 아들의 생일을 위한 행사를 해줬어요,"라고 말했습니다. 그녀가 많은 아들 친구들 위해 액티비티, 음식, 그리고 재미있는 놀이를 준비한 생일 파티를 열었다는 뜻일 거라고 생각했습니다. 하지만 그녀는 무료로 케익을 받고 생일 축하 노래를 들었다고 했습니다. (누군가의 생일이라고 말하면 미국 식당에서는 매우 흔하게 볼 수 있는 일입니다.) 하지만, 미국인들에게는, 이것은 행사가 아닙니다. 미국사람들은 그것을 이벤트라고 하지 않습니다. 이벤트는 많은 사람들과 여러 계획과 자원들이 있어야 합니다.

How Americans use Event:

미국인들이 "Event"를 사용하는 법:

FAMILY NAME 패밀리 네임

Meaning in American English:
미국식 영어로 의미:

> This has the same meaning in Konglish and American English; however, *family name* is not as common in the USA as *last name*. You might find "family name" or "surname" written on some official documents, but "last name" is much more common, especially in everyday speech. If you wanted to ask someone, you would ask, "What's your *last name*?" never, "What's your *family name*?"

> 콩글리시와 미국 영어에서 같은 의미이지만, "family name"은 "last name"만큼 미국에서 흔하지 않습니다. 일부 공식 문서에서 "Family name 이라고 쓰여진 것을 볼 수 있지만, "Last name"은 특히 일상 대화에서 훨씬 더 흔합니다.누군가에게 이름 성을 묻고 싶다면, "last name 이 무엇입니까?"라고 물을 것입니다. 결코 "family name 이 무엇입니까?"라고 질문하지 않습니다.

Say Instead:
미국식 영어로 말할려면:

> Last name

Konglish Sentence	American English
What's your *family name*? ⟹	What's your *last name*?
성이 무엇인가요?	

FIGHTING 파이팅

Meaning in American English:
미국식 영어로 의미:

1. Physical violence or conflict with your actions, for example, in boxing or in a fight or war
   예를 들어 복싱이나 싸움이나 전쟁에서 신체적 폭력이나 행동과의 충돌

2. Disagreement with your words; for example, a couple was fighting and now they are angry and hurt.
   상대방의 말에 동의하지 않을 때 쓰인다. 예를 들어 부부가 싸우고 있었는데 지금 그들은 화가 나고 상처를 받았습니다.

3. A conflict between people, for example, two friends are fighting, so they aren't really talking to each other or hanging out right now
   사람들 사이의 갈등, 예를 들어 두 친구가 싸우고 있기 때문에 그들은 지금 서로 대화를 하거나 어울리고 있지 않습니다.

Say Instead:
미국식 영어로 말할려면:

Go! You got this! You can do it! *(general shout or cheer of encouragement)*
Way to go! *(if you already did it)*

Konglish Sentence	American English
Fighting! You can do it! 	*Go team! You can do it!* (cheering for a team) *You got this! You can do it!* (encouraging a friend or person)
	힘내! 잘 할 수 있어!

MAYBE 아마도

Meaning in American English:
미국식 영어로 의미:

Not yes, but not no. I don't know. I'm not sure. I haven't decided yet.
긍정도 부정도 아님. 잘 모르거나 결정할 수 없을 때 쓰는 단어입니다.

Say Instead:
미국식 영어로 말할려면:

If you are sure, don't say maybe
확실하게 말할 수 있다면 아마도라는 표현을 쓰지 않는 것이 좋습니다.

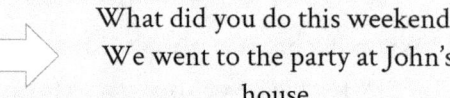

Konglish Sentence	American English
What did you do this weekend? *Maybe* we went to the party at John's house.	What did you do this weekend? We went to the party at John's house.

이번 주말에 뭐 했어?
아마도 우리는 존의 집에서 열리는 파티에 갔을 거야.

Life and Culture in the USA:
미국의 삶과 문화:

Maybe means possibly yes or possibly no in English. It is a 50/50 answer. If a friend invites you to a party and you answer "maybe," your friend is likely to follow up with you a day or two before the party to check whether or not you have decided yes or no. If your son or daughter is invited to a birthday party, it is much more polite to answer "yes" if you are able to go than it is to say "maybe" and keep your host wondering how many people will attend. Specifically in regards to parties, weddings, or specific more formal invitations, it is usually important to give a yes or no answer. Maybe is OK if you are unsure, but if you know the answer is yes or no, it's more polite to answer honestly.

In short, "maybe" does not show a solid commitment. Here are a couple 'maybe' scenarios you may come across:

아마도 영어로는 "예" 또는 "아니오"를 의미할 것입니다. 그것은 50 대 50 의 대답입니다. 만약 친구가 파티에 초대했는데 여러분이 "아마도"라고 대답한다면, 그 친구는 예 또는 아니오를 다시 확인하기 위해 파티 하루나 이틀 전에 연락을 할 것입니다. 만약 아들이나 딸을 생일 파티에 초대 받았을 때, 갈 수 있다면 "예"라고 대답하고 갈 수 없다면 "아니요"라고 대답하는 것이 "아마도" 보다 좀더 예의바른 방법입니다. 특히 파티, 결혼식 또는 더 공식적인 초대와 관련하여, 보통 "예" 또는 "아니오"라고 대답하는 것이 중요합니다. "아마도"는 확신할 수 없다면 괜찮을지 모르지만, "예" 또는 "아니오"라고 솔직히 대답하는 것이 더 예의 바른 것입니다. 공식적인 행사의 경우, 만약 "아마도"라고 대답했지만 결코 "예"라고 대답하지 않았다면, 참석자에 포함되지 않을 수 있고, 참석을 확인하지 않았기 때문에 도착했을 때 자리가 없거나 입장을 허용 받지 못할 수 있습니다.

Birthday Invitation
생일초대

Jennifer creates an online birthday invitation to celebrate a birthday. Three days before the party, there are 10 yes's, 5 no's, and 10 maybes. The host probably wants to know exactly how many people to expect and hopes to have a more accurate count. To Jennifer, "maybe" likely means either the guests who selected maybe have not updated their RSVP yet or they cannot come and didn't want to say "no" directly. Depending on Jennifer's relationship with the "maybe" guests, she might follow up with them by text or ask them when she sees them the week before the party. Nowadays, most online e-invitation systems allow a feature that follows up on the host's behalf and reminds guests to reply yes or no for their attendance. True 50/50 maybes might give a response like, "I have to attend my son's baseball game, and I'm not sure what time it will finish. I will try to make it to the party after we finish his baseball game if it's not too late!" Remaining maybes are probably no's who either forgot to update their response or who can't come but feel bad saying "no" directly.

제니퍼는 생일을 축하하기 위해 온라인 생일 초대장을 준비합니다. 파티 3일 전에, '예'가 10명, '아니요'가 5명, '어쩌면'가 10명 있습니다. 생일 초대자는 얼마나 많은 사람들이 참석할지 정확히 알고 싶어하고 더 정확한 참석자 수를 희망합니다. 제니퍼에게 '어쩌면'이라고 답변한 사람은 아직 RSVP를 업데이트하지 않았거나 올 수 없어서 직접 '아니요'라고 말하고 싶지 않았을 가능성이 높습니다. 제니퍼는 '어쩌면'이라고 답변한 사람들의 관계에 따라, 파티 일주일 전에 문자를 보내거나 그들을 직접 보았을 때 물어볼 수도 있습니다. 요즘에는 대부분의 온라인 전자 초대 시스템에서 초대자를 대신하여 회신 여부를 알리고 참석 여부를 알려달라는 메시지를 보내는 기능을 제공합니다. 사실 50 대 50은 "아들의 야구 경기에 참석해야 하는데 몇 시에 끝날지 모르겠어요. 너무 늦지 않다면 야구 경기가 끝난 후 파티에 참석할 수 있도록 노력할 거예요!"라고 대답할 수도 있습니다. 어떤 사람들은 아마 답변을 알려주는 것을 잊었거나, 올 수 없지만 직접 '아니요'라고 말하는 것을 기분 나쁘게 생각하는 사람일 것입니다.

Casual plans with a friend
친구와의 일상계획

Sue casually asks her friend if she wants to do something on Saturday for lunch. Her friend says, "Yeah, maybe!" If there is no follow-up and no other plans made, Sue can assume they will not be having lunch on Saturday. If someone answers "maybe" with no follow-up, this likely means they are just being polite and either can't or don't really want to. If someone is interested and is expressing maybe 50/50, there will likely be some follow-up or additional confirmation of the plans. Her friend might answer, "Yeah, maybe! I might have something that morning, so I need to check what time I will be finished and I will get back to you." Or "Yeah, maybe! My husband mentioned that he wanted to do something on Saturday, so let me check with him first. I will let you know!"

수는 친구에게 토요일에 점심을 같이 먹고 싶어하는지 물어봅니다. 친구는 "그래, 아마도!"라고 말합니다. 만약 연락이 없고 다른 약속이 없다면, 수는 토요일에 점심을 먹지 않을 거라고 생각할 수 있습니다. 만약 누군가가 연락 없이 "아마도"라고 대답한다면, 단지 예의를 갖추거나 하고 싶지 않다는 것을 의미할 수 있습니다. 누군가가 관심이 있고 아마도

50 대 50 으로 표현하고 있다면, 아마도 그 계획에 대한 연락을 하거나 추가 확인이 할 것입니다. 친구는 "그래, 아마도! 그날 아침에 뭔가가 있을 수도 있어서, 몇 시에 끝날지 확인해 보고 다시 연락드리겠습니다."라고 대답할 수도 있습니다. 또는 "그래, 아마도! 남편이 토요일에 뭔가를 하고 싶다고 말했으니, 먼저 확인해 볼게. 알려줄게!"

How Americans use Maybe:
미국인들이 "Maybe"를 사용하는 법:

 Aunt Emily

> Are you guys going to be able to meet us in Maryland for Thanksgiving with the family?

Maybe! We aren't sure yet because I might have to work at the hospital that week. Hopefully we will have an answer by next week

 Austin

> Do you want to come have pizza with us and watch the basketball game?

Maybe! I have to check our schedule and talk to my wife first, but it sounds fun! I can let you know by tomorrow!

NIGHT 나이트

Meaning in American English:
미국식 영어로 의미:

Never a place; the time from about 8/9 p.m. until about 4 a.m., when it's dark outside.

장소가 아닙니다. 밖이 어두운 밤 8/9 시부터 새벽 4 시까지 뜻합니다.

Say Instead:
미국식 영어로 말할려면:

Nightclub, Club, Lounge

Konglish Sentence	American English
A lot of young people in Korea go to *night*.	A lot of young people in Korea go *to (night) clubs / clubbing*.
한국 젊은 사람들은 나이트에 많이 간다.	

SCHEDULE 스케줄

Meaning in American English:
미국식 영어로 의미:

Your whole schedule or calendar
with all your plans in it
모든 계획이 포함된 전체 일정
또는 달력

Say Instead:
미국식 영어로 말할려면:

Plans

Konglish Sentence	American English
I can't meet you on Monday. I have a *schedule*.	I can't meet you on Monday. I have *plans*.
월요일에 못 만날 것 같아요. 스케줄이 있어요.	

Additional Info:
그 외:

This is a common conversation I have with Korean students:

Me - Do you want to meet me Tuesday at 10am?

Student - I'm sorry. I have a schedule on Tuesday. Can you meet me Wednesday? I don't have any schedule then.

This sentence doesn't make any sense to Americans. The schedule is kind of like the non-specific planner or calendar in which all your plans and events are kept. So if you say, "I have a schedule at that time," or, "I don't have any schedule on Wednesday," people will understand that you simply have a calendar at that time or date, which doesn't make sense. Your schedule is the keeper of all the plans.

But we CAN talk about plans. You put plans in your schedule. In this usage, we always use plans, plural. We say, "I'm sorry. I have plans Tuesday." "I don't have any plans." Plan can be used singularly in other meanings, but for this specific usage, plans will typically always be plural.

제가 한국 학생들과 자주 하는 대화입니다:

나- *화요일 오전 10 시에 만날래요?*

학생 - *죄송합니다. 제가 화요일에 스케줄이 있어서요. 수요일에 만날 수 있나요? 그때는 스케줄이 없어요.*

이 문장은 미국인들이 전혀 이해할 수 없습니다. schedule 은 모든 계획과 행사를 적어 놓은 달력이나 일정표와 같아요. 만약 "그 시간에 schedule 이 있어요" 또는 "수요일에 schedule 이 없어요"라고 말한다면, 단순히 그 시간이나 날짜에 달력을 가지고 있다는 것으로 이해할 것이고, 전혀 말이 되지 않습니다. 여러분의 일정은 모든 계획을 가지고 있습니다.

하지만 계획에 대해 이야기할 수 있습니다. 계획을 스케줄에 넣습니다. 이 용법에서 항상 plan 을 복수형로 사용합니다. "죄송합니다. 화요일에 계획이 있습니다."라고 말합니다. "저는 계획이 없습니다." plan 은 다른 의미로 단수형으로 사용될 수 있지만, 이 특정한 용법의 경우, plan 은 일반적으로 항상 복수형입니다.

How Americans use Schedule:
미국인들이 "Schedule"을 사용하는 법:

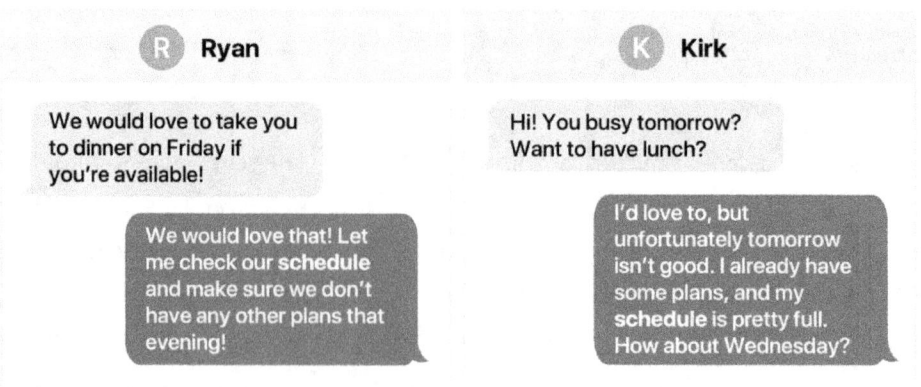

R Ryan	K Kirk
We would love to take you to dinner on Friday if you're available!	Hi! You busy tomorrow? Want to have lunch?
We would love that! Let me check our **schedule** and make sure we don't have any other plans that evening!	I'd love to, but unfortunately tomorrow isn't good. I already have some plans, and my **schedule** is pretty full. How about Wednesday?

SILLY 씰리

Meaning in American English:
미국식 영어로 의미:

It can mean foolish, stupid, and mindless in a negative way, but it is very weak in meaning and not very offensive. Also, it is more often used in a positive, inoffensive way, meaning something closer to playful, lighthearted, and mildly funny or amusing. It can also mean ridiculous, but also in a positive-leaning way. 부정적인 의미로 어리석고, 멍청하고, 무심한 것을 의미할 수 있지만, 아주 경미하고 특히 불쾌하지 않습니다. 자주 모욕적이지 않은 긍정적인 방식으로 사용되는데, 장난스럽거나 가벼운 마음으로, 약간 재미있는 것을 의미합니다. 우스꽝스러운 것을 의미할 수 있지만, 장난스럽고 재밌다는 긍정적인 의미로 쓰입니다.

Say Instead:
미국식 영어로 말할려면:

Foolish, Dumb, Stupid (for negative meanings)

Konglish Sentence	American English
I was too *silly* that I got a warning from my teacher.	I was *acting foolish*, so I got a warning from my teacher.
너무 씰리해서 선생님한테 혼났다.	

American Life & Culture:
미국의 삶과 문화:

Sometimes you can hear an adult call a child, "Silly." This is not an insult. In fact, it's like you're saying that that kid is playful and amusing. For example, a child might tell a joke that doesn't make much sense but that he finds hilarious. Many adults will laugh along and say, "You're so silly!" meaning, "You're so playful, and it's cute and good that you like to find and enjoy funny and amusing things."

가끔 어떤 어른이 아이보고 "어리석다"라고 말하는 것을 들을 수 있습니다..그 아이가 장난스럽거나 웃길 때 씁니다. 예를 들면, 어떤 아이가 말도 안되는 농담을 말할 때 웃기다고 합니다. 그 때 어른들이 "너, 참 어리석구나"라고 하는데, 그 뜻은, "웃기고 귀엽다. 그런 말에 웃기고 재밌어하니"라고 할 수 있습니다.

Real Life Story:
실화:

A friend of mine was dating a terrible guy for several years who cheated on her with a woman in Korea and later again with a third woman. When my friend found out, she found the Korean woman on social media and found that she believed the guy was also *HER* boyfriend. My friend reached out to the woman to let her know that their man was a liar and a cheater in order to hopefully save her from some future pain. The Korean woman did not believe her at all and replied in her message with, "Hello Silly, [angry words about the situation]..." The message felt really confusing. "Hello Silly" sounded light, unoffensive, and even playful to our American English-speaking ears like maybe she was about to send a kind message. But then the message followed with angry, insulting words. If a native English speaker had written that same message, they would have probably used a much stronger word than "silly" in this situation. "Oh stupid" (or perhaps a stronger offensive word). Silly sounds playful and doesn't sound or feel offensive. Instead, it's playful or neutral most of the time.

The other time you might hear silly is when you want to say something negative like "stupid" or something more strong but feel it is inappropriate to use stronger language. For example, someone might say, "These silly bugs!" to express frustration around a child instead of "These stupid bugs!" or "These #%@! bugs!" Stupid is not considered a bad word in English, but still there are some people who do not like to use stronger words around children. Another possible situation would be when talking about something you think is pointless but don't feel so strongly as to call it "stupid."

제 친구 중 하나는 한 명도 아닌 한국 여자 세명과 바람을 피는 정말 나쁜 남자를 만났습니다. 제 친구가 그 것을 알게 되자 SNS 에 자기도 그 남자의 여자친구였다고 올렸습니다. 그 친구는 다른 여자들에게도 SNS 를 통해 그 남자는 바람둥이라고 말해 다른 여자를 도와주려고 했습니다. 그 여자가 답장하기를, "안녕, Silly (화난 언어로)..." 내 친구가 그 것을 읽고 혼란스럽게 느꼈습니다. 우리는 그 메세지를 보고 웃었습니다. 그 이유는 미국사람들은 silly 라는 단어는 장난스럽고 별로 상처가 되지 않는 말이기 때문입니다. 만약, 영어를 모국어로 사용하는 사람이 그 메세지를 보냈다면, silly 라는 단어보단 더 심한 단어를 썼을 것입니다. "오 바보" (또는 아마도 더 심하고 공격적인 단어). silly 는 대부분 장난스럽게 들리고, 불쾌하게 들리거나 느껴지지 않습니다. 그것은 대부분 중립적이거나 장난스럽습니다.

어떤 상황에서는 silly 라는 단어를 바보나 욕, 부정적인 의미의 단어를 대신해 쓰기도 합니다. 예를 들면, 누군가 아이들에게 "이 바보같은 벌레들!"이나 "이 #%@! 벌레!"라고 하는 대신에 "이 silly 벌레들!"이라고 말할지도 모릅니다. stupid 는 영어에서 아주 나쁜 단어로 여겨지지 않지만, 아이들 주변에서 더 심한 단어를 사용하는 것을 좋아하지 않는 사람들이 있습니다. 어떤 때에는 어떤 사람과 대화를 하는데 그 사람이 쓸데없는 이야기만 한다면 stupid 라는 단어를 쓸 정도로 강하게 말하는 것이 아니라면 silly 라는 단어를 쓰기도 합니다.

How Americans use Silly:
미국인들이 "Silly"를 사용하는 법:

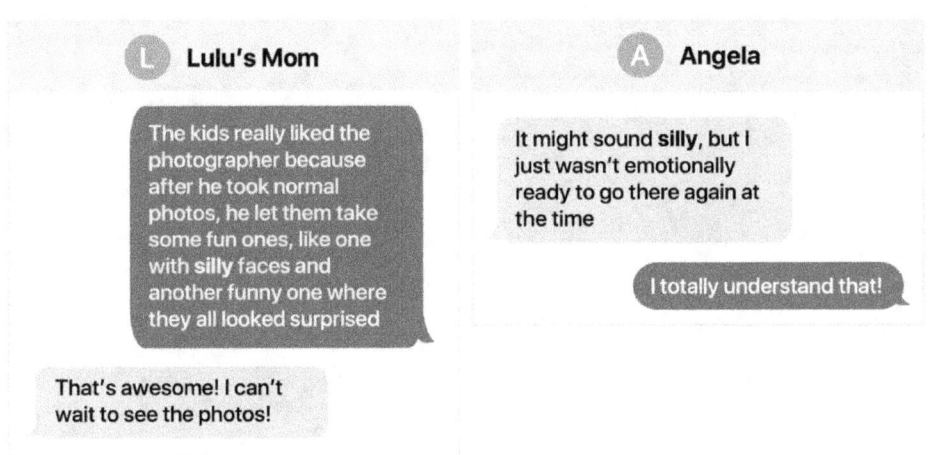

SNS 에스엔에스

Meaning in American English:
미국식 영어로 의미:

Doesn't exist

이 단어는 존재하지 않습니다

Say Instead:
미국식 영어로 말할려면:

Social media

Konglish Sentence	American English
Let's follow each other on *SNS*.	Let's follow each other on *social media*.

우리 SNS 팔로우하자.

UNTACT 언택

Meaning in American English:
미국식 영어로 의미:

Doesn't exist

이 단어는 존재하지 않습니다

Say Instead:
미국식 영어로 말할려면:

Contactless

Konglish Sentence	American English
Nowadays, people use a lot of *untact* machines.	Nowadays, people use a lot of *contactless* machines.

요즘엔 언택으로 된 기계를 많이 쓴다.

WAY TO GO 웨이 투 고

Meaning in American English:
미국식 영어로 의미:

This is only used to express "Good job!" for something that was already completed. It can never be used to express future actions. It is always used as an expression alone, "Way to go!" It can't be used with other verbs like "Do way to go." And it cannot be used to express past tense, "You did way to go!" Lastly, "Way to go!" cannot be used to speak in third person. It can only be said directly to the person you are congratulating. It is never correct to say, "John did way to go!"

이미 완성된 것에 대해 "수고했어!"를 표현할 때만 사용됩니다. 미래의 행동을 표현할 때 결코 사용될 수 없습니다. 이것은 항상 "Way to go!"와 같은 표현으로만 사용됩니다. "Do way to go!"와 같이 다른 동사와 사용할 수 없습니다. 그것을 과거 시제로 표현할 수 없습니다. 마지막으로, 3 인칭으로 말할 때 "Way to go!"를 사용할 수 없습니다. 축하하는 사람에게만 직접적으로 말할 수 있습니다. 우리는 "John did way to go!"라고 절대 말할 수 없습니다.

Say Instead:
미국식 영어로 말할려면:

Good job, Great job

Way to go! (*Only for something you want to congratulate someone on doing* 어떤 일에 관해 다른 사람을 축하해주고 싶을 때만 사용함)

He did a great job! He did a good job! (*For speaking in 3rd person* 제 3 자의 입장에서 말할 때)

You got this! / You can do it! (*For encouragement of something in progress or not accomplished yet* 어떤 일이 진행되어지는 과정이나 아직 완료되지 않았을 때 격려하는 말)

Konglish Sentence		American English
He *did way to go.*		He *did a good job.*
Do *way to go!*		*You got this! You can do this!*
그는 정말 잘했다. 잘했어!		

308

RELATIONSHIPS & DATING
관계 & 데이트

15

Scan for Audio!

BOOKING 부킹

Meaning in American English:
미국식 영어로 의미:

A reservation at a hotel or restaurant

호텔 또는 레스토랑 예약

Say Instead:
미국식 영어로 말할려면:

An introduction to someone at a club

Set up with someone at a club

Konglish Sentence	American English
I had a *booking* at a club last week. ⟹	I was *set up with someone* for a date at a club last week.

저번 주 클럽에서 부킹했다.

How Americans use Booking:
미국인들이 "Booking"을 사용하는 법:

 S Restaurant

Just a reminder you're booked at S Restaurant for lunch today at 1:15 pm. Please reply '1' to confirm your **booking** or '9' to cancel.

---

to: Me <Hotel@FrequentTraveler.com>

subject: Hotel *Booking* Confirmation

Your *booking* is confirmed!

Thanks for *booking* your stay with us! Please find your *booking* details below and use the link to easily modify or cancel your reservation.

Booking Number: XTR389P10

HER/HIS/THEIR EYES ARE REALLY HIGH
눈이 높다

Meaning in American English:
미국식 영어로 의미:

Doesn't exist

이 단어는 존재하지 않습니다

Say Instead:
미국식 영어로 말할려면:

Their standards/expectations are too high/unrealistic.

They are too picky.

Konglish Sentence	American English
Her mom always tells her she will be solo because *her eyes are too high*, but she'd rather be single than settle for someone who doesn't treat her with respect.	Her mom always tells her she will be single because *her standards are too high*, but she'd rather be single than settle for someone who doesn't treat her with respect.

그녀의 엄마는 그녀가 눈이 높기 때문에 솔로로 살게 될 것이라고 했지만, 그녀는 그녀를 존중해주는 사람을 만나지 않을 바엔 솔로로 사는게 낫다고 했다.

HUNTING 헌팅

Meaning in American English:
미국식 영어로 의미:

1. Shooting animals for food or sport (e.g., deer hunting, duck hunting)
   음식이나 스포츠를 위해 동물을 쏘는 것, 예를 들어 사슴 사냥, 오리 사냥

2. Hunting can also mean looking for something intently with focus and purpose (e.g., house-hunting, daycare-hunting, hunting for a new car)
   사냥은 또한 집중력과 목적을 가지고 무언가를 열심히 찾는 것을 의미할 수 있습니다 (예: 집 구하기, 탁아소 찾기, 새 차 구하기 등)

Say Instead:
미국식 영어로 말하려면:

Ask for someone's number, Ask out

Konglish Sentence	American English
I got *hunted* by a guy I do not know at the beach.	I *got asked out* at the beach by a guy I do not know. / A guy at the beach *asked for my number*.

바닷가에서 모르는 사람에게 헌팅당했다.

How Americans use Hunting:
미국인들이 "Hunting"을 사용하는 법:

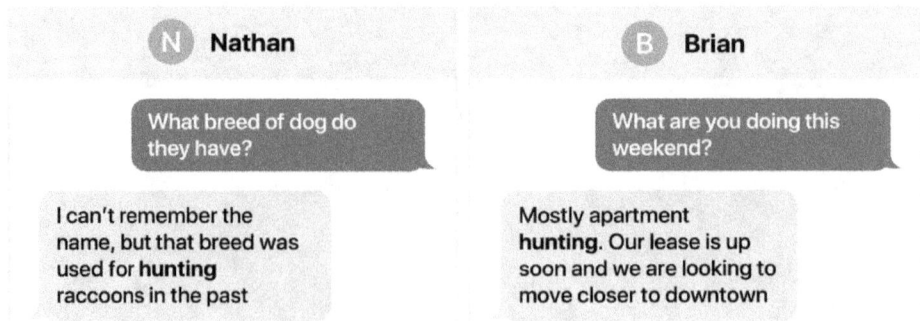

Nathan

What breed of dog do they have?

I can't remember the name, but that breed was used for **hunting** raccoons in the past

Brian

What are you doing this weekend?

Mostly apartment **hunting**. Our lease is up soon and we are looking to move closer to downtown

MEETING 미팅

Meaning in American English:
미국식 영어로 의미:

A gathering of a group of people for some purpose, often to plan or discuss something: for example, a business meeting, a parent meeting for parents at a school, a committee, a meeting for a volunteer activity (to plan and discuss it), a meeting with a lawyer or accountant or other professional providing a service, etc.

어떠한 목적을 위해 사람들이 만날 때 쓰이는 단어입니다. 예를 들어, 사업 회의, 학교의 학부모 모임, 위원회, 자원봉사 활동을 위한 모임(계획하고 논의하기 위한 모임), 변호사나 회계사 또는 서비스를 제공하는 다른 전문가와의 모임 등.

Say Instead:
미국식 영어로 말할려면:

Blind date, Blind double date, Blind group date

Konglish Sentence	American English
I met my husband at a *meeting* through my friends.	I met my husband on a *blind date* that my friends set up. I met my husband on a *blind double date* that my friends set up.

우리 남편을 친구 소개로 미팅으로 만났다.

OUR COUPLE (OUR BOO BOO) 부부

Meaning in American English:
미국식 영어로 의미:

Doesn't exist

이 단어는 존재하지 않습니다

Say Instead:
미국식 영어로 말할려면:

My wife and I

My husband and I

My boyfriend and I

My girlfriend and I

My spouse and I

My partner and I

My significant other and I

Konglish Sentence	American English
Did *your couple* go to the party?	Did *you and your boyfriend/ girlfriend/wife/husband/spouse/ partner/significant other* go to the party?

너희들 파티에 갔었어?

PROPOSE 프로포즈

Meaning in American English:
미국식 영어로 의미:

1. (Verb) To ask someone to marry you
   (동사) 누군가에게 청혼하는 것

2. (Verb) To formally offer an idea or plan
   (동사) 아이디어나 계획을 공식적으로 제안하는 것

   Note: With this meaning, we usually need an object. For example: "He proposed a new plan at the meeting." If we simply say "He proposed," without an object, this sounds like he asked someone to marry him.

   *참고: 이런 의미로 사용할 때 보통 목적어가 필요 합니다. 예를 들어 "그는 회의에서 새로운 계획을 제안했다."라고 말할때 목적어가 있어야 합니다. 목적어없이 "그는제안했다"라고하면, 누군가에게 결혼을 제안했다는 것처럼 들립니다.

Say Instead:
미국식 영어로 말할려면:

Proposal

Konglish Sentence	American English
He *proposed* her at a park.	He *proposed* to her at a park.
그는 공원에서 그녀에게 프로포즈를.	

Konglish Sentence	American English
His *propose* was really amazing.	His *proposal* was really amazing.
했다 그의 프로포즈는 완벽했다.	

How Americans use Propose:
미국인들이 "Propose"를 사용하는 법:

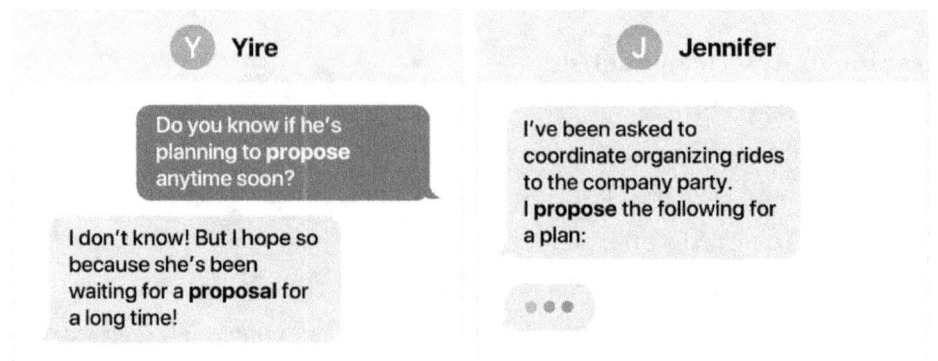

Additional Info:
그 외:

In Konglish, a propose is always a big event. In American English, a *proposal* can be of course, but it is also the same word if someone just proposes spur of the moment at dinner. We would use the same sentence. "He proposed." So it is common to ask, "How did X propose?!" And it might be something simple like, "We were eating dinner, and he asked if I would marry him." Or it might be, "We had some drinks, then he took me to a park with a beautiful lake where a photographer friend was hiding in some trees nearby to take photos as he proposed as the sun set. Afterwards, he brought me to a surprise dinner where the room was filled with flowers and candles and my favorite kinds of food, and our friends were all waiting there to congratulate us."

콩글리쉬에서 'propose'는 항상 큰 이벤트를 뜻합니다. 미국 영어에선 누군가와 저녁을 먹을 때 프로포즈할 수 있습니다. 우리는 같은 문장을 사용할 것입니다 "그가 프러포즈를 했어." 그래서 흔히. "X 가 어떻게 프러포즈를 했어?!"라고 묻습니다. "저녁 먹을 때 결혼하자고 했어"라고 말할 수 있습니다. 또는 "술을 마시고 있었는데 어떤 큰 이쁜 호수가 있는 공원으로 날 데려가는 거야. 해가 질 때 친구 사진작가가 근처 나무에 숨어서 프로포즈하는 모습을 찍었어. 그런 다음에 꽃과 양초, 좋아하는 종류의 음식으로 가득 찬 깜짝 저녁 식사에 데려갔는데 친구들이 우리를 축하하기 위해 기다리고 있었어."

SKINSHIP 스킨십

Meaning in American English:
미국식 영어로 의미:

Doesn't exist

이 단어는 존재하지 않습니다

Say Instead:
미국식 영어로 말할려면:

Physical affection, Physical contact, Physical touch, PDA, Holding hands,
Hugging

Konglish Sentence	American English
My wife loves *skinship*. ⟹	My wife likes *physical affection / physical touch*.

우리 아내는 스킨십을 좋아한다.

SOLO 솔로

Meaning in American English:
미국식 영어로 의미:

Alone, no other people, just one person
혼자, 다른 사람은 없고, 한 사람만

Say Instead:
미국식 영어로 말할려면:

Single

Konglish Sentence		American English
He's *solo*.	⟹	He's *single*.
	그는 솔로이다.	

How Americans use Solo:
미국인들이 "Solo"를 사용하는 법:

L Luke & Tiffany

> Hi! How's parent-life?! Are you guys surviving? Do you need anything?

Our parents helped us a lot with the baby these first 2 weeks. They'll be leaving next week, so after that we'll be flying **solo**

R Raul

> What are you up to this week? Want to go out for a drink with us tomorrow?

Maybe next week... my wife took a **solo** trip to Philadelphia to visit some friends, so I'm at home with the kids this week

WEDDING MARCH 웨딩마치

Meaning in American English:
미국식 영어로 의미:

A specific classical song by Felix Mendelssohn often played during weddings
펠릭스 멘델스존이 지은 결혼식에서 자주 연주되는 특정 클래식 곡

Say Instead:
미국식 영어로 말할려면:

Wedding, Bridal entrance, Bridal procession, Walking down the aisle

Konglish Sentence	American English
People celebrated our *wedding march.*	People celebrated at our *wedding.*
사람들은 우리의 결혼 행진을 축하했다.	

Konglish Sentence	American English
During her *wedding march*, she tripped on her wedding dress.	As she was *walking down the aisle*, she tripped on her wedding dress.
결혼 행진 도중 웨딩드레스에 걸려 넘어졌다.	

How Americans use Wedding March:
미국인들이 "Wedding March"를 사용하는 법:

Customer Review

"Not only does the quartet play traditional wedding music such as Pachelbel's Canon in D and the **Wedding March**, they can also play popular modern music."

★ ★ ★ ★ ★

16

FEELINGS, EMOTIONS, DESCRIBING CHARACTER & PERSONALITY
감정, 기분, 기질 & 성격

Scan for Audio!

CENTI 센치

Meaning in American English:
미국식 영어로 의미:

Doesn't exist

이 단어는 존재하지 않습니다

Say Instead:
미국식 영어로 말할려면:

Centimeter

Sad, Feeling sentimental, Moody

Konglish Sentence	American English
I'm so *centi*.	I'm so *emotional*.

나 오늘 조금 센치해.

CHEER UP 치얼업

Meaning in American English:
미국식 영어로 의미:

> To make someone happier who is feeling a little sad or down
> 슬프거나 우울한 사람을 행복하게 해주는 것

Say Instead:
미국식 영어로 말할려면:

> Cheer (for)

Konglish Sentence		American English
She's going to *cheer up* the football team.		She's going to *cheer for* the football team.
그녀는 풋볼팀을 응원할 것이다.		

How Americans use Cheer Up:
미국인들이 "Cheer Up"을 사용하는 법:

 Roel

> He's been really sad ever since he was laid off from his job. Maybe we can do something to **cheer him up**? Any ideas?

> He likes sports... what if we get tickets to a basketball game next weekend?

 Sue

> If you need something ridiculous to **cheer you up**, watch this video! It's hilarious – I couldn't stop laughing!

CHIC 시크

Meaning in American English:
미국식 영어로 의미:

Stylish and fashionable, mostly a positive meaning

스타일리시하고 패셔너블하며, 대부분 긍정적인 의미

Say Instead:
미국식 영어로 말할려면:

Fashionable, intimidating, and unapproachable

Konglish Sentence	American English
She is very *chic* and cool.	She is *fashionable, intimidating, and unapproachable*.
그녀는 시크하고 멋있다.	

How Americans use Chic:
미국인들이 "Chic"를 사용하는 법:

Customer Review

The hotel blends contemporary chic with their own unique design making it truly one of a kind! We highly recommend staying here!

★★★★★

Aunt Rosa

Beautiful picture! Your outfit is **chic**!

Thanks! I actually borrowed it from my friend

COMPLEX 콤플렉스

Meaning in American English:

미국식 영어로 의미:

1. (Noun) A complex is an unconscious emotional system of thoughts, emotions, and associations that causes a person to act or think in certain (usually unnatural) ways. This is often used with an adjective, for example:

   (명사) 콤플렉스는 무의식적인 감정적 사고 체계로서, 사람이 특정한 (보통 자연스럽지않은) 방식으로 행동하거나 생각하게 만드는 사고, 감정 및 연관성입니다. 이 용어는 일반적으로 형용사와 함께 사용되며, 예를 들어:

   - *"She has an inferiority complex."* This means she typically feels inferior and inadequate compared to the people around her.

     "그녀는 열등감 콤플렉스를 갖고 있다"라고 말하면 그녀가 주변 사람들과 비교해서 일반적으로 열등하고 불만족스러운 느낌을 의미합니다.

   - *"He has a God-complex."* This means someone has a pattern of seeing themselves as better than everyone else and powerful like a god or perhaps not subject to the same rules of others.

     "그는 신의 콤플렉스를 가지고 있습니다." 이것은 누군가가 자신을 신처럼 다른 사람들보다 더 뛰어나고 힘이 있다고 보거나 다른 사람들의 동일한 규칙을 따르지 않는 패턴을 가지고 있다는 것을 의미합니다.

2. (Adjective) Something with many complicated parts, not simple; for example, "That's a really complex topic. We will need a lot of time to discuss it because it's not simple."

   (형용사) 단순하지 않고 복잡한 부분이 많은 것, 예를 들어 "정말 복잡한 주제네요. 단순하지 않기 때문에 토론하는 데 많은 시간이 필요할 것입니다."

Say Instead:
미국식 영어로 말할려면:

Self-conscious about, Insecure about

Konglish Sentence	American English
My *complex* is my low nose.	I *feel self-conscious about* my nose. I *feel insecure about* my nose.
난 내 낮은 코가 콤플렉스이다.	

How Americans use Complex:
미국인들이 "Complex"를 사용하는 법:

 Leah

> I wish she would speak up more often and share her ideas! She is really creative!

> She has kind of an inferiority **complex** and never feels like her ideas are good enough, so I always try to be encouraging about it

 Jayden

> Luna is my favorite character in the show

> Mine too. She is a really complicated and **complex** character and grows a lot over time

FROZEN 프로즌

Meaning in American English:
미국식 영어로 의미:

1. Really cold
   정말 춥다
   "I was frozen during the meeting" =
   I felt so incredibly cold during the
   meeting.
   "회의하는 동안 얼었어요" =
   회의하는 동안 너무 추웠어요.

2. Really scared and can't move because of fear
   정말 무섭고 두려움 때문에 움직일 수 없습니다

When we want to say someone was frozen, it is more than just nervous. It shows
extreme fear or extreme paralyzing anxiety. It expresses a much more extreme version.
누군가가 얼었다고 말하고 싶을 때, 단지 긴장하는 것 이상입니다.
극도의 두려움 또는 극도의 마비 불안을 보여줍니다. 훨씬 더 극단적인
형태를 표현합니다.

Say Instead:
미국식 영어로 말할려면:

Nervous

Konglish Sentence	American English
When the teacher came in, I was *frozen*.	When the teacher came in, I got really *nervous*.

선생님이 들어오자 얼었다.

Additional Info:

그 외:

If you want to express the feeling where you forget what you want to say or you lose your thoughts out of nervousness, you can use the phrase, "I was so nervous that my mind went blank." But "my mind went blank" can be used in other situations, even when you aren't feeling nervous or anxious as well.

하고 싶은 말을 잊어버리거나 초조해서 생각이 나지 않는 느낌을 표현하고 싶다면 "너무 떨려서 마음이 멍해졌다"라고 할 수 있다. 하지만 "마음이 멍해졌다"는 것은 긴장하거나 불안하지 않는 다른 상황에서 사용될 수 있다.

INTIMATE 인티메이트

Meaning in American English:
미국식 영어로 의미:

Something private and shared with only very close people. An intimate relationship is a very close relationship between two people in which they share things that they don't share with everyone else. An intimate group could be a small group of people who are close to each other and can share more personal things with each other because they have more trust. Intimate can also mean private.

사적인 것이고 아주 가까운 사람들과 공유하는 것입니다. 친밀한 관계는 다른 사람들과 공유하지 않는 것들을 공유하는 두 사람 사이의 매우 가까운 관계입니다. 친밀한 그룹은 서로에게 가깝고 더 많은 신뢰를 공유하고 더 많은 신뢰를 가지고 있기 때문에 서로 더 많은 개인적인 것들을 공유할 수 있는 작은 그룹일 수 있습니다. 친밀한 것은 또한 사적인 것을 의미할 수 있습니다.

Say Instead:
미국식 영어로 말하려면:

Open, Makes casual small talk, Friendly, Talkative

Konglish Sentence	American English
She is really *intimate* in the office.	She is really *friendly and talkative* in the office.
그 사람과 사무실에서 정말 친하다.	

How Americans use Intimate:
미국인들이 "Intimate"를 사용하는 법:

 Wine & Convo

We'd love to invite you all to our house for wine and conversation this Friday evening!

Please RSVP so we can know whether we're hosting an **intimate** gathering or a major social event

 Gaby

I can't believe she asked you such an **intimate** question about that!

Yeah, I know. I just politely told her I wasn't comfortable talking about something so private with someone I don't know very well.

MANIA 매니아

Meaning in American English:
미국식 영어로 의미:

1. Excessive or unusual excitement, enthusiasm, or obsession with something. This is usually negative in meaning and never refers to a person.
    어떤 것에 대한 과도하거나 특이한 흥분, 열정, 집착. 일반적으로 의미가 부정적이며 결코 사람을 지칭하지 않습니다.

2. Mania in a psychiatric disorder like in bipolar disorder
    심리학의 마니아 (조울증과 같은)

Say Instead:
미국식 영어로 말할려면:

Connoisseur (*positive, also means you know a lot about the topic too (usually used for the arts and food related topics – a wine connoisseur*) 긍정적인, 어떠한 주제에 대해 박식하다는 뜻도 된다. (보통 예술이나 음식에 관함. 와인 connoisseur)

A (big) fan (*positive* 긍정적임)

To be really into (*neutral* 중립적임)

Obsessed with (*can be positive or negative* 긍정적이거나 부정적임)

Obsession (*for the thing*) (*somewhat negative* 거의 부정적임)

Maniac (*for the person*) (*negative* 부정적임)

Konglish Sentence		American English
She is Korean drama *mania*. She knows almost all the dramas streaming right now.	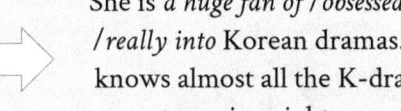	She is *a huge fan of / obsessed with / really into* Korean dramas. She knows almost all the K-dramas streaming right now.

그녀는 한국 드라마 매니아이다. 아마 지금 방송되고 있는 모든 드라마를 알 것이다.

How Americans use Mania:
미국인들이 "Mania"를 사용하는 법:

 Ethan

> Doesn't he have bipolar disorder? Is he still taking his medication?

> Recently he stopped taking them. It's not a good situation. When he is in the manic phase, he doesn't sleep and the **mania** causes hallucinations and makes him think he is a prophet from the Bible...

 Amelia

> Apparently a side effect of the medicine is delusion and **mania**

> Yikes, that doesn't sound very helpful

How Americans use Maniac:
미국인들이 "Maniac"을 사용하는 법:

 Elise

> I told him I wasn't interested but he won't stop messaging me. I've gotten at least 10 DMs from him every day

> OMG he is so creepy! I hate those types of guys on dating apps. He sounds like a **maniac**! Block him!

MENTAL 멘탈

Meaning in American English:

미국식 영어로 의미:

An adjective describing anything related to your mind. Common examples:

정신과 관련된 상태를 표현할 때 쓰이는 단어. 일반적인 예:

- *Mental math* = math done in your head only and not written on paper.
  정신 수학 = 종이에 쓰지 않고 머리속에서 푸는 수학.
- *Mental exercise* = any activity to "exercise" your mind/brain.
  정신 운동 = 마음/뇌를 운동하는 모든 활동.
- *Mental health* = health related to your mind.
  정신 건강 = 마음과 관련된 건강.
- *Mental illness* = illness or sickness related to your mind (like depression)
  정신 질환 = 마음과 관련된 질병(우울증과 같은)

Say Instead:

미국식 영어로 말하려면:

Willpower, Determination, Ability to face a challenge, Mentality, Attitude

- He is unmotivated / not determined / unable to face the challenge / doesn't have very much willpower. = *His mental is weak.*
- He is determined / motivated / able to face the challenge / ambitious / has a lot of willpower. = *His mental is strong.*

Konglish Sentence		American English
My *mental* is really weak.	⇨	I *don't feel motivated.* I *don't have a lot of willpower.* I *feel unable to face a challenge.*

나는 맨탈이 너무 약하다.

How Americans use Mental:
미국인들이 "Mental"을 사용하는 법:

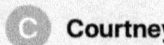 Courtney

Guess what! I got the promotion!!

Congrats!! I'm doing a **mental** happy dance!!

Also, so sorry I forgot to answer your text yesterday. I had a long day and didn't have the **mental** energy to think about which option is best! I wasn't ignoring you!

 Jeff

Did you hear about the soccer player who bit someone during the game?!

YES! So crazy! This was his THIRD time biting another player! He needs actual **mental** help!

MIND 마인드

Meaning in American English:
미국식 영어로 의미:

A person's intellect and area of thinking and consciousness. If you say, "My mind feels tired," that means your brain or thinking area feels tired of thinking.
한 사람의 지성과 사고와 의식의 영역입니다. 만약 누군가가 "내 마음이 피곤하다"고 말한다면, 그것은 당신의 뇌나 사고 영역이 사고에 지쳤다고 느낀다는 것을 의미합니다.

Say Instead:
미국식 영어로 말할려면:

Want to, Intend to, Plan to, Put your mind to, Have your mind set on; Intention

Konglish Sentence	American English
He has a *mind* to learn English. 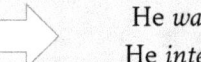	He *wants to* learn English. He *intends to* learn English.

그는 영어를 배우기로 결심했다.

How Americans use Mind:
미국인들이 "Mind"를 사용하는 법:

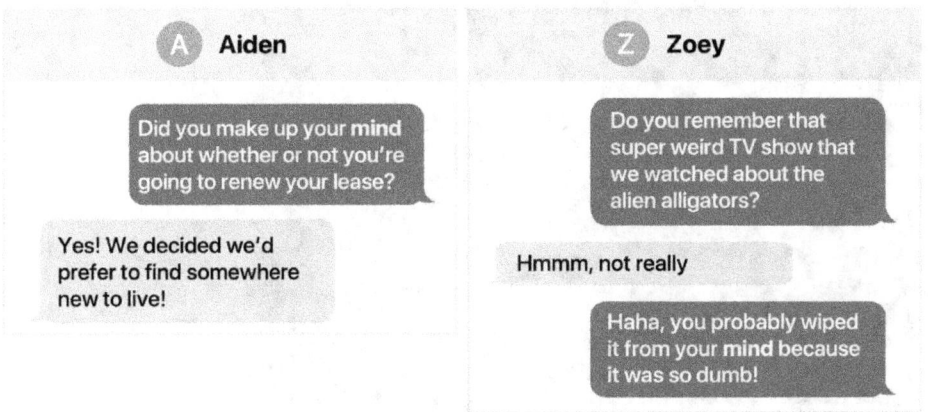

Aiden

Did you make up your **mind** about whether or not you're going to renew your lease?

Yes! We decided we'd prefer to find somewhere new to live!

Zoey

Do you remember that super weird TV show that we watched about the alien alligators?

Hmmm, not really

Haha, you probably wiped it from your **mind** because it was so dumb!

MIND CONTROL 마인드 컨트롤

Meaning in American English:

미국식 영어로 의미:

Controlling someone's mind like in a sci-fi movie or thought-control like brainwashing

공상과학 영화처럼 누군가의 마음을 통제하거나 세뇌와 같은 사고 통제

Say Instead:

미국식 영어로 말할려면:

Work up the courage, Self-motivation, Self-help, Calm yourself down, Keep composure, Get yourself in the right mindset, Pump yourself up

Konglish Sentence	American English
He had to *do mind control* before he gave his speech.	He had to *work up the courage* and *get mentally prepared* before he gave his speech.

그는 강연/연설을 하기 전에 마인드 컨트롤을 해야한다.

How Americans use Mind Control:

미국인들이 "Mind Control"을 사용하는 법:

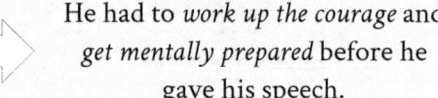

Some Characteristics of a Cult:

- Authoritarian leader
- Manipulative
- Mind Control:
      sometimes Brainwashing
- Emotional Control:
      often shame, fear
- Isolation from outsiders
- Questioning not allowed

SPORTS & ACTIVITIES
스포츠 & 운동

Scan for Audio!

BACK NUMBER 백 넘버

Meaning in American English:
미국식 영어로 의미:

Doesn't exist

이 단어는 존재하지 않습니다

Say Instead:
미국식 영어로 말할려면:

Jersey number

Konglish Sentence	American English
What's his *back number*? It's 13. ⟹	What's his *jersey number*? It's 13.
그의 등넘버가 뭐야? 13 이야.	

BICYCLE HIKING

Meaning in American English:
미국식 영어로 의미:

Doesn't Exist

이 단어는 존재하지 않습니다

Say Instead:
미국식 영어로 말할려면:

Mountain biking

Konglish Sentence	American English
We went *bicycle hiking* on the scenic trail last weekend.	We went *mountain biking* on the scenic trail last weekend.

우리는 지난 주말에 경치 좋은 산책로로 자전거 하이킹을 갔다.

HANDY 핸디

Meaning in American English:
미국식 영어로 의미:

Used as an adjective - convenient, easy to use, close by, useful

Never use as a noun; it has an inappropriate meaning

형용사로 쓰임 - 편리하고, 사용하기 쉽고, 가까이에 있고, 유용함

일반명사로 사용될 때 부적절한 의미를 가지니 절대 사용하지 마십시오.

Say Instead:
미국식 영어로 말할려면:

Handicap (in golf)

Easy to carry

Konglish Sentence	American English
He had a golf *handy* of 7.	He had a *handicap* of 7.
그는 일곱명의 핸디들이 있었다.	

Konglish Sentence	American English
The box is *handy*.	The box is *easy to carry*.
그 상자는 편리하다.	

How Americans use Handy:
미국인들이 "Handy"를 사용하는 법:

 Madison

> Thanks again for giving us your extra at-home COVID tests. They came in **handy** on our trip!

> You're welcome! I'm glad they were useful!

 New Client

> Would you like for me to send you a copy of the tutor's resume?

> A resume would be great if you have it **handy**! If not, a summary here is good!

HIKING 하이킹

Meaning in American English:
미국식 영어로 의미:

Hiking is walking that is usually done by following a marked trail - it can range from a paved trail for an easy hike to a rough natural trail with steep inclines for a more difficult or advanced hike. A hike can be as short as 10 minutes or as long as an entire day. Most hikes are at least an hour, but you can find guidebooks that say, "It is a beautiful 10 minute hike from the parking spot to the viewpoint." *Hiking* is almost always in nature (for example, we don't hike in a downtown area of a city). Depending on the location, this could be a hike through a prairie or forest with flat terrain or a hike in the mountains with ups and downs.

To put it simply, *hiking* is a less-than-one-day walk in a place with nature following some kind of set trail or path. We can also use the phrase *overnight hike* if we want to talk about a hike where you camp for just one night. If you say, "I'm going hiking," it will be assumed you are not staying overnight. If you say, "I'm going on an overnight hike," this means you are going on a hike, camping for one night, and returning the next day. *Hiking* for longer than this is not usually called *hiking* anymore, but is called *backpacking* or *trekking* depending on the details.

하이킹은 일반적으로 표시된 등산로를 따라 걷는 것입니다. 쉬운 하이킹을 위한 포장된 등산로부터 더 어렵거나 발전된 하이킹을 위한 가파른 경사가 있는 거친 자연 등산로까지 다양할 수 있습니다. 하이킹은 짧게는 10 분, 길게는 하루가 걸릴 수 있습니다. 대부분의 하이킹은 최소 한 시간이지만, '주차장에서 전망대까지 10 분 거리 아름다운 하이킹'과 같은 안내서를 찾을 수 있습니다. 하이킹은 대부분 항상 자연에서 합니다.(예를 들어, 도시 시내에서 하이킹을 하지 않습니다). 위치에 따라 평평한 지형이 있는 대초원이나 숲을 통한 하이킹일 수도 있고, 기복이 있는 산에서 하이킹일 수도 있습니다.

간단히 말해서, 하이킹은 자연에서 정해진 오솔길이나 길을 따라 걷는 하루 미만의 산책입니다. 하룻밤만 캠핑하는 하이킹에 대해 이야기하고 싶다면 '밤새 하이킹'이라는 표현을 사용할 수 있습니다. 만약 "나는 하이킹을 갈 것이다"라고 말한다면, 하룻밤을 머무르지 않는 것으로 간주될 것입니다. 만약 "나는 밤샘 하이킹을 갈 것이다"라고 말한다면, 이것은 하이킹 가서 하룻밤 캠핑하고 다음 날 돌아오는 것을 의미합니다. 이것보다 더 긴 하이킹은 보통 '하이킹'이라고 부르지 않고, 세부 사항에 따라 배낭여행이나 트레킹이라고 불립니다.

Say Instead:
미국식 영어로 말할려면:

Biking (*if using a bicycle* 자전거를 사용할 때)

Hiking (*for one day or less* 하루나 더 짧은 시간)

Overnight hiking (*a hike, one night of camping, and finish the hike the next day* 하이킹, 1박 캠핑, 그리고 다음 날까지 하는 하이킹)

Trekking (*for adventurous trips longer than one day following a set route* 정해진 경로를 따라하는 하루 이상의 모험적인 여행)

Backpacking (*for trips longer than one day where you carry all sleeping and food gear with you* 자연속에서 캠핑 용품을 가지고 다니며하는 하루보다 더 긴 여행)

Konglish Sentence		American English
We love to go *hiking* with our bicycle to the viewpoint.		We love to go *biking* to the viewpoint.
우리는 자전거를 타고 등산하는 것을 좋아한다.		

Konglish Sentence		American English
In Colombia, you can take a three-day *hike* through the jungle to the ancient ruins.		In Colombia, you can go on a three-day *trek* through the jungle to the ancient ruins.
콜롬비아에서는 정글을 지나 로스트 시티라고 불리는 고대 도시의 유적지까지 3일간의 하이킹을 할 수 있다.		

How Americans use Hiking:
미국인들이 "Hiking"을 사용하는 법:

 Sister

Dad said he's up for **hiking** tomorrow. The trail I sent you is about 3 hours total

Sounds great! Do we want to pack lunch and eat on the trail or just go out afterwards?

 Mike

Did everyone go **hiking**?

His parents and nephew **hiked** the 2-mile trail with our dog while the rest of us took the 10-mile **hiking** trail to the highest peak

POCKETBALL 포켓볼

Meaning in American English:
미국식 영어로 의미:

Doesn't exist

이 단어는 존재하지 않습니다

Say Instead:
미국식 영어로 말할려면:

Pool, Billiards

Konglish Sentence	American English
He was the *pocketball* champion at his school.	He was the *pool/billiards* champion at his school.

그는 포켓볼 챔피언이었다.

RUNNING MACHINE 러닝머신

Meaning in American English:
미국식 영어로 의미:

Doesn't exist

이 단어는 존재하지 않습니다

Say Instead:
미국식 영어로 말할려면:

Treadmill

Konglish Sentence	American English
We decided to buy a *running machine*.	We decided to buy a *treadmill*.
우린 러닝머신을 사기로 했다.	

SKIN SCUBA 스킨스쿠버

Meaning in American English:

미국식 영어로 의미:

Doesn't exist

이 단어는 존재하지 않습니다

Say Instead:

미국식 영어로 말하려면:

Scuba diving (*the activity* 액티비티)

Scuba diver (*the person doing the activity* 액티비티를 하는 사람)

Konglish Sentence	American English
I like to *skin scuba* in Jeju Island.	I like to *scuba dive* in Jeju Island.

난 제주도에서 스킨스쿠버 하는 걸 좋아한다.

SPORTS DANCING 스포츠 댄싱

Meaning in American English:
미국식 영어로 의미:

Doesn't exist
이 단어는 존재하지 않습니다

Say Instead:
미국식 영어로 말할려면:

Competitive ballroom dancing

Konglish Sentence	American English
She has been doing *sports dancing* for five years.	She has been doing *competitive ballroom dancing* for years.

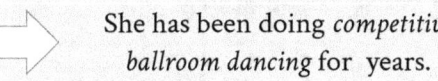

그녀는 스포츠 댄스를 5 년동안 했다.

SPORTSMAN 운동선수

Meaning in American English:
미국식 영어로 의미:

This is not a commonly used term anymore, but it would mean someone who plays sports or who enjoys playing them; however, this can include anyone, not necessarily a professional.

이 단어는 일반적으로 잘 사용되는 용어는 아니지만, 스포츠를 하는 사람 또는 그것을 즐기는 사람을 의미합니다. 그러나 프로 선수가 아닌 보통 사람을 포함할 수 있습니다.

Say Instead:
미국식 영어로 말할려면:

Professional athlete

[Sport name] pro *(e.g., Tennis pro)*

Pro(fessional) [sport] player *(e.g., Pro basketball player)*

Konglish Sentence	American English
He's one of the most famous *sportsmen* in Korea.	He's one of the most famous *professional athletes* in Korea.
그는 한국에서 아주 유명한 운동선수이다.	

TREKKING 트레킹

Meaning in American English:
미국식 영어로 의미:

Trekking is somewhat a mix of backpacking, *hiking*, and walking through towns and villages. Typically, *trekking* lasts for several days or more, includes difficult or adventurous terrain (like crossing raging rivers or waterfalls), and you will often (but not always) bring your sleeping gear and food supplies on your back with you as you hike like you do in backpacking. Each night you will sleep in a different location as part of your trek. For *trekking*, you're usually following a set route from point A to point B, and your journey can be in nature as well as through towns, villages, and rural areas. You might be crossing rivers one day and camping in a forest one night and then walking through a small village the next day. You might camp some nights or stay in shelters or small local inns or lodges along the way. We call this *backpacking* when it is only done in nature rather than going through towns and villages too.

트레킹은 배낭여행, 하이킹 및 도시와 마을에서 걷는 것을 다소 혼합하고 있습니다. 일반적으로 트레킹은 며칠 또는 그 이상 지속되며, (격심한 강이나 폭포를 건너는 것과 같은) 어렵고 모험적인 지형을 포함하며, 배낭여행처럼 하이킹할 때 침구와 음식물을 종종 배낭에 담아 갈것입니다. 매일 밤 트레킹 일정에 따라 다른 장소에서 잠을 잘 것입니다. 트레킹은 보통 A 지점에서 B 지점까지 정해진 경로를 따라가고, 마을, 시내 및 시골 지역뿐만 아니라 자연 속에서 지낼 수 있습니다. 아마도 어느 날은 강을 건너고, 어느 날은 숲에서 캠핑을 하고 그다음 날에는 작은 마을을 걸을 것입니다. 며칠밤은 캠핑하거나 가는 길에 쉼터 또는 작은 지역 여관 또는 숙소에서 묵을 수도 있습니다. 시내나 마을을 지나가는 것보다 자연에서만 지낼 때 이것을 배낭여행이라고 부릅니다.

Say Instead:
미국식 영어로 말할려면:

Hiking (*for one day or less* 하루나 더 짧은 시간)

Overnight hiking (*a hike, one night of camping, and finish the hike the next day* 하이킹, 1 박 캠핑, 그리고 다음 날까지 하는 하이킹)

Trekking (*for adventurous trips longer than one day following a set route*
정해진 경로를 따라하는 하루 이상의 모험적인 여행)
Backpacking (*longer than one day, where you carry all sleeping and food gear*
자연속에서 캠핑 용품을 가지고 다니며하는 하루보다 더 긴 여행)

Konglish Sentence	American English
We *trekked* to the top of Baegundae in the National Park near Seoul. It took us around five hours to go all the way to the peak and back down.	We *hiked* to the top of Baegundae in the National Park near Seoul. It took us around five hours to go all the way to the peak and back down.

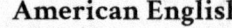

우리는 서울 근처의 국립공원에 있는 백운대 정상까지 트레킹을 했다.
정상까지 갔다가 다시 내려오는데 5 시간 정도 걸렸다.

Additional Info:
그 외:

Backpacking can also mean when you travel to a place (Europe or Southeast Asia) in the cheapest way possible, bringing only a large backpack. This is popular for young adults, especially in their 20s. It allows you to see the world at the cheapest way possible. You stay in cheap hostels, eat cheap local food, and take public transportation like buses or trails (or sometimes even hitchhiking) to get around. It's a dream of many people to spend a month or maybe even a summer in college backpacking through Europe or Southeast Asia. (Those places are popular for backpacking because you can travel to a lot of different countries within a close area easily using cheap public transportation options).

배낭여행은 가능한 가장 저렴한 방법으로 큰 배낭만을 가지고 (유럽이나 동남아시아) 여행하는 것을 의미할 수 있습니다. 이러한 여행은 특히 20 대의 젊은 성인들에게 인기가 있습니다. 가능한 가장 저렴한 방법으로 세상을 경험할 수 있게 해줍니다. 저렴한 호스텔에 머물며, 값싼 지역 음식을 먹고, 돌아다니기 위해 버스나 산책로와 같은 대중교통(때로는 히치하이킹)을 이용합니다. 유럽이나 동남아시아를 배낭여행하며 대학시절 한 달 또는 한 여름을 보내는 것은 많은 사람들의 꿈입니다. (저렴한 대중교통 수단을 이용하여 가까운 지역 내에 많은 다른 나라들을 쉽게 여행할 수 있는 지역이 배낭여행으로 인기가 있습니다.)

18

Music, Movies, TV, & Entertainment
음악, 영화, TV & 연예계

BACK DANCER 백 댄서

Meaning in American English:
미국식 영어로 의미:

Doesn't exist

이 단어는 존재하지 않습니다

Say Instead:
미국식 영어로 말할려면:

Backup dancer

Konglish Sentence	American English
That singer has good *back dancers*.	That singer has good *backup dancers*.

그 가수는 잘하는 백댄서들이 있다.

BACK SINGER 백 싱어(코러스)

Meaning in American English:
미국식 영어로 의미:

Doesn't exist

이 단어는 존재하지 않습니다

Say Instead:
미국식 영어로 말할려면:

Background singer, Backup singer, Backing vocalist

Konglish Sentence		American English
The *back singers* make the music better.		The *backup singers* make the music better.
백싱어들이 노래를 더 좋게 해준다.		

CM SONG 씨엠송

Meaning in American English:
미국식 영어로 의미:

Doesn't exist

이 단어는 존재하지 않습니다

Say Instead:
미국식 영어로 말하려면:

Jingle

Konglish Sentence	American English
That brand is famous for its *CM song*.	That brand is famous for its *jingle*.

그 밴드는 CM 노래들이 유명하다.

Real Life Story:
실화:

The first time I heard this term, I guessed that CM Song meant a country music song, and I was surprised that country music was popular in Korea.

이 용어를 처음 들었을 때 CM 송이 컨트리 노래를 의미하는 것이라고 추측했고, 한국에서 컨트리 음악이 인기가 있다는 것에 놀랐습니다.

Docu 다큐/다큐멘어리

Meaning in American English:
미국식 영어로 의미:

Doesn't exist; people will probably understand "documents."

이 단어는 존재하지 않습니다. 사람들은 아마 '문서'라고 이해할
것입니다.

Say Instead:
미국식 영어로 말할려면:

Documentary

Konglish Sentence	American English
I get mad when I watch a *docu* about the Korean War.	I get mad when I watch *documentaries* about the Korean War.

한국 전쟁에 대한 다큐를 보면 화가난다.

DRAMA 드라마

Meaning in American English:
미국식 영어로 의미:

A specific genre of show, like comedy or horror or drama
코미디, 공포, 드라마와 같은 특정 장르의 쇼

Say Instead:
미국식 영어로 말할려면:

TV show, Show, TV series, K-drama, Korean drama

Konglish Sentence	American English
What kind of *dramas* do you watch? I enjoy comedies.	What kind of *shows* do you watch? I enjoy comedies.

어떤 드라마 보세요? 저는 코미디를 즐겨요.

How Americans use Drama:
미국인들이 "Drama"를 사용하는 법:

 Girlfriend

What do you want to do later tonight?

> Let's watch a movie! Would you rather watch a **drama** or fantasy?

 Elliot

Do you still watch that TV show you were telling me about? It's a comedy **drama** or dramedy...

> Oh, Blue's Anatomy... the show has gotten so (eye roll) with character **drama**, so I stopped watching it

EPISODE 에피소드

Meaning in American English:
미국식 영어로 의미:

1. One episode of a TV show with many episodes.
   많은 분량의 TV 프로그램의 한 방송분

2. Also used for a psychology-related mental-breakdown.
   심리학과 관련된 정신 분열에도 사용됩니다.

Say Instead:
미국식 영어로 말할려면:

Story, Something that happened

Konglish Sentence		American English
I have to tell you an *episode* that happened yesterday.		I have to tell you a *story* about what happened yesterday.

어제 일어난 이야기를 꼭 해야해.

How Americans use Episode:
미국인들이 "Episode"를 사용하는 법:

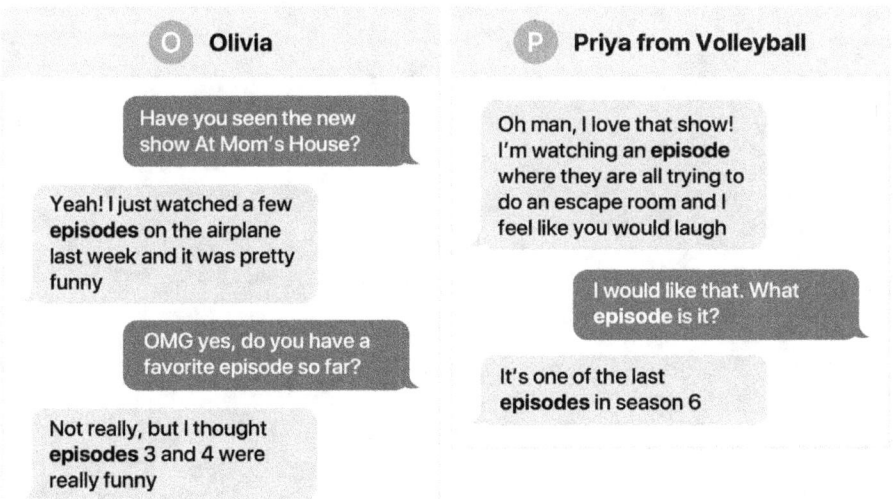

O Olivia

Have you seen the new show At Mom's House?

Yeah! I just watched a few **episodes** on the airplane last week and it was pretty funny

OMG yes, do you have a favorite episode so far?

Not really, but I thought **episodes** 3 and 4 were really funny

P Priya from Volleyball

Oh man, I love that show! I'm watching an **episode** where they are all trying to do an escape room and I feel like you would laugh

I would like that. What **episode** is it?

It's one of the last **episodes** in season 6

FAN SIGN / FAN SIGNING 팬싸인회

Meaning in American English:
미국식 영어로 의미:

Doesn't exist

이 단어는 존재하지 않습니다

Say Instead:
미국식 영어로 말할려면:

Meet and greet

[He] is giving out autographs

Konglish Sentence	American English
I will go to G-Dragon's *fan sign*! 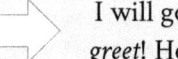	I will go to G-Dragon's *meet and greet*! He's giving out autographs!

나 지드레곤 팬 싸인회에 갈거야.

FANTASTIC 판타스틱

Meaning in American English:
미국식 영어로 의미:

Wonderful

훌륭함

Say Instead:
미국식 영어로 말할려면:

Fantasy

Konglish Sentence	American English
I like *fantastic* movies. ⟹	I like *fantasy* movies.

난 판타지 영화를 좋아한다.

How Americans use Fantastic:
미국인들이 "Fantastic"을 사용하는 법:

Simon

Want to go to Green's Park tomorrow evening?

Sure, what's going on there? Anything specific?

L's Band is playing. It's going to be **FANTASTIC**... and I don't use that word often

Liz

His proposal was pretty much perfect!!!

That's **fantastic**!!! I'm so glad everything was so wonderful!!!! Can't wait to celebrate with you!

GAGMAN 개그맨

Meaning in American English:
미국식 영어로 의미:

Doesn't exist

이 단어는 존재하지 않습니다

Say Instead:
미국식 영어로 말할려면:

Comedian

Konglish Sentence		American English
Son, if you become a *gagman*, I will accept your decision, but you won't make big money.		Son, if you become a *comedian*, I will accept your decision, but you won't make very much money.
아들아, 네가 개그맨이 되는 걸 허락하지만 돈을 많이 못 벌 수도 있어.		

HIGHTEEN STAR 하이틴스타

Meaning in American English:
미국식 영어로 의미:

Doesn't exist

이 단어는 존재하지 않습니다

Say Instead:
미국식 영어로 말하려면:

Teen(age) celebrity, Teen actor/actress

Konglish Sentence	American English
The *highteen star* sings well too!	The *teen celebrity* sings well too!

그 하이틴 스타가 노래도 잘해.

MELODRAMA 멜로드라마

Meaning in American English:
미국식 영어로 의미:

  Drama - a very specific genre of TV show or movie
  드라마 - TV 프로그램이나 영화의 특정한 장르

  Melodrama - anything that is over the top dramatic
  멜로드라마 - 감상적인 드라마

Say Instead:
미국식 영어로 말할려면:

  Romantic drama

Konglish Sentence		American English
She really likes to watch *melodramas.*		She really likes to watch *romantic dramas.*
그녀는 로맨스 드라마를 좋아한다.		

PIERROT 피에로

Meaning in American English:
미국식 영어로 의미:

Doesn't exist

이 단어는 존재하지 않습니다

Say Instead:
미국식 영어로 말할려면:

Clown

Konglish Sentence	American English
I worked part-time wearing a *pierrot* costume.	I worked part-time wearing a *clown* costume.

피에로 옷을 입고 아르바이트를 했다.

Additional Info:
그 외:

There are several Konglish terms that did not actually come from English at all! This is one of them! *Pierrot* is not a word in English at all!

영어에서 유래하지 않은 콩글리쉬 용어들이 몇 개 있습니다! 이것이 그들 중 하나입니다! 피에로는 영어 단어가 아닙니다!

SIGN 싸인

Meaning in American English:
미국식 영어로 의미:

1. (Verb) To sign your signature
   (동사) 서명하다

2. (Noun) A symbol
   (명사) 상징

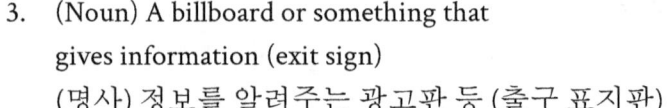

3. (Noun) A billboard or something that gives information (exit sign)
   (명사) 정보를 알려주는 광고판 등 (출구 표지판)

4. (Noun) Forewarning or something that points to something
   (명사) 당신에게 어떤 것을 가리키는 경고나 그 어떤 것

5. (Noun) This can also mean a zodiac sign
   (명사) 여러분의 별자리를 의미할 수도 있습니다

Say Instead:
미국식 영어로 말할려면:

Signature

Autograph (for famous people)

Konglish Sentence	American English
Can I have your *sign* here? ⟹	Can I have your *signature* here?
여기 싸인해주실 수 있나요?	

364

How Americans use Sign:
미국인들이 "Sign"을 사용하는 법:

C Carlo

Have you done the Rainforest Hike in Hawaii before?

Yeah! It's a great hike. There aren't any **signs** for the first 2 miles, but after that the **signs** are good and the trail is clearly marked

B Brandon

Any update on the new house?

We close tomorrow! We are going to **sign** all the papers in the morning and then we get the keys!

TALENT 탤런트

Meaning in American English:
미국식 영어로 의미:

1. The skill or ability that someone has (most common use)
   당신이 가지고 있는 기술 또는 능력 (가장 일반적인 것)

2. A person who has great skill or talent in a specific area
   특정 분야에서 뛰어난 기술이나 재능을 가진 사람

Say Instead:
미국식 영어로 말할려면:

Movie star, actor/actress, celebrity, K-drama actor/actress/star

Konglish Sentence		American English
My favorite *talent* is filming a new drama.		My favorite *K-drama actor* is filming a new K-drama.
내가 제일 좋아하는 탤런트가 새로 드라마 찍는다.		

How Americans use Talent:
미국인들이 "Talent"를 사용하는 법:

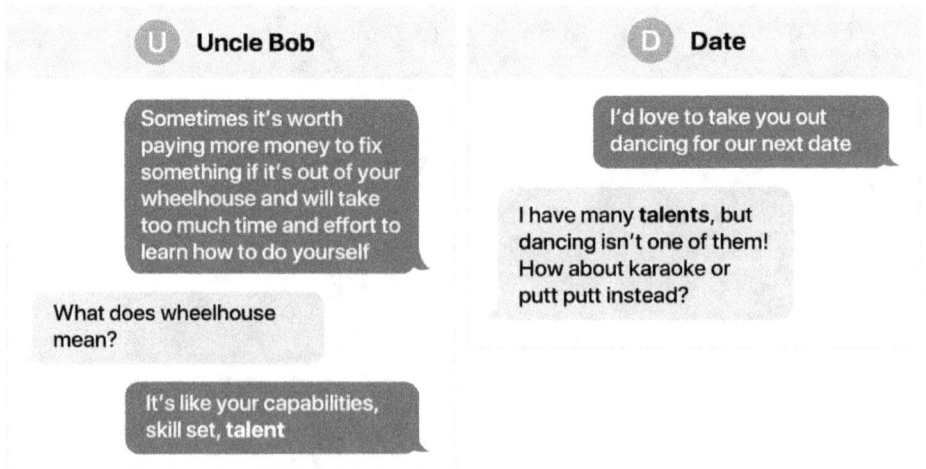

Uncle Bob

Sometimes it's worth paying more money to fix something if it's out of your wheelhouse and will take too much time and effort to learn how to do yourself

What does wheelhouse mean?

It's like your capabilities, skill set, **talent**

Date

I'd love to take you out dancing for our next date

I have many **talents**, but dancing isn't one of them! How about karaoke or putt putt instead?

TELEBI 텔레비

Meaning in American English:
미국식 영어로 의미:

Doesn't exist

이 단어는 존재하지 않습니다

Say Instead:
미국식 영어로 말할려면:

TV

Konglish Sentence	American English
My hobby is watching *telebi*. ⟹	My hobby is watching *TV*.
나는 테레비 보는 게 취미이다.	

TOP STAR 탑스타

Meaning in American English:
미국식 영어로 의미:

Doesn't exist

이 단어는 존재하지 않습니다

Say Instead:
미국식 영어로 말할려면:

A-list celebrity

Konglish Sentence	American English
She is a *top star* in Korea.	She is an *A-list celebrity* in Korea.
	She is a *huge movie star* in Korea.

그녀는 한국에서 탑스타이다.

TV SHOW TV 쇼

Meaning in American English:

미국식 영어로 의미:

TV program or any genre of show made for TV including talk shows, game shows, dramas, news, etc.

TV 프로그램이나 쇼, 예를 들면, 토그쇼, 게임쇼, 드라마, 뉴스 등

Say Instead:

미국식 영어로 말할려면:

Talk show

Konglish Sentence	American English
What *TV shows* do you like? Oh, I don't watch *TV shows*. I only like dramas like This is Us and Grey's Anatomy.	What *talk shows* do you like? Oh, I don't watch *talk shows*. I only like (TV) shows like This is Us and Grey's Anatomy.

-어떤 티비쇼를 좋아하시나요?
- 어, 저는 티비쇼는 보지 않아요. 그레이스 아나토미같은 드라마만 봅니다.

19

TRAVEL & VACATION
여행 & 휴가

Scan for Audio!

CARRIER 캐리어

Meaning in American English:
미국식 영어로 의미:

Someone or something that carries something; a company that transports things

어떤 물건을 들어주는 사람이나 어떤 것; 물건을 옮기는 회사

Say Instead:
미국식 영어로 말할려면:

Suitcase, Carry-on bag

Konglish Sentence	American English
Are you bringing a *carrier* with you on the plane?	Are you bringing a *suitcase* with you on the plane?
비행기 탈 때 캐리어 가지고 갈 것인가요?	

How Americans use Carrier:
미국인들이 "Carrier"를 사용하는 법:

to:	Me <Resident@OurApartments.com>
subject:	Residents at Apartment Green

Attention All Residents:

Our mail *carrier* has requested that we remind you to check your mailbox often. If a mailbox becomes too full, the *carrier* will return the mail to the post office. We have been having some issues with overflowing mailboxes, so please make sure to check your mailbox. We have placed recycling bins in the mail room for your convenience if you wish to throw away any spam mail or newspapers.

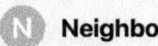 **Neighbor**

How's packing going? Do you have everything ready for the move?

It's good, mostly done... Do you think you could help me put my cat in the **carrier** at some point? I can't put her in by myself

 Food Delivery

Your order has been delivered by the **carrier**

GOODS 굿즈

Meaning in American English:
미국식 영어로 의미:

Usually physical items to be sold, often from another place needing to be transported elsewhere, like merchandise or products. As an example, in studies of business or economics, we often discuss "goods and services," where *goods* talks about any tangible items sold for profit (for example: Korean face cream to sell or English books to sell), and *services* are tasks or jobs provided for a customer (for example: an esthetician giving a facial massage or a tutor teaching you English).

일반적으로 판매되는 물품, 종종 상품이나 제품과 같이 다른 곳으로 운반되어 다른 장소에서 판매됨. 예를 들어, 경영학이나 경제학에서, "상품과 서비스"에 대해 논의할 때 상품은 이익을 위해 판매되는 유형의 물품(예: 판매할 한국의 얼굴 크림 또는 영어책)을 뜻하고, 서비스는 고객에게 제공되는 업무 또는 직업(예: 얼굴 마사지를 하는 미용사 또는 영어를 가르치는 과외 선생님)입니다.

Say Instead:
미국식 영어로 말할려면:

Souvenirs

Konglish Sentence	American English
We need to get some *goods* on our vacation to bring back to our friends.	We need to get some *souvenirs* on our vacation to bring back to our friends.
관광와서 친구들에게 줄 물건을 좀 사야겠어.	

HAND(Y) CARRY 핸드 케리

Meaning in American English:
미국식 영어로 의미:

Doesn't exist

이 단어는 존재하지 않습니다

Say Instead:
미국식 영어로 말할려면:

Carry-on bag

Konglish Sentence	American English
Do you have a *handy carry*?	Do you have a *carry-on bag*?
핸드캐리 있나요?	

HOCANCE 호캉스

Meaning in American English:
미국식 영어로 의미:

Doesn't exist

이 단어는 존재하지 않습니다

Say Instead:
미국식 영어로 말하려면:

Staycation at a hotel that offers a lot of on-site services, food, entertainment, activities, etc.

Konglish Sentence	American English
I really want to have a *hocance*. Do you know any hotels that are good for a *hocance*?	I really want to have an *all-inclusive staycation at a hotel*. Do you know any hotels that are good for this?

나 정말 호캉스 가고싶다. 호캉스하기 좋은 호텔 좀 알고 있니?

MORNING CALL 모닝 콜

Meaning in American English:
미국식 영어로 의미:

Doesn't exist

이 단어는 존재하지 않습니다

Say Instead:
미국식 영어로 말할려면:

Wake-up call

Konglish Sentence	American English
Can I get a *morning call* at 7 a.m.?	Can I get a *wake-up call* at 7 a.m.?
아침 7 시에 모닝콜 해주실 수 있나요?	

OUTING 아우팅

Meaning in American English:
미국식 영어로 의미:

A small day trip or activity (outdoors or to an interesting place like a museum)
짧은 당일 여행 또는 활동 (야외 또는 박물관과 같은 흥미로운 공공 장소에 갈 수 있음)

Say Instead:
미국식 영어로 말할려면:

Picnic

Konglish Sentence	American English
We had an *outing* at the park this weekend.	We had a *picnic* at the park this weekend.

요번 주말에 공원에서 아우팅을 했다.

How Americans use Outing:
미국인들이 "Outing"을 사용하는 법:

 Ladies' Group

Let me know if any of you ever want to try a pilates class – I'm allowed to bring friends for their first class for free! Could be a fun activity for us to do together!

Oh, I'd totally go! That would be a fun girls' **outing** for us!

M **Mother-in-Law**

Would you guys be interested in going to the zoo sometime this weekend?

Good idea! I'll pass it on to the family and see if we can make a fun **outing** of it!

ROUNDING 라운딩

Meaning in American English:
미국식 영어로 의미:

1. (Verb) To round - in math, to take an exact number and estimate it up or down to a whole number. For example, we might round the number 49 to 50, or when talking about the cost we paid for something, we might round the cost $232.15 to $230. (E.g., "How much money do I owe you? -$23.29, so let's just round it to $23.")

    (동사) 반올림하다 - 수학에서 정확한 숫자를 더 다루기 쉬운 숫자로 반올림하는 것. 예를 들어, 숫자를 49 에서 50 으로 반올림할 수도 있고, 어떤 것에 대한 비용을 말할 때, 232.15 달러에서 230 달러로 반올림할 수도 있습니다. (예를 들어, "내가 얼마 갚아야해? 23.29 달러니깐 23 달러로 하자.")

2. (Noun) Rounding - the gerund form of the verb above. (E.g., "We are learning rounding in math at school." "Please write your answer to the math problem, rounding all answers to 3 decimal places.")

    (명사) 반올림 - 위 동사의 동명사형. (예. "학교에서 수학 반올림을 배우고 있습니다." "수학 문제의 답을 소수점 3 자리까지 모두 반올림하여 작성해 주세요.")

3. (Verb) To round - to go around something. (E.g."Horse number 5 is rounding the bend on the racetrack, and it looks like he is moving into 1st place!")

    (동사) 돌아가다: 무엇을 돌아 가는 것. ("5 번 말이 경주로에서 굽이굽이를 돌고 있는데, 마치 1 등으로 달리는 것처럼 보입니다!")

Say Instead:
미국식 영어로 말할려면:

Tour, Take a tour

Play golf

Konglish Sentence		American English
Guests from Korea will visit our hospital. We will give them a *rounding*.		Guests from Korea will visit our hospital. We will give them a hospital *tour*.

한국에서 손님들이 우리 병원에 올 것이다. 우리는 병원 라운딩을 해드릴 것이다.

TOP/TAP 탑

Meaning in American English:
미국식 영어로 의미:

Top 위, 위쪽

Tap 수도꼭지, 톡톡 두드리다

Say Instead:
미국식 영어로 말할려면:

Tower

<table>
<tr><th>Konglish Sentence</th><th></th><th>American English</th></tr>
<tr><td>We didn't go to the top of the Eiffel top.</td><td></td><td>We didn't go to the top of the Eiffel Tower.</td></tr>
</table>

에펠탑 위에 가진 않았다.

Real Life Conversation:
실생활 대화:

I once had this confusing conversation with a student:

학생과의 대화:

Me - How was your trip to France?!

나 - 프랑스 여행은 어땠어요?

Student - It was great! We visited so many places, but we didn't go to the top.

학생 - 정말 좋았어요! 많은 곳을 방문했지만, 정상에는 가지 않았어요.

Me - The top of what?

나 - 무엇의 꼭대기?

Student - We didn't go to the top in Paris.

학생 - 우리는 파리에서 정상에 오르지 못했습니다.

Me - ?? but the top of what?

나 - ?? 근데 뭐 위에?

(Student looks up a picture of the Eiffel Tower and shows me)

(학생이 에펠탑 사진을 구글링해서 보여줍니다)

Me - Ohhhh, you didn't go to the top of the Eiffel Tower. Did you go to the bottom and take pictures around it?

나 - 아, 에펠탑 꼭대기에 가지 않으셨군요. 아래 주변에서 사진을 찍으셨나요?

Student - No, we didn't go to the Eiffel.

학생 - 아니요, 에펠탑에 안 갔어요.

20

CARS & TRANSPORTATION
자동차 & 운송기기

ACCEL 악셀/액셀

Meaning in American English:
미국식 영어로 의미:

Doesn't exist; sounds close to Excel

이 단어는 존재하지 않습니다. Excel 에 가까운 소리로 들립니다

Say Instead:
미국식 영어로 말할려면:

Accelerator, Gas pedal

Konglish Sentence	American English
There is a problem with my car. When I press the *accel*, my car doesn't move.	There is a problem with my car. When I press the *accelerator* / *give it gas* / step on the *gas (pedal)* my car doesn't move.

내 자동차에 문제가 있어. 내가 악셀을 밟을때 차가 움직이지 않아.

AUTOBI 오토바이

Meaning in American English:
미국식 영어로 의미:

Doesn't exist

이 단어는 존재하지 않습니다

Say Instead:
미국식 영어로 말할려면:

Motorcycle, Motorbike

Konglish Sentence	American English
It's fun to ride an *autobi*.	It's fun to ride a *motorcycle*.

오토바이 타는 건 정말 재밌어.

BACK MIRROR 백미러

Meaning in American English:
미국식 영어로 의미:

Doesn't exist

이 단어는 존재하지 않습니다

Say Instead:
미국식 영어로 말할려면:

Rearview mirror

Konglish Sentence	American English
I looked at my kids in the *back mirror*.	I looked at my kids in the *rearview mirror*.

백미러로 내 아이들을 봤어.

CAMPING CAR 캠핑카

Meaning in American English:
미국식 영어로 의미:

Camping car doesn't have a clear meaning in American English. It is clear that you are taking some kind of vehicle to do some kind of camping, but other than that, this term would be unclear for most Americans.

캠핑카는 미국 영어에서 명확한 의미를 갖지 않습니다. 캠핑을 하기 위해 어떤 종류의 차량을 타고 가는 것은 분명하지만, 대부분의 미국인들에게 이 용어는 불분명할 것입니다.

Say Instead:
미국식 영어로 말할려면:

Camper, RV

Konglish Sentence	American English
Let's go camping in a *camping car*! ⟹	Let's go camping with an *RV*!
캠핑카을 타고 캠핑 가자!	

CARAVAN 카라반

Meaning in American English:
미국식 영어로 의미:

1. A type of minivan, like a Dodge Caravan
   닷지 카라반과 같은 미니밴의 한 종류

2. A group of people traveling together in cars or by animals (e.g., traditional nomadic groups in the North African desert travel in caravans from one place to another on camels bringing their belongings and livestock)
   차를 타거나 동물을 타고 함께 여행하는 한 무리의 사람들 (예: 북아프리카 사막의 전통적인 유목민 집단들은 낙타를 타고 한 곳에서 다른 곳으로 이동하며 그들의 소지품과 가축을 가지고 이동합니다)

Say Instead:
미국식 영어로 말할려면:

Camper, RV

Konglish Sentence	American English
Let's go camping in a *caravan*! ⟹	Let's go camping with an *RV*!
카라반을 타고 캠핑가자!	

CAR CENTER 카센터

Meaning in American English:
미국식 영어로 의미:

This doesn't exist as a specific term. Depending on the situation, *car center* could be used to mean an auto shop, a new car dealership, a used car dealership, a museum that showcases different types of cars, etc. It could cause confusion if used without context.

이 용어는 구체적인 용어로는 존재하지 않습니다. 사용 방법에 따라 자동차 정비소, 새로운 자동차 대리점, 중고차 대리점, 여러 종류의 자동차를 전시하는 박물관을 의미하는 데 사용될 수 있습니다. 맥락 없이 사용하면 혼란을 일으킬 수 있습니다.

Say Instead:
미국식 영어로 말할려면:

Auto shop, Mechanic shop, Car shop, Auto repair shop, Mechanic

Konglish Sentence	American English
I'm going to the *car center* to fix my car today.	I'm going to the *auto shop* to get my car fixed today.
오늘 차 고치러 카센터에 갈거야.	

How Americans use Car Center:
미국인들이 "Car Center"를 사용하는 법:

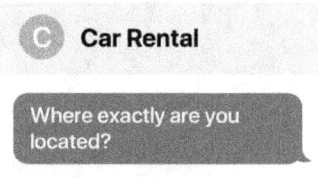

C **Car Rental**

Where exactly are you located?

Take the sky train from the airport to the rental **car center**. Follow the signs from there to find your car rental company.

CLAXON 클락션

Meaning in American English:
미국식 영어로 의미:

Doesn't exist

이 단어는 존재하지 않습니다

Say Instead:
미국식 영어로 말할려면:

Horn

Konglish Sentence	American English
I hate driving here because people always use the *claxon*.	I hate driving here because people always honk the *horn*.
난 여기서 운전하는게 싫어 사람들이 너무 크락션을 울려.	

HANDLE 핸들

Meaning in American English:
미국식 영어로 의미:

Anything to control or open with your hand (e.g., bicycle handle, door handle)
손으로 제어할 수 있는 것 (보통 열거나 닫거나 잡습니다). 자전거
손잡이, 문 손잡이, 바구니 손잡이 등.

Say Instead:
미국식 영어로 말할려면:

Steering wheel

Konglish Sentence		American English
I took my car to the auto shop because my *handle* has a problem.		I took my car to the auto shop because there's a problem with my *steering wheel*.
자동차 핸들이 고장나서 자동차를 수리센터에 가지고갔어.		

How Americans use Handle:
미국인들이 "Handle"을 사용하는 법:

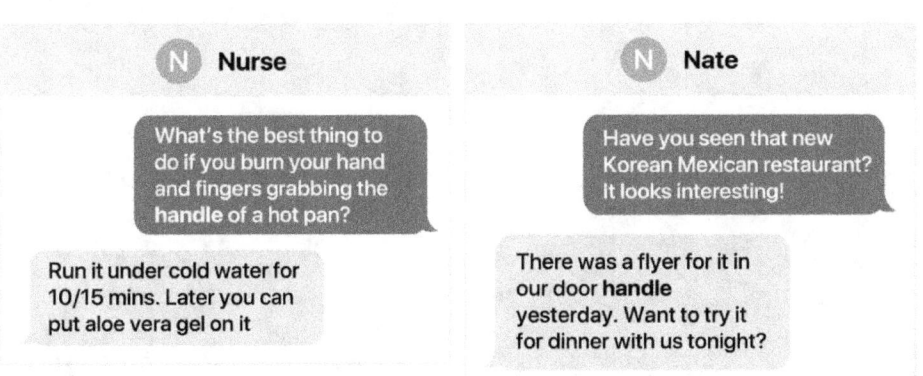

Nurse

What's the best thing to do if you burn your hand and fingers grabbing the **handle** of a hot pan?

Run it under cold water for 10/15 mins. Later you can put aloe vera gel on it

Nate

Have you seen that new Korean Mexican restaurant? It looks interesting!

There was a flyer for it in our door **handle** yesterday. Want to try it for dinner with us tonight?

KICKBOARD 킥 보드

Meaning in American English:
미국식 영어로 의미:

A board for swimming to hold onto
and kick
잡고 발차기 위한 수영용 보드

Say Instead:
미국식 영어로 말할려면:

Scooter

Konglish Sentence	American English
My kids ride their *kickboards* to their friend's house.	My kids ride their *scooters* to their friend's house.
아이들은 친구집에 킥보드를 타고 간다.	

MISSION 미션

Meaning in American English:
미국식 영어로 의미:

Life goal or overall goal or number one calling
인생의 목표 혹은 전체적인 목표 혹은 최고의 사명

Say Instead:
미국식 영어로 말할려면:

Transmission

Konglish Sentence	American English
My car *mission* is broken, so I need to fix it.	My car *transmission* is broken, so I need to get it fixed.

미션이 나가서 수리해야해.

How Americans use Mission:
미국인들이 "Mission"을 사용하는 법:

to:	Me <Employee@ArtandCoffee.com>
subject:	December Service *Mission*

I'm very excited to share with you about our December social/service *mission*. Our company will be working alongside The Children's Charity to help give them a special Christmas celebration. We plan to host a nice evening for them filled with good food, games, crafts, and music. You can expect more details in the next week.

Beatrice Goodman
Owner of Artz&Coffee
"Furthering the *mission* of connecting people through art and coffee"

OPEN CAR 오픈 카

Meaning in American English:
미국식 영어로 의미:

Doesn't exist

이 단어는 존재하지 않습니다

Say Instead:
미국식 영어로 말할려면:

Convertible

Konglish Sentence	American English
I want to buy an *open car*.	I want to buy a *convertible*.
나 오픈카 사고 싶어.	

PUNK 펑크

Meaning in American English:
미국식 영어로 의미:

1. Punk can mean an inexperienced trouble-maker (often youth causing trouble - this can range from something harmless like someone with a bad attitude to something more serious and dangerous like criminal-behavior)

    펑크는 가치가 없거나 경험이 부족한 문제아를 의미할 수 있습니다. (흔히 문제를 일으키는 청소년들 - 이것은 나쁜 태도를 가진 사람과 같이 무해한 것에서부터 범죄 행위와 같이 더 심각하고 위험한 것에 이르기까지 다양할 수 있습니다.)

2. It can also be a small piece of wood used to help start a fire or light something on fire like fireworks.

    불꽃놀이와 같은 불을 지르거나 불을 붙이는 데 사용되는 작은 나무 조각일 수 있습니다.

3. Punk-rock is a style of music

    펑크록은 음악의 한 스타일입니다.

Say Instead:
미국식 영어로 말할려면:

Flat tire

Konglish Sentence		American English
She had a *punk* this morning, so she'll be late to class today.		She had a *flat tire* this morning, so she'll be late to class today.
그녀는 오늘아침에 펑크나서 오늘 수업에 늦을 거야.		

How Americans use Punk:
미국인들이 "Punk"를 사용하는 법:

 Fred

> Do you know anything about the Greenwood area? Is it safe?

Well, I read recently that there have been some incidents of 'punks with guns' in the evenings around the mall and park. So I would probably stay away from there for now

RADIATOR 라디에이터

Meaning in American English:
미국식 영어로 의미:

1. Car Radiator
   자동차 라디에이터

2. Radiator can have the same meaning
   as in Korean (라디에이터); however,
   in American English, radiator usually
   only refers to a specific type of heating
   device that is attached to the wall, pipes, and boiler in an older building or

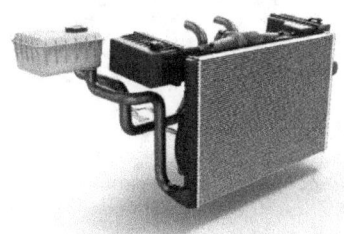

home. It does not usually refer to the smaller, portable, electric heaters.
한국어 라디에이터와 같은 의미일 수 있지만, 미국식 영어로
라디에이터는 오래된 건물이나 집의 벽이나 파이프, 보일러에
붙어있는 특정한 종류의 난방기구만을 말합니다. 보통 작고, 휴대가
가능한 전기 히터를 말하지 않습니다.

Say Instead:
미국식 영어로 말할려면:

Space heater, Portable heater, Electric heater

Konglish Sentence		American English
American office buildings are so cold because of the aircon, but you can buy a *radiator* at HMart, the Korean store.		American office buildings are so cold because of the air conditioner, but you can buy a *space heater* at HMart.
미국 빌딩의 사무실은 에어컨 때문에 너무 추워요 하지만 한인마트 H.Mart 에서 라디에이터를 구입 할 수 있습니다.		

How Americans use Radiator:
미국인들이 "Radiator"를 사용하는 법:

G Grandpa

> There is likely a leak somewhere in the cooling system of the car, maybe the **radiator**

> If the leak is in the **radiator** and they want to replace it, I recommend asking about the warranty. Some places have a warranty for only 3 months, but others have a lifetime warranty.

B Brittany

> Do New York apartments still have **radiators**?

> Yes, but I only know a few people who do

SCOOTER 스쿠터

Meaning in American English:
미국식 영어로 의미:

A non-motorized scooter that you use with
your foot
킥보드

Say Instead:
미국식 영어로 말할려면:

Moped, Motorbike

Konglish Sentence	American English
It's comfortable riding a *scooter*.	Riding a *moped* is comfortable.

스쿠터를 타면 정말 편하다.

How Americans use Scooter:
미국인들이 "Scooter"를 사용하는 법:

B Babysitter

When the kids wake up from their naps, they might want to play outside. You can play in the backyard or walk to the park nearby. If they want to ride their **scooters** to the park, that's ok too. Thank you!!!

SIDE BRAKE 사이드브레이크

Meaning in American English:
미국식 영어로 의미:

Doesn't exist

이 단어는 존재하지 않습니다

Say Instead:
미국식 영어로 말할려면:

Parking brake, Emergency brake

Konglish Sentence	American English
When I park my car, I set up my *side brake.*	When I park my car, I use the *parking brake / emergency brake.*

내가 주차할 때 사이드 브레이크를 채워놓았어요.

STICKER 벌금딱지

Meaning in American English:
미국식 영어로 의미:

An adhesive sticker to stick on things
물건에 붙이는 스티커

Say Instead:
미국식 영어로 말할려면:

Speeding ticket, Parking ticket, Ticket, Fine

Konglish Sentence		American English
I feel upset about getting a *sticker*.		I'm upset about getting a *speeding ticket*.

나 벌금딱지 받아서 화나.

Life & Culture in the USA:
미국의 삶과 문화:

In the USA, stickers are very common! Stickers are often used as rewards for younger children at home and school, and many children's doctors and dentists have special stickers for kids after a visit. After Americans vote in an election, they receive an "I voted" sticker to proudly show they participated in their civic duty.

미국에서 스티커는 매우 흔합니다! 스티커는 종종 집과 학교에서 어린 아이들을 위한 보상으로 사용되기도 하고, 소아과 의사들과 치과 의사들은 치료 후 아이들에게 특별한 스티커를 줍니다. 미국인들이 선거에서 투표를 마친 후 시민의 의무에 참여했다는 것을 자랑스럽게 보여주는 '나는 투표했다'스티커를 받습니다.

WINDOW BRUSH / WIPER
윈도우 브러시 / 와이퍼

Meaning in American English:
미국식 영어로 의미:

Doesn't exist

이 단어는 존재하지 않습니다

Say Instead:
미국식 영어로 말할려면:

Windshield wipers

Konglish Sentence	American English
It could be dangerous if your *window brush / wiper* is too old.	It could be dangerous if your *windshield wipers* are too old.

와이퍼가 오래되면 위험할 수 있어.

21

TOOLS &
OTHER USEFUL ITEMS
도구 & 유용한 것들

Scan for Audio!

DRIVER 드라이버/도라이바

Meaning in American English:
미국식 영어로 의미:

1. A person who drives
   (e.g., a bus driver)
   운전하는 사람(예: 버스 운전사)

2. A type of golf club
   골프채의 일종

Say Instead:
미국식 영어로 말할려면:

Screwdriver

Konglish Sentence	American English
He bought a *driver* at L's Hardware.	He bought a *screwdriver* at L's Hardware.

그는 타겟에서 드라이버를 샀다.

Real Life Conversation:
실생활 대화:

I once had this confusing conversation with a student:
한 학생과 이런 혼란스러운 대화를 나눈 적이 있습니다:

Student - My husband needs a driver. Do you know where he can buy a driver?
학생 - 제 남편은 드라이버가 필요해요. 어디서 드라이버를 살 수 있는지 아세요?

Me - What do you mean? He needs a taxi?
나 - 무슨 말씀이세요? 우버나 택시가 필요하다고요?

Student - No.
학생 - 아니요.

Me - He needs to rent a car? Is there something wrong with your car?
나- 차를 빌려야 한다고요? 차에 무슨 문제라도 있나요?

Student - No. The car is fine. He doesn't need a ride anywhere.
학생 - 아니요. 차는 괜찮아요. 태워다 줄 필요가 없어요.

Me - But you said he needed a driver. What does he need?
나- 드라이버가 필요하다고 했잖아요. 뭐가 필요하죠?

She then acted out the motion of using a screwdriver and explained that he needed to fix something.
"Ohhhhh," I said, "A screwdriver!
그녀는 스크루 드라이버를 사용하는 동작을 연기했고 남편이 무언가를 고칠 필요가 있다고 설명했습니다.
"오," "스크루 드라이버!

How Americans use Driver:
미국인들이 "Driver"를 사용하는 법:

 Delivery Service	Hotel in NYC
Your delivery **driver** has arrived and will be dropping off your order momentarily	The **driver** will wait for you at the passenger exit at the airport with a sign with your name

to: Me <Volunteer@schoolevent.com>

subject: Information for Volunteers

Thank you so much to everyone who has volunteered to help out with our school event this weekend!

Information for *Drivers*:
If you are under 21, sorry, but you cannot transport students under our insurance. But we are taking care of making sure there will be enough *drivers* to transport everyone. If you are under 21 and volunteered to drive, we will assign you as an assistant to a *driver* for the weekend!

MACGYVER KNIFE 맥가이버 나이프

Meaning in American English:
미국식 영어로 의미:

Doesn't exist

이 단어는 존재하지 않습니다

Say Instead:
미국식 영어로 말할려면:

Pocketknife, Swiss Army knife

Konglish Sentence	American English
You can't bring a *MacGyver knife* on an airplane. They might confiscate it.	You can't bring a *pocketknife* on an airplane. They might confiscate it.
맥가이버 나이프를 공항에 가져갈 수 없다. 압수당할 수 있다.	

Additional Info:
그 외:

MacGyver was a popular TV show in the 1980s. There is also a recent remake of the show. Mac MacGyver is the main character who works for the U.S. government. He uses unusual items to solve problems in a creative way. He always has a pocketknife with him. There is a phrase in American English from this TV show and character. To "MacGyver something" means you fix it in a creative and innovative way using unorthodox items. For example, imagine your phone charger cord is bent and the wires are exposed, so now it only charges when the cord is bent exactly a specific way. If you find exactly the right angle where it works well and then use duct tape and a rubber band to secure it at that angle, you can say, "My phone cord wasn't working, but I MacGyvered it. Now it's working great."

맥가이버는 1980 년대에 인기 있는 TV 프로그램이었습니다. 최근에 그 프로그램의 리메이크 버전도 있습니다. 맥가이버는 미국 정부를 위해 일하는 주인공입니다. 독창적인 방식으로 문제를 해결하기 위해 특이한 물건들을 사용합니다. 항상 주머니 칼을 가지고 있습니다. 이 TV 프로그램과 캐릭터에 유래한 미국 영어로 된 문구가 있습니다. '맥가이버 한다'는 어떤 문제를 독창적으로 해결한다는 뜻을 가지고 있습니다. 예를 들어, 여러분의 핸드폰 충전기 코드가 구부러지고 전선이 밖으로 노출되었다고 상상해 보세요. 그것이 잘 작동하는 정확한 각도를 찾은 다음 테이프와 고무 밴드를 사용하여 그 각도로 고정시킨다면, 여러분은 "제 핸드폰 코드가 작동하지 않았지만 맥가이버 했습니다. 지금 잘 작동하고 있습니다"라고 말할 수 있습니다.

PINCHER 삐찌

Meaning in American English:
미국식 영어로 의미:

1. Someone or something that pinches (e.g., crab claws can be called pinchers)
   핀처"는 누군가나 무언가가 뭔가를 집어 끌기 위해 사용되는 것을 나타냅니다 (예: 게의 집게발은 때로 "핀처"라고 부릅니다).

2. A breed of dog (pinscher)
   견종(핀셔)

Say Instead:
미국식 영어로 말할려면:

Pliers

Konglish Sentence	American English
I need a hammer and *pinchers*.	I need a hammer and some *pliers*.
나는 망치랑 삐찌가 필요하다.	

How Americans use Pincher:
미국인들이 "Pincher"를 사용하는 법:

 Selena

> Awww cute picture at the beach, but why is your daughter crying?

She stuck her finger in the **pincher** because she wanted to touch the crab, but then it closed its claw and got her good and wouldn't let go lol

POKLAIN 포크레인

Meaning in American English:
미국식 영어로 의미:

Doesn't exist

이 단어는 존재하지 않습니다

Say Instead:
미국식 영어로 말할려면:

Excavator

Konglish Sentence	American English
There were many *poklains* building a big mall.	There were many *excavators* building a big mall.

큰 몰을 짖는 포크레인이 많이 있었다.

TUPPA 타파

Meaning in American English:
미국식 영어로 의미:

Doesn't exist

이 단어는 존재하지 않습니다

Say Instead:
미국식 영어로 말할려면:

Tupperware

Konglish Sentence	American English
The water bottles made from *tuppa* are smooth.	The *Tupperware* bottles are smooth.

타파로 만든 물병은 부드럽다.

VINYL 비닐

Meaning in American English:
미국식 영어로 의미:

1. Record 레코드
2. Specific material (raincoat or floor) 특정 재질(우비 또는 바닥)

Say Instead:
미국식 영어로 말할려면:

Plastic (bag)

Konglish Sentence	American English
We need to stop using *vinyl bags* to save our environment.	We need to stop using *plastic bags* to save our environment.

비닐 봉지를 안써야 환경 오염이 되지 않는다.

How Americans use Vinyl:
미국인들이 "Vinyl"을 사용하는 법:

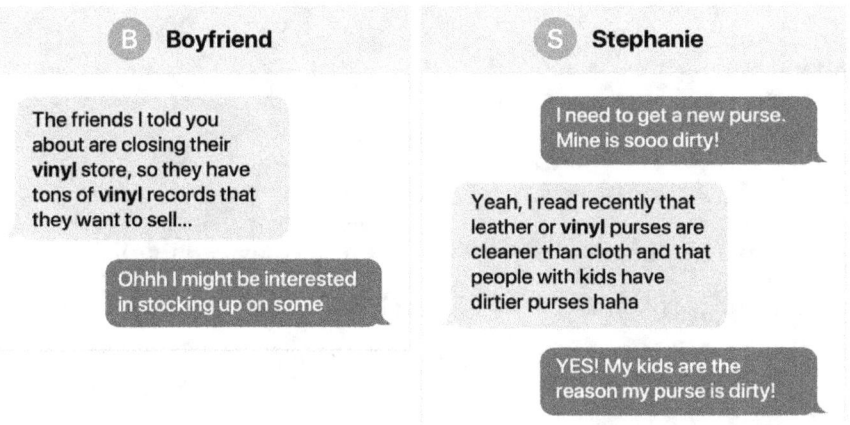

B Boyfriend

The friends I told you about are closing their **vinyl** store, so they have tons of **vinyl** records that they want to sell...

Ohhh I might be interested in stocking up on some

S Stephanie

I need to get a new purse. Mine is sooo dirty!

Yeah, I read recently that leather or **vinyl** purses are cleaner than cloth and that people with kids have dirtier purses haha

YES! My kids are the reason my purse is dirty!

WRAP 랩

Meaning in American English:
미국식 영어로 의미:

1. (Verb) To fully cover something in paper or plastic, like to wrap a gift or wrap up some bread so it doesn't get stale
   (동사) 종이나 플라스틱으로 무엇인가를 싸는 것. 예를 들면 선물 포장, 빵을 신선하게 보관하기 위해 랩을 싸는 것.씌워서 마르지 않게 한다

2. (Noun) A loose skirt or dress that's made by wrapping a large piece of fabric around the body (like a sarong)
   (명사) 큰 천 원단을 몸에 감아 만든 헐렁한 치마나 원피스 (사롱처럼)

3. (Noun) Similar to a sandwich, but the main ingredients are wrapped with a flatbread like a tortilla instead of put between two slices of bread
   (명사) 샌드위치와 비슷하지만, 주재료를 빵 두 조각 사이에 넣는 대신 토르티야처럼 납작한 빵으로 감싼다.

Say Instead:
미국식 영어로 말할려면:

Plastic wrap, Saran wrap, Cling wrap

Konglish Sentence	American English
The *wrap* is made of plastic. $\Longrightarrow$	The *plastic wrap* is made of plastic.

랩은 플라스틱으로 만든 것이다.

How Americans use Wrap:
미국인들이 "Wrap"을 사용하는 법:

G Gal Pal

> I found a really cute **wrap** dress you might like! I'll send you the link in a min

> Awesome! I can't wait to see what it looks like!

B Bridesmaids

> I bought the gift from us for the bridal shower. Do you want me to **wrap** it and bring it to the shower?

> Sure, that's perfect!

ZIPPER BAG 지퍼 백

Meaning in American English:
미국식 영어로 의미:

Doesn't exist

이 단어는 존재하지 않습니다

Say Instead:
미국식 영어로 말할려면:

Ziplock bag, Sandwich bag, Freezer bag, Snack bag

Konglish Sentence	American English
I put some fruit in the *zipper bag.* ⟹	I put some fruit in the *ziplock bag.*
지퍼백에 과일을 넣었다.	

22

MISCELLANEOUS
그 외

Scan for Audio!

DRY 드라이

Meaning in American English:
미국식 영어로 의미:

The opposite of wet

마른

Dry   Wet

Say Instead:
미국식 영어로 말할려면:

Dry cleaning

Konglish Sentence	American English
I need to *dry* these clothes. I need to take these clothes to *dry*.	I need to *dry clean* these clothes. I need to take these clothes to be *dry cleaned*.
이 옷들을 드라이해야한다. 이 옷들을 드라이하러 가야한다.	

JOURNAL 일지

Meaning in American English:
미국식 영어로 의미:

1. A journal is where you write your thoughts or feelings or ideas
   생각이나 느낌이나 아이디어를 쓰는 곳입니다

2. Journal can be a professional or academic magazine or publication; but it's not used like this in everyday conversation
   전문적이거나 학술적인 잡지 또는 출판물이 될 수 있지만 일상적인 대화에서 이와 같이 사용되지는 않습니다.

Say Instead:
미국식 영어로 말할려면:

Newspaper, Magazine

Konglish Sentence	American English
My friend loves fashion *journals*.	My friend loves fashion *magazines*.

내 친구는 패션 저널을 좋아한다.

Additional Info:
그 외:

We can call some specific technical types of magazines "journals." For example: Medical journals or science journals. "Good doctors try to spend some of their free time reading medical journals to learn about new innovations in medicine."

특정 기술 유형의 잡지를 '저널'이라고 부를 수 있습니다. 예를 들어: 의학 저널 또는 과학 저널. "좋은 의사들은 의학의 새로운 혁신에 대해 배우기 위해 그들의 자유 시간 중 일부를 의학 저널을 읽는데 보냅니다."

ONE SHOT, ONE KILL 원샷 원킬

Meaning in American English:
미국식 영어로 의미:

Only used in video gaming

비디오 게임에만 사용됩니다

Say Instead:
미국식 영어로 말할려면:

Zero tolerance, One strike and you're out

Konglish Sentence	American English
The company policy on drinking alcohol on the job is *one shot, one kill.*	The company policy on drinking alcohol on the job is *zero tolerance / one strike and you're out.*
우리 회사 술자리에선 원샷 원킬을 해야한다.	

OVER 오버

Meaning in American English:
미국식 영어로 의미:

1. Above
   위에
2. Finished
   끝났다

Say Instead:
미국식 영어로 말할려면:

Over-exaggerating

Over the top

More/better than I expected

Konglish Sentence	American English
She is always *over*.	She is always *over-exaggerating*.

그녀는 항상 오버한다.

Konglish Sentence	American English
The party was really *over*.	The party was really *over the top*.
	The party was *better than I expected*.

파티가 끝났다.

PARADIGM 패러다임

Meaning in American English:
미국식 영어로 의미:

A usual example of something or the usual way something is done. This doesn't describe a physical example or model, only a pattern, standard, method, or usual way of doing things or thinking about something.

어떤 것의 일반적인 예 또는 어떤 일이 수행되는 일반적인 방식입니다. 물리적인 예나 모델을 설명하지 않고, 단지 어떤 것을 하거나 생각하는 패턴, 표준, 방법 또는 일반적인 방식을 설명합니다.

Say Instead:
미국식 영어로 말할려면:

Model

Konglish Sentence		American English
Here is a digital *paradigm* of the new medical complex that will be finished next year.	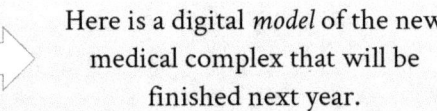	Here is a digital *model* of the new medical complex that will be finished next year.
내년에 완공될 신의료복합단지의 디지털 패러다임을 소개한다.		

420

PICK ME UP 픽미업

Meaning in American English:

미국식 영어로 의미:

Pick someone up - To physically lift someone/something up or to go get someone in your car from a place to bring to another place

누군가를 태우는 것 - 누군가를 물리적으로 들어 올리거나 다른 장소로 데려가기 위해 차에 누군가를 태우기 위해 가는 것

Pick something up – to physically lift something or to go buy or gather something from one place and bring it to another place

물건을 집어 드는 것 – 물건을 물리적으로 들어 올리거나, 물건을 사러 가거나, 모아서 다른 곳으로 가져 가는 것

Say Instead:

미국식 영어로 말할려면:

Pick, Choose

Konglish Sentence		American English
I'm going to *pick up* salad for dinner.		I'm going to *choose* salad for dinner.
저녁 식사로 샐러드를 가지러 갈 것이다.		

Note: In English, I'm going to pick up salad for dinner means I am going to buy a salad for dinner. 저녁으로 샐러드를 살 것이라는 것을 의미한다.

Real Life Story:

실화:

A student recently told me that she and her husband were planning to paint a room. She said she wanted to pick up blue paint but her husband wanted to pick up white paint. I was confused and clarified, "Do you mean you are going to buy the blue paint, and your husband is going to buy the white paint?" No. "Do you mean you are going to paint all the blue parts, and he is going to paint all the white parts?" No. She meant that they couldn't paint yet because they hadn't agreed on which color to pick. She wanted to paint the room blue, and her husband wanted to paint the room white. So they had to decide which color to choose before they could paint.

최근에 한 학생이 그녀와 그녀의 남편이 방을 칠할 계획이라고 말했습니다. 그녀는 파란색 페인트를 고르고 싶었지만 그녀의 남편은 흰색 페인트를 고르고 싶어했다고 말했습니다. 저는 혼란스러웠고, "당신은 파란색 페인트를 살 것이고, 당신의 남편은 흰색 페인트를 살 것이라는 말인가요?" 아닙니다. "당신은 모든 파란색 부분을 칠하고, 그는 모든 흰색 부분을 칠한다는 말인가요?" 아니요. 그들이 어떤 색을 선택할지에 대해 합의하지 않았기 때문에 아직 페인트를 칠할 수 없다는 것을 의미했습니다. 그녀는 방을 파란색으로 칠하기를 원했고, 그녀의 남편은 방을 흰색으로 칠하기를 원했습니다. 그래서 그들은 그들이 페인트를 칠하기 전에 어떤 색을 선택할지 결정해야 했습니다.

Another student explained that he had entered a competition and was hoping they would "pick him up for the winner." At first, I thought maybe they were going to arrive at his house, pick him up in the car, and then take him somewhere special to celebrate.

또 다른 학생은 그가 대회에 참가했고 그들이 "우승자를 위해 그를 데리러" 오기를 바란다고 설명했습니다. 처음에, 저는 아마 그들이 그의 집에 도착해서 그를 차로 태우고 나서 축하하기 위해 다른 특별한 장소로 데려갈 거라고 생각했습니다.

How Americans use Pick Me Up:
미국인들이 "Pick Me Up"을 사용하는 법:

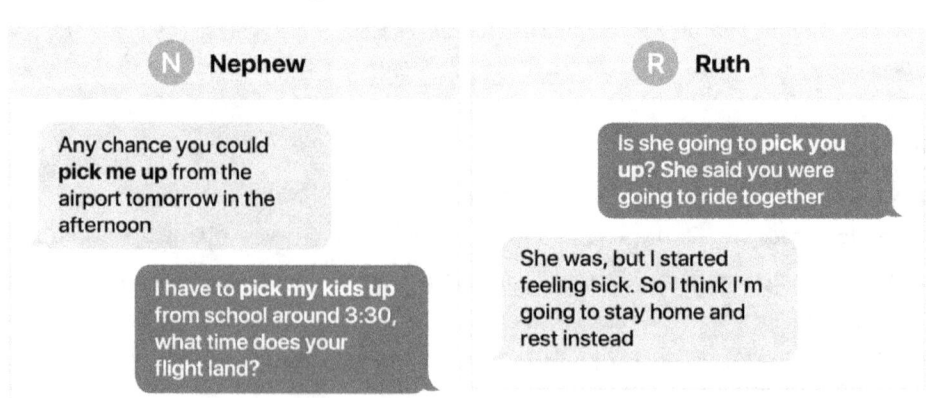

REVIVE 리바이브

Meaning in American English:
미국식 영어로 의미:

To bring something back to life
무엇인가를 되살리는 것

Say Instead:
미국식 영어로 말할려면:

Repeat

Konglish Sentence	American English
I'm sorry, I didn't hear that. Can you *revive*, please?	I'm sorry, I didn't hear that. Can you *repeat it*, please?

죄송해요. 잘 못들었어요. 한 번만 다시 말씀해주실래요?

How Americans use Revive:
미국인들이 "Revive"를 사용하는 법:

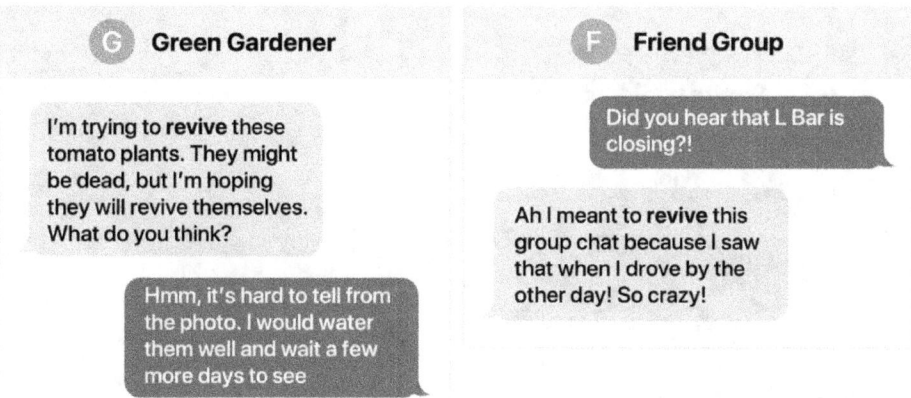

G Green Gardener

I'm trying to **revive** these tomato plants. They might be dead, but I'm hoping they will revive themselves. What do you think?

Hmm, it's hard to tell from the photo. I would water them well and wait a few more days to see

F Friend Group

Did you hear that L Bar is closing?!

Ah I meant to **revive** this group chat because I saw that when I drove by the other day! So crazy!

SHADOW 샤도우

Meaning in American English:
미국식 영어로 의미:

The shade formed by the sun being blocked by an object, often in a cool shape (like a tree)

태양이 물체에 의해 가려져서 생기는 그늘. 종종 시원한 모양으로 (나무처럼)

Say Instead:
미국식 영어로 말할려면:

Shade

Konglish Sentence	American English
There is some *shadow* under that tree where we can have an outing.	There is some *shade* under that tree where we can have a picnic.

저기 나무 밑 그늘이 있어서 그 곳에서 아우팅하면 된다.

How Americans use Shadow:
미국인들이 "Shadow"를 사용하는 법:

 Xavier

> Wow! Look at your shadow on the wall! It looks like a monster!

> Woah! And the cat's **shadow** looks like she's a big lion!

424

SPEAK OUT 스픽 아웃

Meaning in American English:
미국식 영어로 의미:

To use your voice and influence to speak publicly about a difficult topic or a
topic that needs to change in society
목소리와 영향력을 이용하여 어려운 주제나 사회의 변화가 필요한
주제에 대해 공개적으로 말하는 것

Say Instead:
미국식 영어로 말할려면:

Speak, Speak up, Speak louder

Konglish Sentence	American English
Speak out, Susie, we can't hear you.	*Speak up*, Susie, we can't hear you.

조금 더 크게 말해, 수지. 안들려.

Konglish Sentence	American English
I was surprised when Karen *spoke out* Korean.	I was surprised when Karen *spoke* Korean.

케런이 한국어로 말했을 때 난 놀랐다.

How Americans use Speak Out:
미국인들이 "Speak Out"을 사용하는 법:

 History by Text

After the movement, many
women started to **speak
out** about their experiences
with harassment and
discrimination in the
workplace

UNISEX 유니섹스

Meaning in American English:

미국식 영어로 의미:

Something that someone of any gender could use or wear (unisex bathroom, unisex clothes)

남녀 공용으로 사용하거나 착용할 수 있는 것(남녀 공용 화장실, 남여 공용 옷)

Say Instead:

미국식 영어로 말할려면:

Co-ed (*usually used for things, events, places where men and women are mixed together (schools, sports teams, etc.)* 일반적으로 물건, 행사, 남녀가 함께 섞여 있는 장소 (학교, 스포츠팀 등)에 사용됩니다.)

Unisex (*usually used for items that can be used or worn by either men or women (clothes)* 일반적으로 남성이나 여성 모두가 사용하거나 입을 수 있는 아이템(의류)에 사용됩니다)

Gender-neutral (*also an increasingly common way to refer to something that can be used by any gender* 모든 성별이 사용할 수 있는 것을 지칭하는 점점 더 일반적인 방법입니다)

Konglish Sentence	American English
She plays soccer on a *unisex* team.	She plays soccer on a *co-ed* team.
그녀는 남녀 축구팀에서 축구를 한다.	

How Americans use Unisex:
미국인들이 "Unisex"를 사용하는 법:

 Amanda

If you're still looking for birthday present ideas, she really wanted this shirt. Here is the link. They are **unisex** and any color is ok.

> Thanks! Yes, I'm still looking for a gift for her!

 Gene

For the Christmas gift exchange, go out and buy a **unisex** gift for around $10-15 that you would like to receive yourself. No crappy gifts!

> Sounds fun! I'm looking forward to it!

ACKNOWLEDGMENTS

To Yire, first and foremost, thank you for all your hard work and the hours you put into discussing, consulting, and translating in order to help make this book and its counterpart a reality. Thank you for being my first Korean friend. Thank you for teaching me to read and write Hangul, the Korean alphabet, for introducing me to Korean food and culture, and for taking me to beautiful Korea with your family so many years ago. Thank you for showing me life there and patiently translating everything back and forth until you probably didn't want to talk anymore at all. I'm honored to still call you a close friend after 20+ years! There aren't enough words to express my gratitude to have had your help with this book.

To Jaeeun, thank you for believing in this idea with contagious excitement even from the very beginning before it became anything close to a book. I'll never forget those roommate times laughing, telling stories, and sharing our cultures and languages in that old crappy apartment, especially that one summer we camped out under the living room fan when our air conditioner went out in the middle of a hot Houston summer. This book would not have happened if it weren't for those days, all the laughs, the friendship, and the stories we shared. Thank you for all the brainstorming sessions years later, even from half a world away!

To my husband, Kurt, thank you for supporting me throughout this process, for believing in me and reminding me to trust my gut when I doubted myself. Thank you for your extensive help in developing the audio resources for this book, for humoring me the many times I leaned over and asked, "Hey, what does this word mean to you?" and for looking through unending piles of variations of layouts, fonts, and photos to give me your thoughtful opinions.

To all my Korean students, past and present, thank you for letting me enter your world, sometimes even your homes and offices; for sharing fresh brewed tea and espresso and cookies like couque d'asse 쿠크다스; for sharing your culture with me as you learned mine, explaining everything from Korean birthing traditions and methods of making kimchi to modern politics and business norms; and for being brave and humble enough to continue the ambitious journey of learning and perfecting a new language as adults. Never let yourself feel ashamed of your English mistakes – they are essential for learning!

To all my Korean and Korean American high school students at the hagwon-style tutoring center from 2010-2012, who have since grown up, thank you for all your hard work, your great senses of humor and the laughs during our lessons, and your sharing all the delicious Korean snacks like hyeonmi-nokcha 쿠크다스, corn hair tea 쿠크다스, Korean chestnuts, rice cakes, and more. Even more so, thank you for trusting me with vulnerable pieces of your lives as you learned to turn lived experiences into well-written essays. You are inspirations as incredible humans who have walked the often-challenging road straddling two cultures, sometimes each with different expectations of you. As you grow in life, always remember that who you are is always enough. Your experiences, your opinions, and your stories matter.

To my brother, Daniel, thank you for your valuable help as audio engineer, for taking the time and effort to clean up all the recorded audio for the audio resources to make it all sound pristine. Thank you also for your and Larissa's valuable input along the way regarding style and design.

To everyone else who believed this book was possible and gave encouragement along the way, thank you! Your kind words and support made this book possible.

IMAGE CREDITS

The authors and publishers acknowledge the following sources of copyright material and are grateful for the permissions granted. While every effort has been made, it has not always been possible to identify the sources of all the material used, or to trace all copyright holders. If any omissions are brought to our notice, we will be happy to include the appropriate acknowledgments on reprinting and in the next update, as applicable.

Photographs, Images, & Graphics

The following images are from **Adobe Stock Photos**:

Cover (flags): Aroastock; p. 16 (apple): Dionisvera; p. 28 (goldengate): UVAconcept; p. 34 (coffee): olllikeballoon; p. 40 (chicken): MovingMoment; p. 48 (hops): osoznaniejizni; p. 50 (hot dog): venski; p. 52 (jelly): alter_photo; p. 54 (dancing beer): sabelskaya; p. 55 (lunchbox): soupstock; p. 56 (menu): Vector Tradition; p. 58 (sand): New Africa; p. 63 (yogurt): HstrongART; p. 72 (dress): Hein Nouwens; p. 77 (dress): Kathleen; p. 77 (hospital patient): Joseph Kirsch; p. 77 (night gown): JUSTDZINE; p. 81 (school jumper): viktorijareut; p. 81 (jumper cables): romiri; p. 82 (muffler): sveta; p. 84 (one piece): Magdalena; p. 88 (school jumper): viktorijareut; p. 92 (slippers): MichaelJBerlin; p. 101 (two piece): Vita; p. 102 (walker): Destina; p. 107 (hair band): sasimoto; p. 108 (bobby pin): Aninka; p. 110 (sack of potatoes): mbongo; p. 110 (sack of groceries): SkyLine; p. 110 (santa): James Steidl; p. 118 (suitcase): Pixel-Shot; p. 118 (boxes): Aleks Gedeiko; p. 118 (pencils): Zonda; p. 120 (rinse): bignay; p. 124 (black eye): MaskaRad; p. 129 (hip): laschi adrian; p. 143 (disk golf): Shanvood; p. 143 (spinal disk): vonuk; p. 147 (full person): pathdoc; p. 160 (chip clip): Terence Keller; p. 160 (hair clip): pixarno; p. 172 (sad worker): Jiw Ingka; p. 180 (magic rabbit): Ljupco Smokovski; p. 190 (note): sean824; p. 193 (notebook): nata777_7; p. 194 (police officer): Flash concept; p. 212 (desktop computer): Denis Rozhnovsky; p. 214 (flash): DEFMORPH; p. 220 (video gamers): drawlab19; p. 228 (large money): Szasz-Fabian Jozsef; p. 230 (money in pocket): Kenishirotie; p.

233 (small money): W.Scott McGill; p. 241 (groceries): SkyLine; p. 258 (consent form): hvostik16; p. 265 (outside scene): Stockgiu; p. 266 (rocks): BillionPhotos.com; p. 276 (veranda): the8monkey; p. 280 (dryer): BlureArt; p. 283 (induction): Zern Liew; p. 285 (hand mixer): Denis Gladkiy; p. 285 (blender): nito-stock.adobe.com; p. 295 (fighting): Christos Georghiou; p. 300 (night scene): Colorfuel Studio; p. 301 (calendar): vernstudio; p. 327 (cold person): Ирина Горбунова р. 360 (man gagged): Emrah_Avci; p. 388 (minivan): Yuri Schmidt; p. 388 (camels): Mieszko9; p. 391 (bicycle): thanapun; p. 391 (cabinets): fotoru; p. 392 (kickboard): makiaki; p. 395 (punk rocker): Boris Riaposov; p. 399 (scooter): pioneer111; p. 401 (sticker roll): 24K-Production; p. 402 (window brush): snike; p. 408 (dog): DoraSett; p. 411 (records): hiten666; p. 412 (wrap present): Di Studio; p. 412 (wrap skirt): jill; p. 412 (burrito): Mara Zemgaliete; p. 416 (wet and dry): Nizova Tina; p. 421 (pick someone up): nakedcm; p. 424 (cat shadow): FedotovAnatoly

The following images are from **Pixabay**:

p. 22 (capitol and flag): OpenClipart-Vectors; p. 81 (guy jumping): OpenClipart-Vectors; p. 109 (ribbon): MAKY_OREL; p. 143 (disks): OpenClipart-Vectors; p. 199 (knife): OpenClipart-Vectors; p. 202 (glasses): Clker-Free-Vector-Images; p. 212 (laptop): Clker-Free-Vector-Images; p. 364 (vegas sign): lindsayascott; p. 404 (driver): Clker-Free-Vector-Images

The following images are from **Shutterstock**:

p. 143 (gargling): IROHA – Brush Art; p. 160 (office clips): udaix; p. 175 (diary): StockSmartStart; p. 275 (music stand): wacpan; p. 278 (rice cooker): pomxpom; p. 285 (stand mixer): M. Unal Ozemn; p. 397 (radiator): NosorogUA

Other Image Credits:
p. 437 (author photo): Nate Messarra Photography
p. 439 (logo): design by Renee Blodgett

BIBLIOGRAPHY

Ahn, Soojin. "Perceptions of Konglish by English Language users: An analysis of a reaction video and its comments on YouTube*." *Linguistic Research (KHU ISLI)*, vol. 40, 2023, pp. 151–169, https://doi.org/10.17250/khisli.40..202309.006.

Charles, Quanisha. "Native Korean speakers' attitudes toward *Konglish* as a standardized variety of English." *International Journal of Literature and Arts*, vol. 3, no. 6, 2015, p. 136, https://doi.org/10.11648/j.ijla.20150306.12.

General, Ryan. "Why South Koreans Say 'Hwaiting!'" *NextShark*, 20 Dec. 2021, nextshark.com/south-koreans-say-hwaiting.

Hagens, Sheilagh A. "Attitudes toward Konglish of South Korean Teachers of English in the Province of Jeollanamdo." *Brock University*, 2009.

Jeong, Chan Hee. "The Roles Konglish Plays in the Korean American Community." *Bryn Mawr College*, 2021.

Kim, Hwan-bae. "하이킹 vs. 트레킹, 무엇이 다를까?" 데일리스포츠한국, 2 Aug. 2017, www.dailysportshankook.co.kr/news/articleView.html?idxno=187227.

Lee, Hyon-soo. "Follies of Konglish." *Koreatimes*, 10 June 2014, www.koreatimes.co.kr/www/news/opinon/2016/06/162_158502.html.

McPhail, Sean A. "South Korea's linguistic tangle: English vs. Korean vs. Konglish." *English Today*, vol. 34, no. 1, 7 Aug. 2017, pp. 45–51, https://doi.org/10.1017/s0266078417000244.

Ow, Victoria. "41 Konglish Words You Need to Know to Level up Your Korean Skills." *TheSmartLocal South Korea - Travel, Lifestyle, Culture & Language Guide*, 1 June 2022, thesmartlocal.kr/konglish-words/.

Song, Pyeong-in. "The Evolution of English." 동아일보, www.donga.com/en/article/all/20121226/405367/1.

"South Korea's Hiking Culture Reflects Its Social Pressures." *The Economist*, The Economist Newspaper, www.economist.com/christmas-specials/2020/12/16/south-koreas-hiking-culture-reflects-its-social-pressures.

Tse, Jennifer. "Evolution of Konglish based on the current prevalence and South Korean public attitude towards Konglish." *The George Washington University Undergraduate Review*, vol. 3, 2020, https://doi.org/10.4079/2578-9201.3(2020).10.

INDEX

ABOUT THE AUTHOR
저자 소개

 Lauren is the owner and founder of Lauren's Language Lessons, LLC and has been teaching English for over 15 years. She has a degree in International Studies and certifications in TEFL/TESL/TESOL for teaching English as a Second Language. Lauren has worked with numerous Korean businesses and students of various ages and levels from a variety of fields and professions including business, trading, medicine, research, education, music, oil & gas, law, and technology. Lauren is passionate about language and culture and travels every chance she gets. She lives in Houston, Texas with her husband, cat, and dog and enjoys playing soccer and spending time with friends and family.

로렌(Lauren)은 Lauren's Language Lessons, LLC 의 소유주이자 설립자이며, 15 년 이상 영어를 가르치고 있습니다. 국제학 학사 학위를 가지고 있고, 영어를 제 2 외국어로 가르치기 위한 TEFL/TESL/TESOL 자격증을 보유하고 있습니다. SK 와 같은 기업부터 비즈니스, 거래, 의학, 교육, 음악, 석유 및 가스, 기술을 비롯한 다양한 분야와 직업에서 다양한 나이와 수준의 한국 학생들과 함께 일해 왔습니다. 언어와 문화에 대해 열정적이며 여행을 즐깁니다. 남편, 고양이, 그리고 강아지와 함께 텍사스 휴스턴에 살고 있으며, 또한 축구를 즐기고 친구 및 가족과 시간을 보내는 것을 즐깁니다.

ABOUT THE TRANSLATOR
번역가 소개

Yire emigrated from South Korea to the United States in 2003 as a high school student in Houston, Texas. She graduated from Klein High School and earned a BA in Education from the University of Texas at Austin. Since then, she has resided in Austin, Texas with her husbands and two sons.

이레는 2003 년 고등학교 때 휴스턴, 텍사스, 미국으로 오게되었습니다. Klein 고등학교를 나오고 오스틴 주립 대학에서 교육학을 공부했습니다. 이후, 오스틴에서 남편과 두 아들과 살고 있습니다.

ABOUT THE AUTHOR & TRANSLATOR

Many years before the writing of this book, Lauren and Yire met in high school and quickly became close friends. Yire was Lauren's first Korean friend, and Lauren was Yire's first American friend. They are honored to have this opportunity to work together to promote better understanding of their cultures and languages through this book.

이 책을 집필하기 전부터 로렌과 이레는 고등학교에서 친한 친구가 되었습니다. 이레는 로렌의 첫 한국 친구였고 로렌은 이레의 첫 미국 친구였습니다. 이렇게 책을 발간하면서 서로의 문화와 언어를 이해할 수 있어 기회와 시간이 주어져 너무 좋았습니다.

ABOUT LAUREN'S LANGUAGE LESSONS
로렌의 언어수업에 대해서

Lauren's Language Lessons is an online language school offering private tutoring and small group English classes as well as lessons in 9 other languages including Korean, French, German, Italian, Portuguese, Japanese, Mandarin, Arabic, and Spanish. With Lauren's Language Lessons, you can learn English from scratch, pick up where you left off, or perfect where you are now. All language instructors are native speakers or speak with native level fluency and accent and hold relevant qualifications and teaching experience. Private English lessons are customized to the needs and goals of each student to achieve the best results and can focus on anything including academic English, business English, conversational English, or casual everyday English as well as tailored topics such as accent reduction, pronunciation, reading, writing, listening, speaking, grammar, test prep, cultural fluency, and more. We also offer small group classes on specific topics such as pronunciation and business English periodically throughout the year.

Please visit our website at LaurensLanguageLessons.com or send us an email at LaurensLanguageLessons@gmail.com to learn more!

로렌의 언어 수업은 영어뿐만 아니라 한국어, 프랑스어, 독일어, 이탈리아어, 포르투갈어, 일본어, 만다린어, 아랍어, 스페인어를 포함한 9 개의 다른 언어를 개인 과외와 소규모 그룹 수업을 통해 제공하는 온라인 어학원입니다. 영어를 기초부터 배울 수 있고, 놓쳤던 부분이나 지금 현제 레벨에서 시작하실 수 있습니다. 모든 언어 강사들은 원어민이거나 원어민 수준의 유창함과 억양으로 말하고 관련 자격과 수업 경험을 가지고 있습니다. 영어 개인 수업은 최상의 결과를 얻기 위해 각 학생의 필요와 목표에 따라 맞춤화되어 억양 감소, 발음, 읽기, 쓰기, 듣기, 말하기, 문법, 시험 준비, 문화적 유창성 등과 같은 맞춤형 주제뿐만 아니라 학업 영어, 비즈니스 영어, 회화 영어 또는 일상 생활 영어를 포함한 모든 분야를 제공해드립니다. 또한 일년 내내 주기적으로 발음과 비즈니스 영어와 같은 특정 주제에 대한 소규모 그룹 수업을 제공합니다.

더 많은 내용은 웹사이트 LaurensLanguageLessons.com 를 방문하거나 LaurensLanguageLessons@gmail.com 으로 문의하세요!

www.ingramcontent.com/pod-product-compliance
Lightning Source LLC
Chambersburg PA
CBHW060851120626
46553CB00001B/43

*9 7 9 8 9 8 9 9 0 7 8 0 9 *